REFLECTIONS OF
A LIFE IN MEDICINE

REFLECTIONS OF A LIFE IN MEDICINE

The Ups, Downs, and All Arounds

GARY Z. LOTNER, M.D.

BOOKLOGIX®
Alpharetta, GA

ISBN: 978-1-63183-989-4 - Paperback
eISBN: 978-1-63183-990-0 - ePub
eISBN: 978-1-63183-991-7 - mobi

Printed in the United States of America   040921

♾This paper meets the requirements of ANSI/NISO Z39.48-1992 (Permanence of Paper)

ACKNOWLEDGMENTS

There are many people I would like to thank for their help and encouragement in the writing of these memoirs. First and foremost is my wife Sandra, who has graciously put up with my stories for our 45 years together. She was the heart and soul of this project. Indeed, I would like to thank my entire family for their encouragement over time, and with particular kudos going to my daughter Jessica, who for many years, would laugh so vigorously at my tales (a few of which are contained in this volume) and was so constantly encouraging that she would often inspire me to start writing again after I would invariably bog down.

I would like to thank my staff in my medical offices over the years, not only for their help in my practice, but also for encouraging me to memorialize some of the tales I would tell during breaks. In particular, I would like to thank a nurse, Lynn Garrett, whom I've not seen in at least 15 years. An excellent nurse and a better person, she encouraged me so frequently and repetitively to write down various anecdotes that I actually wrote the first one down (the "romantic" tale about how Sandy and I first met) almost two decades ago, where it sat untouched and unread for many years until my grandkids came along.

Indeed, I would like to thank all of my grandchildren, ranging as of this date from age ten down to one month. They were the real inspiration for this book. During the initial wave of the COVID-19 pandemic in early 2020, as I contemplated my son's family with my three youngest grandchildren, all under the age of three, and with thoughts of my own mortality, my desire for my grandchildren to remember me prompted much of my writing. I hesitate to thank the COVID-19 virus—for anything!— and I hope it mysteriously and rapidly disappears just as it started, but in a weird way, the necessity of self-isolating and social distancing for months on end certainly sped along the physical writing of this book.

And lastly as regards the actual process, although certainly not last in importance, I would like to thank my excellent editors, Justin Spizman and Caitlin Walsh, for their encouragement and invaluable assistance along the way.

As I hope I've made amply clear, I loved my patients and appreciated the chance to assist in their care and their lives. Regarding them, any names or identifying characteristics have been changed or obscured to render individuals unidentifiable, except in one case, where the patient is a close friend and I presented her in a way that made her look smarter than me in figuring out the cause of her own mysterious problem. Way to go, Mary.

Lastly, for other physicians, only a few are specifically identified in this book, usually from earlier on in my medical career. If they were identified, it is because they were excellent physicians or friends who I have nothing but respect for and I am grateful for their help in making me a better physician. Thank you all.

CONTENTS

INTRODUCTION

I wasn't always old.

In fact, there was a time when my youth and inexperience were at the forefront of my life. Those were different times, and in many ways some of the fondest of my life. This book was originally intended for the next generations of my family as a way to introduce myself to them through recounting different stages of my life. As I write this, I have five wonderful grandchildren who I love dearly. Their ages range from the youngest at one month to the oldest at ten years.

While we are great friends and share a wonderful relationship together, I realize that the youngest will only know me as a relatively old man and never during my youth or during my long and satisfying career in medicine. They hadn't the opportunity to know the younger version. Yet, it is certainly not as an old man that I see myself. As they get older, I anticipate the grandchildren will strive to learn more about their heritage and hopefully, about me earlier in life. To help them accomplish that, I have written a collection of stories, vignettes really, to try to give them a sense of who I was as when younger, particularly during the phase of life I spent as a physician in training and then as an actual doctor.

As I started getting more deeply involved in my writing, I asked a few selected acquaintances to read sections. They were so encouraging that these memoirs expanded in range and scope as they urged me to write for a larger audience. I was pleased that they enjoyed the episodes and eventually I ended up with far more stories than originally anticipated. This is the compilation of those stories. As hopefully will become obvious to the reader, I've always enjoyed humor and have been able to find humor and irony sometimes in the most unlikely places or stressful situations. However, not surprisingly in stories focusing on a medical career, while I generally sought humor, not all tales lend themselves that way.

This is not intended to be a medical book. I have purposely not included many challenging cases or brilliant diagnoses that I have made. What I've tried to do is give a sense of the humor, joy, and emotions I have experienced in my early career and—hopefully—a small glimpse into my life as a younger man.

I hope you don't mind my efforts. Please read on and please enjoy.

Chapter 1

Welcome to Medical School

I started medical school in 1969, a tumultuous year for the country and myself. The Vietnam War was raging, and the country was in turmoil. In the craziness of the times, I arrived as a fumbling uncertain medical student. I arrived feeling lost to the core, but six weeks later, I found myself appointed the acting vice-president of the Student Government for the entire medical school.

I had always been fairly sure I wanted to be a doctor, I think. Why not? It certainly had been drummed into me. My mother had always told me that I wanted to be a doctor, starting with lullabies about doctors as I was rocked in the cradle. Of course, was there a Jewish mother of the era not genetically primed with that goal in her innermost soul? Apparently, I believed her. On a more serious note, my younger brother, Larry, three years my junior, had been born with a severe congenital heart condition and hadn't been expected to live more than a few years. A fighter, he would eventually surprise everyone by living into his early thirties, but his condition had a tremendous impact on our family and on my eventual orientation towards medicine. Unfortunately, I had no experience in medicine, unlike many of the friends I was to later make throughout my medical training. But I knew I was smart, especially in science and math. And I liked people, even if I was sometimes awkward and had little self-confidence in those years.

As the last stages of college rapidly approached, I had to decide on a career. Growing up relatively poor (my parents would optimistically describe it as lower middle class), I had no personal heroes or knowledge to guide me towards either business or medicine. But my mom had ingrained inside of my head that medical school would always be a good choice. Even then, I needed some confirmation.

Thus, when it was offered during senior year in college, I availed myself of the opportunity to take an aptitude test offered through my college guidance office. What a joke! Looking back, I've always suspected I could have written the results myself and saved several hours of troublesome forms and testing. At the time, I was a rather gawky 20-year-old, majoring in chemistry and attending some pre-med classes, was also a confirmed atheist (in later years, I would say an agnostic) and as an interest, had much less appreciation for the loud rock music that permeated the era than did most of my classmates. So the results were probably not surprising: after several hours of testing, I was informed I should plan a career as a chemist, the president of a large corporation or as a doctor. On the negative side, the results strongly recommended that I should not consider becoming a minister or a rock star. I felt they had certainly correctly nailed the "Don'ts." With no musical abilities whatsoever and an ear approaching total tone deafness, Rock Stardom was certainly out, and the Ministry seemed an unlikely calling for a Jewish atheist. As for the positive choices, I had considered becoming a chemist until I had taken an advanced course in Physical Chemistry, sadly deciding I could not comprehend any of even the major principles in the subject, making a career in chemistry seem far less enticing. (In retrospect, I may not have been fair to myself. That course was so tough that, on the open-book final, to which the student could bring texts, old tests or any other source materials, I scored a 39. This was by far the highest mark in the class, an "A" with the curve. I only achieved this mark because I had used a friend's final exam from a previous year, legal under the rules. Amazingly, I received the

Chemistry Department's award that year for Physical Chemistry, the very subject that had dissuaded me from a career in the field.) The second recommendation was a little more intriguing. I admit I did like the idea of becoming President of a Large Corporation, but a few calls were enough to convince me that few companies seemed to consider that as an entry-level position.

That seemingly left medicine, which presumably was where I was headed all along. (Yes, Mom, I heard you.) If I needed any persuasion, 1969 was a great year to enter medical school. Medical school offered an automatic exemption from being drafted into the Vietnam War. I didn't need much of a prod in that direction, but the draft helped. In later years, I sometimes would wonder whether I would have made the same choice had there not been the war. But in the end, I turned out to love my career in medicine and could not have envisioned a more satisfying profession.

Applying to several schools in the area, I was accepted at most and delighted to enroll at Albert Einstein College of Medicine (AECOM), a relatively young school with an excellent reputation. Located in the Bronx, the borough of my birth and my home for the first two months of life, Einstein was part of Yeshiva University, situated in Manhattan. It was founded largely with a mission of providing medical education for Jewish students in an era in which top medical schools had unofficial (but widely acknowledged) quotas to limit the numbers of Jewish students. At AECOM in its earlier years (the school was founded in 1955), the student body was almost entirely Jewish and entirely male; by 1969, when I was enrolled, the school was still about 80 percent male and predominately Jewish, but with at least ten percent minorities. Nowadays, like most medical schools, the student body is majority female and with a large percentage of Asians, Hispanics and African Americans.

In the earliest days of school, it was hard to avoid the War and even harder to avoid politics. We had, as I was later told by faculty members, a student class that was considered quite radical, and very different from previous classes. We tended to be a scruffy-looking group with beards, long hair, and worn-out jeans. (Many years later, when I had been married for eight years and shaved my beard my beard for the first time, I realized my wife Sandy had never previously seen my face beardless.) I considered myself to be far more conservative in outlook than most of my classmates, many of whom had been active college radicals, presidents of their local SDS chapters (one of the most revolutionary anti-war groups of the era), and constantly organizing strikes, protests, and demonstrations. While I felt I was attending medical school to get a medical education, an expectation I feared not shared by some of my more radical classmates, the earliest weeks of school seemed to be an endless series of improvised meetings to organize the class into varied protests and political activities.

It was at one of these political organizing meetings that someone came running in and announced that the school administration demanded we name a representative from our freshman class to serve as an executive on the Student Government (SG) executive committee. I was sitting toward the back of the room as our most active class members were busily assigning tasks for varied large anti-war rallies. Someone volunteered my name for this mundane position, as none of the more active leadership groups considered it to be all that important. Before I could say otherwise, I found myself nominated and named as Secretary of Student Government two weeks into my freshman year. Less than a month later, when it turned out that the third and fourth year students recently elected the organization's President and Vice-President were to be engaged in out-of-town electives for the majority of the year and unable to actively run SG, I found myself promoted to Acting Vice-President and a few months later, Acting President. In those positions, I had to make important decisions for the entire student body. Even more fortunately, for someone who could never afford previously afford to travel, the Dean of Student Affairs sent me to represent our school in Los Angeles at the national meeting of Medical School Student Governments! Whew! Things moved quickly back then.

Medical school teachings and a career in medicine were also in a state of flux. Typically and conceptually, medical school was divided into two distinct portions: an academic portion of the first two years, largely in classroom and laboratory settings, and the latter two-year period spent seeing patients in hospitals, with courses (called rotations) in many specialties. In my era, there were many changes to this established curriculum—some that were to prove amusing, and others a little frightening.

Chapter 2

The Cab Driver Medical Student

In a sense, I started my medical school career as a New York City taxicab driver. My father had spent most of his life as a cab driver; similarly, my Uncle Irving had been a cab driver; my Cousin Marvin also a hack; and several other relatives shared the same "calling." You get the picture. Naturally, I became a cab driver when I needed a little money before medical school. I was paying my own way after all and without parental assistance. Although my driving career was short-lived, it was certainly memorable.

I began the process of obtaining a hack license with some paperwork and a test of New York geography. Recall, this was an era before cell phones, GPS, or the like. Negotiating the five boroughs of the city of New York required a huge Atlas with intricate maps. Although 50 years have passed, I still vividly recall the geography test. The prospective cabby received a booklet containing the addresses of ten of New York's best-known landmarks. You'd have to memorize these. One was Shea Stadium and the only answer required was "Queens," an area roughly the size of Rhode Island, and no more specificity was required. Another entry was the Bronx Zoo and you've already guessed the answer to that one—The Bronx. I could easily picture getting to the Bronx and driving for hours before hitting the zoo. Then came two of my favorites on the list: Penn Station (34th and Eighth Ave) and Madison Square Garden (again, 34th and Eighth Ave), the Garden sitting on top of the station. If you could remember one, only a total imbecile would fail to know the other. Several weeks prior to the actual test, the prospective driver would be given a booklet with the answers. To pass the exam, the applicant then only needed to correctly answer six questions. If he failed, he would have the opportunity to take the test twice again. This was a test designed for total morons, most certainly not the MCAT exam for medical school applicants. To any readers who may have endured seemingly endless New York cab rides in the past, now you know. It confounded my brain to realize that only 70 percent of applicants passed this test the first time.

The second obstacle in obtaining a hack license involved a visit before a recently installed psychiatric review board. Apparently in those days, road rage had taken on a new meaning and some cabbies had attacked or even murdered their passengers (as opposed to a few years later, when passengers had taken to attacking and killing the drivers). Thus, the City had established a new panel to ensure the prospective drivers were no more psychotic than the average New Yorker. I had taken an afternoon off to go before the Board, waiting in a large room with others even more unkempt than myself. After more than two hours, I was finally summoned before the panel. I entered a rather foreboding room with a long table and was beckoned to sit at the opposite end from three well-dressed, very bored-looking men. The harried lead person introduced himself as Doctor Someone, a psychiatrist, flanked by two psychologist colleagues. He explained that they were to interview me to establish my mental fitness to drive a cab. This was somewhat of a surprise to me—I hadn't realized that any fitness, mental or otherwise, was required. He said, "Mr. Lotner, tell us, why do you want to drive a taxi?" I started to answer, "Well, I start Medical School in the Fall and ….." Before I could complete the sentence, the leader cut me off and said, "Well, gentlemen, I think we've heard enough. Thanks for coming in, Mr. Lotner. You pass." That was the entire process before the vaunted Psychiatric Review Board. If the shrink was to meet some of my crazy medical classmates a few months later, I'm not sure that he would have been quite so confident with this blanket appraisal.

It was a memorable first day on the job that summer. I was headquartered out of a garage in the Bronx, and picked my cab up at 5:30 A.M., truly an ungodly hour. The dispatcher directed me to get on the Deegan, an elevated highway with an entrance a block away, travel south via connecting parkways into Manhattan, and eventually get off the West Side Highway downtown and start hunting fares. The West Side Highway was also elevated and had a fairly steep series of off-ramps. As I descended, putting my foot on the brakes for the first time since picking up the car thirty minutes earlier, I noted a car stopped at a light at least 70 yards in front of me. I pressed on the brakes—and nothing happened. I pressed harder, with a similar lack of results. By this time, frantic, I had both feet desperately jamming down on the brakes and briefly considered jumping out. Luckily, I had slowed to about ten miles an hour before I piled into the rear of the other vehicle.

I had initially judged it a station wagon but closer inspection revealed it to be a floating Puerto Rican hotel. Inside was a father, a mother, a grandmother, three kids, several chickens, and assorted crates and suitcases. Heck, with all the commotion, the kids hadn't even noticed that I'd plowed into them. The father jumped out and understandably started ranting, cussing at me in Spanish and running several laps around his car. He jumped up and down, pointing to some of the hundreds of dents and scratches on his old wreck of a vehicle, trying to figure out which of the many I had just added to.

Finally, before I could get in a word edgewise, he jumped back into his car and drove off, cursing even more vociferously as he left. I abandoned the brakeless cab, ran to a nearby phone booth and called my garage. I explained what had happened and that they needed to get me as I wasn't going anywhere in this deathtrap. I heard the dispatcher, hand partially over the mouthpiece, yelling at someone, "Harry, did you give the new kid the one with no brakes?" I may be the only cabbie in New York history to have had his first accident before his first fare.

A week later, in a different vehicle, on a very hot New York summer day, I sat stuck in traffic with a Wall Street-type riding in the back seat, fancy suit and reading the *Journal*. It was sweltering and the cab had no air conditioning. The traffic was unbelievable. We were headed crosstown in the mid-60s at lunch hour and it was taking four or five lights to travel just one avenue. I was dying, but my fare just sat and read his paper. We were totally stopped and hadn't moved for minutes. Suddenly, I noticed a plume of gray smoke coming out from under the dash. I turned to Mr. Wall Street and said, "Excuse me, Sir, but the cab is smoking, and I think you may want to jump out."

He looked past me at the dash, where flames now started to appear and yelled, "What are you going to do? Go down with the ship?" We both jumped out, and watched the damned thing going up in smoke. I ran up the block to a phone booth, and again called the garage, all the time with my eyes glancing behind me as the flames enlarged. "Help! This is Gary Lotner, one of your drivers. My cab just caught on fire and is going up in flames!!!"

Again the dispatcher at the other end partially covered the mouthpiece as he bellowed, "Harry, 'nother one!"

Despite these episodes, I made relatively good money as a cab driver. While I was terrified to cut drivers off or veer across multiple lanes of traffic like the more seasoned cabbies (maybe if you were going to be a cabdriver, it paid to be a moron), I was terrific at working tips. My specialty was elderly Jewish women. I would spend the entire ride telling them how I was starting medical school in a few weeks—at Einstein, a Jewish medical school, no less—and the tips rolled in. Once I got a twenty-dollar tip on a $1.75 fare. They also gave me the phone numbers of several of their daughters and granddaughters, amazingly all of them beauties, brilliant and with wonderful personalities.

My cab-driving career was to be a short one. I learned to live with the exploding, careening cars and I survived being robbed twice in the first four weeks. I even tolerated the famous Hollywood actor who stiffed me (and, no, I didn't bask in the glory of meeting him enough to make up for his lack of a tip). Eventually, it was the endless traffic, sitting and not moving, that got to me.

I began to have the same repetitive nightmare night after night—that I would be crawling on Madison Ave, not moving at all in outrageous traffic, my hot smelly cab wedged between a bus and a truck. Every night, I envisioned myself stuck there for hours on end with no break in sight. I would finally awaken from this dream, drenched in perspiration. After almost a week of the same horrible nightmare, I had a passenger in the car who identified himself as a psychiatrist. To pass time and eager to talk, I regaled him with the tale of my repetitive dreams.

He didn't even stop for a second before chiming in. "Your dream is painfully obvious." (Yeah, tell me.) "A bus is an obvious mother symbol; a truck is an obvious father symbol, and you're obviously having a great deal of conflict right now with your parents." He departed almost immediately afterward from his short trip, leaving me pissed off with his blithe explanation. I wanted to smack the guy. Not only was he a total ass to put this spin on my very transparent dream, but he was a heckuva lousy tipper to boot.

Sometime later, I thought about what he had said. I had recently moved back in with my parents a few weeks earlier, before I would start medical school. Prior to this, I had spent the past two years living in a fraternity house in Harlem in the bad old days. The house had been broken into on seven separate occasions, with me personally being mugged twice. Now at home, I was treated as an infant, with my parents yelling at me to make a bed or to wear socks on summer days bordering 100 degrees. I was fed up with the nit-picking living at home. Damned if the shrink wasn't right with his interpretation! I wanted to hit him even more.

My third taxi dropped an engine the next afternoon. Guess

that's better than no brakes or a fireball for a car. It was very clear to me that I wasn't destined to be carrying on the family tradition of driving a cab as my future career.

Chapter 3

"Vake" Me Up

I've always enjoyed humor and pride myself on finding amusement when things might otherwise be bleak. I've told so many stories over the years that sometimes, it's proven hard to pinpoint the border between actual truth and my embellishments. One story, relating to my earliest months in freshman year, has been repeated so often that I'd convinced myself I invented it. To my surprise, several years ago, at my 40th class reunion from AECOM, as we (very-much older) former medical students spent time catching up with each other, several old friends informed me that this story was real, not invented. The episode involved a memorable histology course lecture, the lecture itself being quite unremarkable. What was notable was my response, or lack thereof, and my friend's quick reaction.

It was early in the first year in schooling, and our lecturer was a famous, very elderly gentleman, who was undoubtedly brilliant but whose lecturing style was anything but so. There were several of his ilk teaching at the school. As mentioned previously, the board of Yeshiva University had established AECOM in large part as a response to the "Jewish Quota" that many medical colleges practiced before and after the Second World War, with significant caps on the number of Jews admitted. The situation in some ways is similar to the caps limiting Asian students today, although the number of Jews allowed at top schools then was far lower.

At the same time, there were also many brilliant European Jewish physicians and researchers who, after the War, found themselves displaced and unable to continue with their previous stellar careers. While I don't know this for a fact, it seemed that Einstein made it a mission to give some of these incredible people positions on the faculty. The problem was that some of them may have been intellectually stellar but were not skilled at teaching, at least not for American students in the raucous times of the Sixties and Seventies. Their demeanors were suited to a more formal and respectful group of European students of a bygone era. Often, their thick accents further complicated the situation.

Our histology professor fit into that category. He was a famous, elderly Eastern European with a thick Slavic accent, conducting a lecture in a large tiered hall, one with no assigned seats or seating plan. Histology, the study of healthy tissues that comprise the organs of the body, was one of the subjects that even early on, I knew I would never use during my forthcoming clinical career. While the material might be important, it was basically endless microscope work that pathologists (not clinicians) would perform at hospitals. I knew after medical school and testing, I was unlikely to personally ever perform this tedious work again. At times, the course seemed to be an endless series of microscope slides that, after a while, all seemed to look alike.

In the warm bowl-like classroom, where I sat a few rows above the lecturer's eye level, the combination of his monotonous, droning, deeply accented voice and the repetitive slides had worked their magic. I drifted off …. and awoke to raucous laughter. Apparently, there was a short exchange between the lecturer and my very close friend, Don Kotler. Don was an outstanding medical student who would go on to become a brilliant physician, the head of Gastroenterology at St. Luke's Hospital at Columbia for many years, and later the head of GI at our alma mater, Montefiore-

Einstein. He also had and still owns a fierce wit and great sense of humor.

As I dozed and my head fell, the little gnome-like professor (think a much shorter Mel Brooks with a much thicker Yiddish accent) apparently yelled at Don, sitting next to me, "Hey, You! Vake that man up!" And, Don, just before he hurriedly ran out the rear of the amphitheater, yelled back, "Hey, You! You put him to sleep. You vake him up!"

Chapter 4

But I Haven't Seen One Yet

Beginning the second week of medical school, we were placed in a recently started course with a pretentious name, something like the Family Familiarization Program. It was a new idea, well-intentioned in concept, although not necessarily so in execution. Traditional medical education consisted of two years of strict academics, teaching classes and labs such as anatomy (dissecting cadavers) and my personal non-favorite, the aforementioned histology (looking at endless microscope slides of normal body tissues). This meant that it was only in the third and fourth year of medical school that students would traditionally begin to have contact with real living patients.

The Family Familiarization Program was an attempt to introduce the student, at least in a small way, to live patients at an earlier stage with the goal of encouraging them to view patients in a larger context from a societal viewpoint, as part of a family unit. In an interdisciplinary program, students were assigned in pairs to follow an expectant mother in the last trimester of her pregnancy. Initially, they'd follow the woman at her Obstetric clinic visits, and then subsequent to delivery, the infant and mother together would be seen through the first several Pediatric clinic visits. The coordinators scheduled the visits in advance and notified the pair of students so they might attend. The patients were generally indigent, thus being seen in Clinic rather than having private physicians. Many of them in that area were Puerto Rican, speaking little English. Our roles as students were to be purely observational—we were barely a few weeks removed from college and lacked even the most basic introductory medical courses at this juncture.

The initial section of the course went well. Jeff Abrams and I had been assigned to a patient, Maria, a pleasant young woman who spoke no English (matched by our total lack of Spanish). Once a month, we would attend the OB clinic with her. Again, our role was to be that of observer—her actual care was provided by the OB resident physicians. I enjoyed the somewhat unexpected chance to meet a real patient this early in my medical career, even if language left me barely able to communicate with her directly. Not really able to help, Jeff and I spent much time smiling at Maria. She smiled back at us.

As the program progressed, ideally students were to be notified when their patient went into labor. I say ideally because this was somewhat subject to chance and circumstance. We were not the physicians who would be delivering the patient; there was no guarantee where we would be or that we would in fact be available at the appropriate time. Remember, this was many years before the advent of cell phones or personal computers, thus communication was uncertain. Accordingly, on what turned out to be Maria's delivery day, our freshman class was having comprehensive quarterly exams. As I sat in the large classroom completing a lengthy test, I glanced up and saw on the blackboard, someone had written, "Students Abrams and Lotner, report to Jacobi Hospital Labor Floor." It turned out that Jeff was still toiling over his test work, so I raced off by myself the half mile to the hospital, hoping to arrive in time for the delivery. I made it. Unfortunately.

In medicine, there is a standard rule of teaching in place for many years: See one. Do one. Teach one. However this rule had no application in the Family Familiarization Program. As noted, we, as raw first-year students, were there strictly to watch and learn. There would be no active participation.

As I entered the Maternity ward, Maria was already far into labor. A nurse instructed me to scrub and immediately rush into the Delivery Room, joining the OB intern and resident, both already actively at work. Delivery was imminent, the head crowning. I had never before been in an actual delivery room and had certainly never seen a live birth. I was understandably excited at the prospect. Suddenly spying me, Dr. Schwartz, the senior resident who had taken a liking to me over several clinic visits, noted my presence, turned and yelled, "Dr. Lotner, please come here and deliver this baby!"

In shock, I turned and said, "No! What are you talking about. I don't know how to do that. I've never even seen a delivery!" But Schwartz clearly liked me and was insistent, despite my protestation. "Lotner, get over here. This is simple stuff. Women have been delivering since long before there have been doctors or hospitals. All you do in an uncomplicated delivery is catch the baby and slow it down."

Again, my protests were fruitless. Thus, having never attended a live birth before and only three months into my medical schooling, I now found I was the starting "catcher" that day. I was very glad the patient understood so little English, understanding none of our exchange and was in her own little very painful world, repeatedly screaming, "Dios Mio!" I will admit I was excited; delivering the first baby I had always envisioned as one of the seminal moments in a medical career.

However, I was terrified as I assumed the "catcher's" position, trying to catch and slow, whatever that meant. The baby came within seconds, on the very next contraction. I did a great job with the catching but sadly, apparently failed miserably at the slowing. The baby had come out so quickly that Maria suffered what was termed a fourth-degree laceration. The area between the vaginal opening and the anus, roughly an inch long, is called the perineum. Maria had not had an episiotomy and the baby had thrust so vigorously that the force had torn into and beyond this area. The degree of laceration was assigned a termination of severity depending on how far it extended. The very worst case was a so-called a fourth-degree laceration and extended across the entire length of the perineum, actually into the anal mucosa and muscle. I knew none of this.

Amazed and thrilled that I had successfully delivered my first baby and having never been near a birth, my initial exhilaration soon turned to horror as I looked at the panicked faces of Schwartz, the resident, the OB intern and the nurse. Where I saw a thriving, screaming, squirming infant, they stared at the long laceration that I had not even paid any mind to. The obstetrics intern had never previously seen one of this magnitude and Schwartz, more senior, had just seen a single case in his several years of training.

Schwartz, who had insisted on my participation, was the one left suturing the damage, a repair that required over forty minutes of attention, softly muttering and cursing under his breath the entire time. Even though Dr. Schwartz placed me into a position that I should never have been in, I felt badly about Maria for several years afterwards and hoped that she had no residual discomfort. Part of me wished I had been slower like Abrams and had missed the delivery and part of me screamed, "I delivered a baby!"

See One. Do One. Teach One. But in the end, don't forget the See One!

Chapter 5

This is Sensitivity?

There was no way around it—medical school was a stressful experience. I remember people were running around like headless chickens, with much too much to study and much too much to do when we first began the semester. You could find students hanging out in the library all hours of the night. It was not unusual to see lights on beneath dormitory doorways at 3:00 in the morning.

Before one test, I remember a nervous little classmate, who we had nicknamed Duke, running up and down the hallway at 1:00 A.M. before a quiz, screaming that he could only remember 28 of the 31 arteries arising from the aorta. He ran reciting names of smaller vessels I had never even heard. He wailed banshee-like, in a high-pitched voice calling out names of obscure arteries. I remember how nervous his yelling made me, not even familiar with some of the vessel names he was screaming out.

The school had instituted some new programs to help with the tensions faced by medical students. One of them came in the form of a sensitivity training program, probably not so unusual in current days but certainly new in 1969, my first year in medical school. The faculty offered this to help us share with each other and provide channels to deal with our concerns and emotions. The class had been divided into groups of ten or 12 that would meet regularly in different discussion groups, exercises that were usually led by a trainee in the psychiatry department.

Our pod met regularly for two hours every other week and was semi-enjoyable at times. The group contained two or three of the closer friends I had established early that freshman year; a few others I was somewhat friendly with and several who I knew in passing but really had not spent much time with. I can't say I was big on opening up and letting my emotions flow out—I'm not sure most of us were, particularly the guys—but some of the discussions were relatively interesting and the sessions certainly more benign than many other activities we were involved in. The young shrink-in-training leader of our group was pleasant but uninspiring. Early on, I recall wondering how he would ever handle a true psychiatric emergency.

One negative fact about our mandatory group sessions was that we were just so terribly busy that finding the hours for these sessions sometimes meant taking time from our precious and constant studying or our little personal time, perhaps even from our very limited sleep.

This particular evening was one of those I would have preferred to be someplace else. Almost anyplace else. I was really tired to the point of being cranky—we had just completed a big quarterly test and all of us had been studying until the wee hours for many nights in a row. This afternoon we had had the test and I feared I had not done well (damned, there were 31 branches of the aorta!), and in the 90 minutes between test and sensitivity session, two of my friends had suggested we chill out and smoke a little weed. I went along with this but must say I didn't enjoy smoking pot as much as many of my friends—while sometimes it was great, too often it made me unacceptably tired or even paranoid. This particular evening, it did a little of both.

The session started under the direction of our young psychiatric intern and was pleasant enough to begin, even if not particularly exciting. After some inane chitchat, our leader said he felt it was time we moved on a little. Our group had been meeting for several weeks; we had gotten familiar with each other; we had started to open up a little. It was now time to start the more challenging work: digging deeper and really exposing ourselves more, baring emotions even if it was difficult for many of us.

He asked for volunteers to begin, a request not surprisingly met with a profound silence. After a brief period of failed cajoling, the leader picked one of the students, Bruce, to start things off. Phew! Glad it wasn't me; I really was starting to feel a little paranoid that evening. Bruce was one of those people that I mentally put into the category of minor friends. Seemingly a nice-enough guy, I didn't know him that well. We had sometimes been together in larger groups and always seemed to get on well enough.

The psychologist asked Bruce to pick someone in the group and just tell that person what he thought about them. Bruce looked around, carefully avoiding looking anyone in the eye and not making a choice. The leader persevered. Pick someone across from you, Gary for instance, and tell Gary what you feel about him. Naturally, my head and my defenses went up at this one, but Bruce smiled inanely and reiterated that there wasn't much to say. The leader went on, stressing the importance of us all opening up and sharing our feelings. "Come on, Bruce. Look Gary in the eye and just tell him what you feel about him."

So, Bruce looked over at me, as I presumably sat there with a benign smile. "Okay. Gary, I .... I hate you! I don't know why; I just hate you!"

What? From my semi-stupor, this was not right. What was this attack seemingly arriving from nowhere, that wasn't supposed to be happening? My head started to buzz, I felt like it was constricting around me. Our leader knew this response wasn't right! He tried to redirect Bruce, telling him that feelings like that weren't really helpful, particularly without anything to back them up. Did he want to elaborate on what he meant or say anything about anyone else?

"No," Bruce responded. "I'll stick with Gary. I'm not sure why but since the first day of school I think I've hated you and every time I see you I think I hate you."

My head was reeling, swimming in circles. I had been emotionally attacked. The session broke up shortly afterwards—or maybe I just left it mentally at that time. I staggered back to my dorm room and in a deep paranoid funk, lay there, staring at the ceiling for hours.

Given the insecurity I felt about myself at that stage of life, it took me weeks to get over that one. I never spoke to Bruce again during the remaining three years of medical school. Perhaps not surprisingly, I heard he became a psychiatrist.

I ruled psychiatry off my list of specialties to later pursue.

Chapter 6

Quick I Need A Scalpel

While medical school was almost all-encompassing, there was still a lot going on in the real world. The seemingly ever-enlarging Vietnam War could not be ignored. Nixon had expanded the war into Cambodia and young America had responded with protests. There was to be a March on Washington about six weeks into medical school, to be attended by hundreds of thousands of people. My very activist class was not to be left out.

While the class leaders were busily involved in the protest itself, some of us lesser lights took to more practical tasks. Don Kotler, my friend, and I took on the task of coordinating putting medical teams onto buses heading to Washington. From across the New York area, on fleets of rented buses, tens of thousands of college students headed down to Washington for the big march. Confrontations between students and police, perhaps even National Guardsmen, were to be anticipated.

As the distinct possibility for violence could not be ruled out, we envisioned pairs of medical students accompanying each of these buses and their unprotected students. In discussions, several of the other medical schools from the New York area had students who wanted to attend as well. Somehow, Don, I and a few others emerged in charge of the logistics of pairing a team of medical trainees from these various schools onto each and every bus. It involved a lot of calls and a lot of effort.

When the big day arrived, Don and I headed toward our own assigned bus, with a bunch of enthused and rowdy young college students, setting out for a very long ride. Donning our brand-new short white coats, we each brought our little bag of medical equipment, never before used, plus some extra supplies like bandages for those protestors who would be injured by police, or ophthalmic drops to wash out the eyes of those subjected to tear gas. Don, likewise a freshman (but with more experience around hospitals), looked enthused. I was terrified—what if someone seriously needed me? Heck, it was October of freshman year. I was taking a class in Embryology—what did I know about treating major injuries? At that stage of my career, it was a challenge to even remove a splinter.

After our arrival in Washington, and as the day wore on, two things were apparent: it was incredibly hot, and there was nothing going on from a medical viewpoint. Luckily, there were no major confrontations between police and protestors, no tear gas, no lacerations, wounds, or serious trauma. Don and I wandered through the dense crowds, sweating like pigs, wearing our now sweat-drenched and wrinkled white coats, toting our ridiculous medical bags. Students approached us several times seeking salt pills we didn't have, as the temperature continued to climb into the high nineties.

Finally, after wandering aimlessly and with a sense of relief but also of disappointment, through the crowd, we could hear a young woman screaming as she came running towards us. "Doctors! Doctors!" As she approached, she blurted, "You guys are doctors, right?" Well, sort of. "Quick, I need help. Do you have scissors or one of those scalpel things?!"

We did have a pair of scissors, but she didn't look injured nor did anyone around her.

"Oh, thank God! It's so hot, I'm dying in these jeans and want to cut them down and make them into shorts!" Which she proceeded to do, using my surgical scissors, while sitting on the grass at our feet.

And so ended my first day as an unsupervised doctor.

Chapter 7

Now That's a Mixer

I had been to a couple of mixers in college. But this one was to be nothing like them. To those uninitiated few, a mixer is a dance in which unattached male and female students would attend in a usually futile attempt at meeting their match of the opposite gender. I'm not sure that latter qualification would be included in a mixer in today's politically correct and gender-fluid world. Such affairs were uniformly hideous in my limited experience in college, a roomful of totally nerdy guys with ill-fitting clothes and eyeglasses, often with three pens in their shirt pockets, a total lack of social skills, and the dancing styles of epileptics in the midst of grand mal seizures. They would be joined in a large gymnasium by a mere handful of young women who likewise could not find dates. The women were usually allowed in for free and they still knew better than to come. Cool it wasn't. These were truly grotesque affairs.

So, I wasn't terribly excited when Einstein posters announced a mixer for the second week of school. However, seeing as it was being held one building over from my dorm on campus, and with nothing else to do, I wandered over with a friend. We were floored as we approached the building with the gym. A seemingly endless line of women stood by the door. Unlike college mixers, which sometimes had men paying small entrance fees and women entering for free, here the students (mostly men) were free and the outsiders (all women) paid. The line stretched on for over a block. Some of the women were gorgeous. What gave, I thought to myself with sheer excitement?

In those days, every Jewish male was programmed beginning in utero to be a doctor. While there were some exceptions to be made for lawyers or an occasional business tycoon, the career path was generally determined at birth. But how about the women? Why, of course they had to find a nice Jewish doctor to marry. And where did one go to find a nice Jewish doctor? To a largely Jewish medical school, of course! How simple a concept! I was staggered by the plentitude and pulchritude of the women who excitedly gathered before me. It had the makings of a feeding frenzy.

As I entered the gym where the dance was to be held, I noted that while many attractive women were already inside, there was a much greater talent pool still waiting outdoors in line. A relatively few of my fellow students stood around in the gym. The gender ratio was totally reversed from the two college mixers I had attended in the past. Now, for a lousy dancer like myself, what would be a good way to meet some of these women? I might not be a great dancer, but I had other ideas.

The building was shaped in an "L" arrangement. Out of sight of the dance organizers, around a corner and near the gym entrance, sat a long unused table. In my brain, a light bulb turned on. I pulled up the table, a chair, and drew some columns on a lined pad of paper. As the guests (read: women) came in and had to pass my table, I told them we were collecting information for future mixers, and asked them to enter their name, phone number and address. To my amazement, they eagerly lined up to comply. After a few minutes, impressed by the early success of my rather simplistic scheme, I realized the need for an important modification. I had no way of identifying the more attractive ones. Happily, another light bulb suddenly illuminated, and I was inspired to introduce a rating system, a one to five scale would suffice. But the plan was complicated by the fact that the women were doing all the writing. So, as the next girl entered her data, I asked her where she lived. She replied with "the Bronx," and I instructed her to enter a four next to her name. The next answered "Manhattan" and I asked her to place a five, the next "the Bronx," a three, and so on and so forth.

Finally, one cute young woman, a solid four, smiled wickedly at me and said, "I know what you're doing!" She sat down beside me, laughing as I proceeded to sign people up. Several names later, as my line stretched down the hall, now longer than the official admission line, other women started to catch on to my totally transparent rating scheme and balked at entering info. I thought my plan would come to a crashing end. At least until an unlikely source emerged to save me.

My new best friend, Laura, the first young lady who had figured out my shenanigans and now sat sitting and giggling beside me, realized my plight and immediately grabbed the pad. To my delight, she sat on my lap without a word, and took upon herself the task of enticing the new entrants to give their data to her, which she would duly enter. Women who balked at the obviousness of the ruse when I had been the one requesting information readily provided it to Laura, who entered the data herself, and supplied her own ratings, usually pretty close to mine. Laura would turn to me every once in a while, smiling, and say, "Queens. That's a four, right?" And I would look at a smiling, very attractive woman standing in front of us, and say, "No. Queens, that's a five." I eventually collected over 100 names of women with ratings and was able to supply a large part of the freshman medical school class with dates for the next two months. No, definitely not your typical City College mixer!

As for me, I should have stuck with the delightful and vivacious Laura but sadly opted for Susan T., a beautiful young woman who was one of the few five-pluses on the list. Dazzled by her rating, I somehow was oblivious to the geographical undesirability of a woman who lived 90 minutes away in Brooklyn and the even more general undesirability of a girl totally lacking a sense of humor. Hey, just because I was creative didn't mean I knew anything about picking women. I ended up with a total of three dates with Susan, while other freshmen were sometimes going out for months. At least I made a lot of friends out of my new classmates and gathered some well-earned respect.

Chapter 8

A Common Diagnosis

I woke up that morning with abdominal pains, a little nausea and a sense of dread. I knew what I had. In our second-year pathology class, we had recently covered appendicitis and now, ironically, just days later, I was developing all the classic symptoms. The pain had started centrally when I slept, but slowly seemed to shift to the lower right side, the classic progression of peri-umbilical pain gravitating to the lower right quadrant.

Since the pain was only moderate and the nausea not severe, I foolishly risked going to class rather than heading promptly to student health or the Emergency Room. Somehow I made it through the 9 A.M. Pharmacology class, but all I was able to think about was the worsening discomfort and whether my delay in seeking care might endanger me, risking a much more serious condition if my appendix were to rupture. Having no thermometer available, I felt my forehead. I thought it felt warm.

By 10:30, I knew that I had made a mistake. Both the pain and the nausea had intensified, and while earlier, I was not certain of the pain's migratory and telltale path, now I was sure. Or, at least, pretty sure. Reluctant to miss a class, I nonetheless headed to Student Health. As I waited in line, I saw one of my classmates, John, being waved into an office ahead of me. While I was sitting and filling out forms, I realized I had never actually been to

Student Health before. As I sat there, I spied another one of my classmates, Janice, who was leaving an exam room.

I asked her in passing if she were OK and she seemed embarrassed as she quickly nodded affirmatively and walked on. I was glad someone was feeling good because I was getting more and more ill the longer I waited. I thought of how much time I would likely miss from class if I needed an appendectomy and the subsequent surgical recovery. This was time I could ill afford to lose. As I stewed about my semi-desperate situation, John finally emerged from an office and I was called in behind him. As we passed, I looked at him and he quickly said he was okay and didn't have any major problems to report. I entered the room and a pleasant but harried young physician met me. She appeared just a few years older than me.

By this point, I'm pretty sure I was holding my abdomen. The young infirmary physician glanced over my forms and looked at me. She said, "Abdominal pain. I'm guessing it has migrated down to your lower right quadrant, correct?" That was a little rude. "Yes," I answered. "It started out periumbilically but now it's in the RLQ." I'd hit her with some of my recently acquired medical jargon.

"And I'm guessing that you feel warm and are nauseated." She was leading me, not asking me. No question about it. She may have initially seemed nice, but this was bordering on being down-right nasty.

She asked a few more questions, did an abbreviated exam, and asked me to come and join her by her desk which was half-covered by a large calendar in front of her.

Pointing to her desktop, she said, "Mr. Lotner, do you know what this is?"

Obviously it was a calendar but with a lot of information printed in each box. I looked more closely. It looked somehow familiar. She went on. "This is a list of the lectures in the second year Pathology class and the various disease entities that are covered on each date." I knew it looked familiar! "Do you see these little tick marks next to the disease names?"

I did. It was the usual check-off method, with lines added through the first four, then a cross hatch to make a group of five. There were a number of these next to various diagnoses.

She went on, "If you will notice, on Tuesday, your class had a lecture on Appendicitis. Do you see the tick marks next to that diagnosis?" Hard to miss. There were nine. I would complete the second box for a total of ten. I suddenly had a different kind of sick feeling in the gut and the realization where this was going.

"Don't feel too badly. Your friend just before you was number nine, and my colleague across the hall, who I just ran into between patients, said he just had seen a young woman in your class who was number seven on his own calendar." No wonder Janice had looked embarrassed, just as I was undoubtedly looking now.

I became aware that my pain had rapidly subsided. So had my self-esteem.

She went on a little kindlier, "I could draw some blood to be sure. Do you think we should?" I replied it probably wasn't necessary, I was feeling better and would come back later if it seemed worse. She thought that a good plan. We both smiled, me sheepishly. She added, "Don't be too harsh on yourself. Last year, when the course covered urinary tract infections, almost every female student in the class was here within a week."

As I walked out, I saw a friend David sitting there, looking a little queasy. I didn't ask him what was wrong. Instead, I turned and said, "David, just leave. Now! Trust me, you'll be fine."

Chapter 9

Best Blind Date Ever

Don Kotler, my closest friend in medical school, had a problem. His 18-year-old cousin was visiting in town, and Don and the girl he recently started dating, Barbara (now his wife of nearly 50 years), needed someone to go out with her. As you could imagine, I was the victim. He told me his cousin (I'll call her Katie) was fun and he thought she was "cute." He was right.

What would we do for the evening? We tossed out the usual activities—grabbing pizza, a movie, maybe a club. But I finally turned to Don and said, "I know what we need to do. Let's head for the airport and act out tender departing love scenes." Where I came up with this absurd idea I'll never know. We'd grab the girls along with a couple of suitcases, head to LaGuardia Airport—and then wing it from there. Don looked at me like I was crazy, but then, smiling wickedly, agreed to my insane scheme only after a couple of minutes arguing.

The weekend came, and much to my surprise, Katie was indeed very cute, effervescent and very much fun. She was up for any of the plans we chose for the evening. To my everlasting gratitude, she did not bat an eyelash when informed of the evening's itinerary, somehow deciding that this ridiculous scheme made perfect sense. We threw a couple of rags into some time-worn bags and made it to LaGuardia in record time. For today's readers, accustomed to beautifully large well-lit airports, amazing crowds and the ever-annoying TSA with check-ins, bag-checks, body-checks, strip-searches and shoe-removals, the facility and tenor of 1970 was far different. LaGuardia was a smaller, seedier place, seemingly dating back to the Wright brothers, and it was possible to park close to the terminal and walk directly in, heading right up to any gate one might choose.

Our first activity had us walking down a long corridor between gates until we found one where a crowd huddled awaiting a flight. With suitcases at our sides, Don and I loudly told our respective women how much we would be missing them, then hugging and kissing (yes, Katie definitely was up for anything) and doing this so noisily that it was hard for the actual passengers not be drawn into our little drama. As we departed, we received many appreciative smiles and even a few claps from the assembled masses.

The evening was proceeding quite nicely, thank you, but the setting was not quite right. Suddenly, I had another flash of inspiration (any more flashes and I think Don would have killed me). So, we waited until we found a flight that was just landing. As the passengers began to disembark and make the long walk to the baggage claim area (no significant overhead bins in those days so almost everyone had luggage to pick up), Don and I ran ahead by a few minutes and parked ourselves by the carousel for the appropriate flight. This was where a crowd awaited most of the arriving passengers. Positioning ourselves centrally among the expectant throng, the two of us started talking to each other in comically loud voices. Using tones that would have roused the dead, we described how excited we were to be awaiting our young and brand-new wives.

The annoying and conspicuously loud story line: we had each only been married for a few months, had never previously been apart from our beautiful and wonderful brides who were now returning from a trip to their families. Were we excited! By the time we finished embellishing in loud tones that could have filled an auditorium, everyone in the waiting throng was probably excited for us as well.

Shortly, the passengers started to arrive, each greeted by a loved one or friend. After a few moments, in strolled our two extremely animated and attractive "brides," looking as excited to see us as we were to see them. Don and I let out loud whoops, the girls came running and flung themselves into our arms. The next minutes included fierce hugs, passionate kisses, loud professions of love and finally, each of us picking up our respective woman and spinning them around. People had to clear space to give us room. The crowd loved it! Isn't love grand? And finally, to top it off, my last inspiration: I looked at the very attractive Katie in my arms (too bad she was only 18!) and yelled, "Wait a second! You're not my wife."

Don looked at Barbara, yelled something along similar lines, and we proceeded to swap partners, repeating the same charade, although not quite as passionately or as long. When we finished, someone in the crowd started clapping, the applause picked up by most of the throng. We picked up our suitcases, and departed, turning once to offer small bows. Our first standing ovation!

The evening would have been perfect even if it had ended there, but we had one more airport touch that made it even better. Having left the baggage area, we decided we were hungry and searching around, found the one tiny, jammed coffee shop that existed in the terminal. Small and seedy, it was the only restaurant and very crowded. There were no tables, only stools along an undulating counter. When some other patrons left, we were lucky to grab four seats together. We were all somewhat exhilarated by our unexpectedly terrific evening and a little full of ourselves.

I glanced to my right and in the adjacent stool, found a young GI in uniform, who in contrast to our exuberance, looked like the world had just collapsed on his head. Now, this was a difficult time for the country politically and for military personnel in particular. The extremely unpopular Vietnam War raged on, dividing the country to its very core, and if it was hard on the general populace, it was much worse for our poor military personnel. They were doomed to fight a war that most did not believe in, half a world away, against an enemy they did not intrinsically hate.

The war was waged in ways that our superior military was not adept at, and soldiers were killed or maimed in jungles or tunnels or rice paddies. Then they would return home to find that they were hissed and screamed at by their fellow countrymen, not looked at as heroes or warriors. They were seen as criminals, even murderers. No, this was not a war akin to the World War two decades earlier with clear-cut good guys and bad guys. Our military was treated as the heroes they were during that battle. This was the opposite and, at least to me, it was shameful.

My own feelings were very different. While I was very much against the war, I was always in support of our soldiers. They were risking their lives for our country. Most had been drafted, not volunteered, and I was well aware that but for the grace of God (and for exemptions for medical students), that could have been me. I started chatting with the GI, whose name was John, a sadly appropriate name. I inquired about his story. I commented that he looked pretty stressed and guessed from his dour appearance that he must be heading out on a military tour. Surprisingly, he told me he was actually returning home but the situation was even worse—he had just finished a year-long tour, one that had been terrible with several of his friends dying, and he was finally returning home, looking forward to seeing his fiancée, the only thing that had served to keep him going much of the time. Finally, just before his departure from Nam, he had received a letter from the fiancée breaking it off ("Dear John," I'm sure) and, even worse, she was now with one of his ex-buddies. He was heading home, all right, but was heartbroken, not gleeful. What a homecoming!

The four of us listened to his tale, tears brimming in eyes, and shortly after he asked us what we were doing in the airport. I'm not sure who started the crazy story/charade that followed (probably Don) but between the two of us, we started on a tale and it just kept expanding and feeding on itself. We were the managers of our university bowling team ("what school?"—um, Michigan State, Um, University of Michigan, um, yeah, that's what I meant, University of Michigan, and yeah, of course, colleges have bowling teams) and we were going to a match to catch up with the team in some city.

These lovely young women were not only our girlfriends, but they just happened to be the cheerleaders for the team—no, the assistant managers, the girls added, getting into the farce. John, not surprisingly, was more than a tad skeptical about the whole concept of college bowling teams and cheerleaders or managers or whatever and we began to improvise further, elaborating on the proper techniques of bowling. I got up and in the middle of this very cramped little coffee shop, started to demonstrate the proper form of releasing a bowling ball, swooping down as I finished and almost knocking over some poor schnook with his coffee.

Not to be outdone, Don arose and started to expound on the virtues of the four-step approach versus the three, repeatedly demonstrating ridiculous techniques and lunges amidst the swirling customers. The girls, having no idea what they were doing, got into the act. They looked markedly cuter than us as they also exhibited various techniques. The shenanigans went on for another few minutes. Most of the restaurant, including our previously morose buddy, loudly cracked up. Before we left, John almost hugged us goodbye, adding that before that evening, he wasn't sure he would ever smile again. Go, Michigan!

We returned to our dorm, Don off with Barbara and I with Katie. While I pondered if I should try to kiss her goodnight (this young woman who I had kissed so passionately to a crowd in an airport) Katie was suddenly on top of me, leaving no doubt that mere kissing was not what she had in mind. I was sorely tempted—she was very pretty and very well proportioned and left no doubt as to her intentions. But somehow, part of my brain won out and I kept remembering that she was my best friend's cousin and only 18. (I would long regret this act of presumably misplaced nobility.)

Yup, no doubt about it—best blind date ever!

Chapter 10

You Haven't Died Yet, Have You?

At the time I attended Medical School, there was a huge disconnect between book and classroom learning. The educational journey eventually progressed and moved on to actual clinical experience with live patients. Sometimes, even the brightest students could have difficulties with that transition.

We were mid-second year students, taking a course in physical diagnosis. In that class, we learned a unique set of skills: what to look for in examining the skin or in viewing the ear or the retina of the eye, what to listen for when examining the heart, what a normal abdomen should feel like, and how to palpate an enlarged liver. For each of these, you had to learn the "normal" (i.e., the usual heart sounds and variations); the various "abnormals" (i.e., what a heart murmur or gallop sounded like); and how to use a variety of instruments (i.e., which end of the stethoscope went in the ear, or how to use an otoscope to effectively examine the ear while not injuring the patient, or immobilizing a screaming infant).

After learning these skills in a theoretical fashion, we would next try them on some willing victims, initially the fellow student sitting next to us in the classroom. This alone could cause some embarrassment ("Sorry, Jonas, I didn't mean to give you a nosebleed while pushing too hard with the nasal speculum"). Even then, at least there was the sense of joint purpose and knowledge that we were all novices in this together. The training was unusual and some of the processes were quite difficult. For example, many physicians may have little skill at examining the retina of the eye or ascertaining anything other than gross abnormalities in listening to faint cardiac sounds.

We were introduced to live patients shortly thereafter, which proved to be a major complicating factor. Some of the problems were quite obvious from the patient's viewpoint. While everyone understood that doctors must be trained somewhere, almost no one was excited about being poked and prodded by groups of students who were so clearly beginners. This antipathy was multiplied when the students were released en masse in a city hospital ward where all the patients were quite ill and already unhappy.

We were equally apprehensive as the students performing the procedures. It had to be painfully obvious that we were the rawest of novices. We were to examine real patients with real findings (most of which we'd never seen or heard or felt in person previously), on people who were already sick and uncomfortable. We needed to interact with them, trying desperately not to make total fools of ourselves. Our first practice run wasn't easy and was even mentally terrifying for some.

The old city hospitals had large wards with two parallel rows of eight beds on each side, the only "privacy" afforded by flimsy sliding curtains separating them. Conversations were easily audible up and down the line. Our first experience in physical diagnosis was to be a limited one, with each student to perform a partial exam only on a particular organ system of the patient's body. For example, the treating physician might tell a student her patient had a gastrointestinal condition.

She would then be expected to ask her patient a few questions related to GI ("Do you have abdominal pains and if so, where?" Then, "Describe your bowel movements," etc.) and get on to the main task—feeling the abdominal organs, listening for bowel sounds, and perhaps checking other body parts for signs of gastrointestinal issues. It was not hard to imagine students being intimidated, particularly in these very earliest of patient encounters.

Our supervising doctor told me and the student next to me, David, that our patients both had cardiac issues. We were to focus exclusively on their heart exams by examining patients in adjacent beds. I was nervous. David, a very bright guy but exceedingly shy, looked like he was ready to die. He was sweaty and shaky as we walked in.

I gathered my thoughts for the minute before the instructor led us to our mutual bedsides, focusing on the different heart sounds I would try to listen for, the pulses I needed to feel, and also the few questions I was allowed to ask. Our most recent lecture in cardiology had been on aortic stenosis and flashing through my mind were the three cardinal signs we had learned for this condition: chest pain, syncope (fainting), and sudden death.

I tried to confidently introduce myself to my patient, a pleasant elderly woman, and make a little chitchat to break the ice. The patient smiled and was very pleasant, if less than excited. Just before I could start asking questions, from the next stall barely five feet away, we heard David almost cry out in a voice that was way too loud:

"Did you ever have chest pain?" A weak tremulous voice rasped, "No."

(Uh-oh, I think I know where this is going.)

More loudly, "Did you ever have syncope?" No answer. Dave was too far gone to realize the patient had no idea what syncope was.

(Oh, no. Don't do it, Dave. Don't do it. Come on, man, pull yourself together and don't do it!)

Oh, no, here it comes. He almost screamed it.

"Did you ever have sudden death?"

I really wanted the old guy to answer, "Yeah, Doc, I had that one several times and I hated it each time."

David would become an excellent physician in the future. Cardiology would not be his specialty.

Chapter 11

Let's Draw Blood

Before heading to medical school, I remember one of my old friends had murmured something to me about how he'd hate to be the first patient I ever drew blood on. He was probably right, but I soon was to find out something worse—to be the first student that other students would actually learn to practice on. You see, well before they would let us practice on patients, we had to practice on ourselves. I turned out to be reasonably good at it. My first partner, later to specialize in psychiatry, probably a good choice given his lack of proclivity in most things clinical, certainly was not.

The process of drawing blood consisted of jabbing a syringe into an engorged vein, then stabilizing the syringe with one hand and slowly pulling the plunger out with the other, the resulting suction syphoning blood into the syringe cylinder. That was the theory. And it generally worked very well. (This was the age before vacuum tubes simplified the process.)

We were divided into pairs. I teamed with Bob, a well-intentioned, goofy-looking guy with thick coke-bottle eyeglasses. By luck, I would draw his blood first. While we were both nervous, the procedure went smoothly. As instructed, I brought the needle in from a high angle and entered quickly (the pain nerve endings are all in the skin; going in with a shallow approach or going through the skin too slowly will markedly increase friction and the discomfort of the procedure), hit the vein speedily and drew the sample. Pretty easy. Now it would be my turn to lend an arm. I'm pretty good about pain and wasn't too concerned as we exchanged places. However, I could tell Bob was more than a little anxious as he approached me with his syringe, holding it at a weird angle like a Frenchman holding a cigarette in a World War II movie.

While I should have been the one sweating, Bob was the one with perspiration on his brow and lips, looking vaguely like he was about to pass out. After crossing himself, not a reassuring gesture for a Jewish kid, he came at me ever so slooooowly and at such a low angle that the sticking part seemed to go on forever. I feared I might eventually need sutures to close the resulting wound. Finally getting through the skin, with all my arm's nerve endings maximally firing, he somehow was not yet it my vein. While some people have notoriously small or fragile veins, that was not an issue for me. I have huge veins, sometimes called "ropes" or "rivers" by people drawing blood. Indeed, at a later stage in my career, when doing research and needing blood samples on a daily basis, I learned to easily draw my own blood without any difficulty.

I wasn't sure if Bob was going to make it. My arm was about to give out. He was advancing so tentatively that I did the only thing I could think of—I reached over with my own free hand, and hit him gently behind his elbow, the resultant pressure advancing the needle and forcing it into my vein! At last, we were in.

Now, all he had to do was draw the sample of a few milliliters of blood. Normally, as described above, he'd accomplish this by stabilizing the syringe and retracting the plunger. Inadvertently, Bob tried a different and distinctively less optimal approach. He tried holding his free hand with the top of syringe in place, advancing the needle further and further into my arm, creating a negative pressure that way. In short order, he was not only through the far side of the vein but I was fearful that if he kept advancing, the needle might soon appear through the far-side of my elbow, and in my fevered brain, I imagined potentially severing nerves, tendons and whatever other structures might be in its path. Fortunately, I was able to stop him before permanent damage was done and the resultant hematoma, or leakage of blood, soon to be the size of a small grapefruit, subsided shortly before the end of medical school.

That was unquestionably my most difficult experience with drawing blood. It was surprising how quickly, as a group, we would become proficient at this, a procedure fairly alien to everyday life. As we spent some time over the next few weeks intermittently drawing blood and starting IVs, I found that I, like many of my fellow classmates, had developed an obsession with veins. I would look at my own arms, imagining fifty different places I might start an IV in a pinch.

Similarly, while bored in epidemiology class, I would find my concentration wandering and focusing on the arms of my fellow students, again imagining the optimal places to insert a catheter. I remember one time a friend caught me apparently staring at Lois, one of the more attractive female students in our class. Seeing my attention, he said something about Lois being quite the looker. I replied, "That she is. But in honesty, what I've been staring at have been her veins."

The culmination of this phase came a few weeks later for me on a New York subway. I found myself seated across from three burly muscular young Puerto Rican men. They probably were construction workers; the one in the middle, clad only in a muscle shirt, had a physique worthy of Mr. Universe. This guy had arms the size of a rhinoceros's legs, each with an extensive network of veins that would have made the Nile River envious. As the subway slowly moved past several stations, my gaze traced the meandering path of his veins, mentally drawing blood here, inserting IVs there. Man, those arms were heaven for a medical student or aspiring phlebotomist.

My reverie was interrupted when the three of them suddenly

arose and slowly paced the few steps between us, now towering over me. "Hey, señor. You got a problem with me, man?" It was Mr. Universe, looking even larger now that he stood over me. This guy was definitely not happy. Oh, crap, what were they thinking?

"No, friend. I was just admiring your arms." Had I really said that?

"My arms, Hombre?" They were moving in closer now, definitely inside my personal space. I tried to stand; their closeness forced me back down. "You think I'm a junkie, man? Do I look like a f**king junkie to you?"

Ah, now I knew where we were going. I tried to laugh, unsuccessfully I'm sure. "No, friend. I'm actually in medical school and we're just learning to draw blood. I've been drawing blood all morning and every patient seemed to be a fat little old lady with terrible veins. Then I saw your arms, which are the best arms I've ever seen for drawing blood. I kept thinking about ..." I tried to keep talking, hoping I was getting through.

The train came to a jolting stop in the next station. They looked skeptically at each other and back at me, as they slowly exited, all with swaggering gaits.

A close one. I can still remember that guy's veins a lifetime later.

Chapter 12

Fred, Fred, Has Anyone Seen Fred?

We began anatomy lab in the second year of medical school. It is certainly one of the memorable moments in a student's medical career. The idea of actually dissecting the cadaver of a real human being is a difficult one for many, although necessary in the training of physicians. Many students who have had little experience with actual human bodies prior to this point anticipate the course with a degree of dread and unease. Understandably, they are unsure how they will respond and react to such a remarkable experience.

My first afternoon of the course came with major anxiety, as we entered a rather gruesome room. Grayish cadavers rested upon several slab-like tables, accompanied by the formidable, overwhelming odor of formaldehyde. The professor divided our group into teams of four students each. We were then introduced to the bodies in front of us. Many of the cadavers had been homeless individuals whose bodies remained unclaimed, while others were donated by their families. We were instructed that we should think of the cadavers as people, not objects, and to treat them at all times with respect. I would have to say that at the time, it would have been far easier psychologically to be cutting into an abstract object than a fellow human being. To help ease our discomfort, we all took to nervous joking and to naming our bodies. Our nameless cadaver somehow became Stanley; at the next table, my friend Neil's foursome anointed their body as Fred.

The student groups seemingly experienced different degrees of discomfort that first day. Some, like that of my friend Don with significant previous experience in operating rooms and hospitals, jumped right in with enthusiasm and with no qualms. Others, such as one with three female students at the next table, were considerably more squeamish and made little progress that first day. I was not certain of my own reaction and was happy that after initially reeling at the overpowering formaldehyde odor, was moments later able to concentrate on the abdominal dissection with little discomfort and much more concern over our seeming inability to identify appropriate structures. The two-hour class passed quickly and was less discomforting than I had expected. My major unease seemed to come with the memory of the nauseating formaldehyde stench, not the actual dissection of the body.

By the second class, I realized I would make it through anatomy with at least physical ease (if not the best knowledge of anatomy—a surgeon I'm not!). When I entered the lab, my first thought was again with the formaldehyde odor. But after a few minutes, as I stared at Stanley's newly exposed liver, I was suddenly overwhelmed with pangs of hunger and an inexplicable urge to run to the cafeteria and grab a roast beef sandwich. Wow! Talk about unanticipated results.

The class proceeded over the next several weeks, as we familiarized ourselves with dissecting the organs and structures of the abdomen, chest and extremities. I was amazed at how much we learned of the body in a short period of time. In fact, I was a little disappointed that our class was somewhat abbreviated. In earlier years, medical training had always taught anatomy very extensively, to a degree that was far more detailed than required for many medical specialties. For my year, using a "revised" curriculum, the course had been shortened and we skimmed areas considered less essential. In particular, I remember that we spent only one session on the very complicated structures of the arms and legs.

While I appreciated the brevity at the time (a lot less to memorize!), years later, I would come to rue this abbreviated study. On occasion as a pediatric intern, when staffing the Emergency Room, a parent would bring a child in with a complaint that she had hurt her knee, pointing to the affected area. I felt like saying, "Yup, that's the knee all right." In retrospect, that extra knowledge would have been much appreciated.

After a while, we had all formed a type of weird bonding with our respective cadavers. At this point, most of us appreciated the cadavers for what they were and for their role in our education, having imbued them with personalities that they probably never had. At the onset, I could never have imagined a sense of attachment to a dead body. But there was no doubt that we developed these ties, nonetheless. Thus, it was with chagrin that halfway through the course, upon entering one afternoon, while all tables held their bodies, one table remained conspicuously empty. Neil and his group entered, looked at their empty slab, and cried, "Fred! Fred! Where's Fred?"

It turned out that after several months of absence, the family of Fred (actual name unknown) had discovered that this itinerant vagrant had been missing longer than usual, somehow learned his whereabouts and had claimed the remains of his largely dissected body (minus several organs and irrevocably imbued with the unmistakable and presumably permanent odor of formaldehyde).

As Neil and his group morosely joined our quartet dissecting Stanley, their sense of loss was palpable. Fred, we thank you for your service and hope you're doing well, wherever you are.

Chapter 13

My First Solo Patient

Harvey said to me, "Lotner, today's your big day. I'm going to let you have your own patient."

Harvey was Harvey Aiges, the pediatric intern I was assigned to in my core Pediatric rotation as an early third-year medical student. Harvey was a great intern and would go on to become a terrific and respected pediatrician, the Chief of Pediatrics at a major New York medical institution. Although I hadn't decided for sure, I strongly suspected I would go into Pediatrics myself. Thus, this was a rotation I eagerly awaited. I wanted to do well, and it was important to my future success to excel.

Compared to some of the other interns, some of whom gave their medical students tons of scut work (drawing blood work, running down lab tests and X-rays in the days before computers), no matter how busy he was, Harvey always made time to teach and wanted his students to love pediatrics as much as he did. While many interns never gave students their own patients, Harvey was known to do just that if he thought you were capable.

To explain: the intern is the actual physician and the patient is his responsibility. Teaching medical students is certainly a goal, but definitely a secondary goal. The intern typically sees the patients, with students in tow. After the intern would take the patient's history and perform a physical exam, the students might then get to examine the patient. In a pattern I tried to adapt for myself two years later when I became the intern, Harvey would allow students to work up some patients before he did, presenting the patients to him with the student's assessment, and only later would he, the intern, go in and do it all again. It usually meant more work and time for the harried interns—the delay might cause them to get even farther behind because the new students were just learning and very slow in their performance. However, it was an invaluable opportunity for the students to advance their skills and thinking. Certain pediatric interns on the ward never let their students take over their own cases, not willing to be slowed down further with their overwhelming schedules. However, I was lucky to have been assigned to one known to eagerly do this. I was quite honored that Dr. Aiges deemed me competent enough to do so and even mores that he chose me to be the first student in that particular rotation who would be offered the opportunity. Honored, but nervous as hell.

"Don't look so worried, Lotner. I'll look for an easy patient for you to see the first couple of times. I'll take the hard ones."

Sure, Harvey, and who's nervous? Why, instead of just reading books and playing at doctor, I'd be taking care of a real live child, sick enough to be admitted to a major hospital. Worry? No, not me.

Harvey stuck his head in early that afternoon as he headed to the emergency room. "Lotner, we've got two kids being admitted simultaneously. I'm going down to the ER to get mine—kid's supposed to be pretty sick. You've got a bean in the ear coming up."

A bean in the ear? A BEAN in the EAR? What the heck? Harvey quickly explained that this five-year-old had shown up in the ER because his brother apparently shoved a bean in his ear. Beans tend to swell up when lodged in the ear canal and downstairs, the ER resident was unable to retrieve it with his otoscope and cuvette, so the kid was to be admitted for a very short surgery, which basically meant an ENT surgeon would fish it out under anesthesia. The procedure was minimal, probably to last no more than 30 seconds, but at Einstein Medical School, which had a superb Pediatric department (the chairman, Lewis Fraad, had written THE pediatric textbook), it was a rule that all elective surgical admissions had to be first seen by a pediatrician to be cleared for surgery.

Harvey explained the kid was apparently to go to the operating room very shortly, so all I needed to do was take a minimal history, a very quick physical, and then write a short note saying it was OK for him to have surgery. "You don't need to spend more than fifteen minutes on this!" Yeah, right. And that was it. It seemed very unlikely to me that I was going to risk killing my first patient. And with that, Harvey was off to see his own "real" patient in the ER.

A few minutes later, the nurse told me that my patient and family had arrived and were sitting in an exam room. I went in to introduce myself. In doing so, an overwhelmed and uncomprehending Puerto Rican mother, a bawling five-year-old, his laughing four-year-old (the notorious bean shover) brother, and a shrieking three-year-old sister met me. In her arms, the rather stoic and uncomprehending mother held an 18-month-old of indeterminate gender, who cried constantly and spit up frequently. The three kids who weren't being held, including my patient, were rambunctious, in constant motion. The room vaguely resembled a World War II movie I had recently seen.

All right, well, let's get on with it. History first. Ah, turns out Mom speaks no English. Not a great start and this could be a problem. I know Harvey said I didn't have to do a full history, but certainly I had to obtain SOME history. I did know a few words of Spanish but not a chance to remember any between the yelling, the crying, the laughing, and the damned four-year-old now kicking me in my shin.

Well, maybe I'll do the physical exam first and hopefully a Spanish-speaking nurse will show up later and I'll get a history (and maybe I'll win the lottery, too). Better get the ears out of the way since that was the source of today's problem. However, this kid was all over the place and I didn't think I could actually see in his ears without a nurse to hold him down, and the mother was holding el bambino, who had just vomited on her blouse. Instead, I figured I would start with something that seemed easier, listening to the chest with my stethoscope. The kid was having none of this, however, crying louder when I came near and flinging his arms all over the place. He managed to kick my little black bag off the gurney with all the new and expensive instruments that I had been forced to buy just a few months earlier. No time to deal with that right now. All right, kid, I've got this. I think if I can get my right arm around you then I can use my left hand to put my stethoscope somewhere near your chest. Of course, I wouldn't hear anything meaningful with all the screaming. But I would try.

Oh, damn it. I saw Mr. Four-Year-Old Bean-Pushing Laughing Boy out of the corner of my eye pick up my portable sphygmomanometer (blood pressure cuff) and start to hightail it down the corridor to the right. As I gave up any pretense that I would actually examine this kid's chest and took off after him, I saw three-year-old sister shrieker grab my expensive otoscope/ophthalmoscope and head in the opposite direction. I gave chase, glancing briefly at the vomit-covered mother, whose expression had remained unchanged. These kids had grabbed the tools of my trade. For a very broke medical student, they had cost a lot of dinero.

The four-year-old was fast and squirmy. I found him diving into small places and laughing at slow medical students running in ill-fitting white jackets. Eventually I got the little bugger and got my cuff back. Now where was Sister Shrieker? I had seen her general direction but lost track. She had the real expensive equipment—screw the patient! Now, where was she? I searched and searched, looking on all the wards on the floor, and eventually had to accept ignominious defeat. My first patient, and I had already lost my medical equipment.

I slithered back to the exam room to complete my task somehow—only to find it empty! No patient, no bean shover, no siblings, no mother. Just the scattered contents of my medical bag, minus the otoscope. I ran to the nursing station frantically. I had to do something with this kid so he could have his surgery. The nurses seemed to be laughing as they told me the surgeon had come up for the patient, decided he couldn't wait any longer, and whisked the kid off to the OR. And no, they hadn't seen the young kleptomaniac with the otoscope.

I sat there dejectedly for quite a while. What a total fiasco! Eventually, the unflappable Dr. Aiges appeared, smiling broadly as he put his arm around me. "Harvey, I screwed up big time. I never saw the kid, didn't do any of the stuff I was supposed to do, don't even know if the kid was able to have surgery without me writing a note. Heck, I don't even know which ear the bean was in." I looked at the ground as I talked.

"Don't fret, Lotner. The surgeon was passing by and grabbed me in the ER and I did a quick exam on the kid, wrote the note, and the kid has had his surgery and he has already been sent home.

"And the little girl was playing with this and I suspected the otoscope was more likely yours than hers, so you can have this back."

I thanked him for saving my ass. As he turned away, he looked at me and said, "Right."

Right, I asked. Right? What's right?"

"Right ear. You wanted to know where the bean was."

It felt good to have had a patient of my own. Maybe tomorrow, he'd let me move on to a tougher case.

Chapter 14

Get to the Back of the Line

I had a short rotation in Dermatology as a senior medical student. I was at a clinic at the Jacobi Municipal Hospital that tended to be markedly less busy than some of the other nearby clinics. From where I sat in an exam room with a flimsy curtain that never quite closed, I could look out at the waiting area to the very busy surgical clinic across the hall.

One day, as I glanced out, I watched a small drama unfold. The line to the surgical clinic was very long with a wait time of several hours to be seen. There was also a long line of standees just waiting to sign in. The patients in this line were all bored and tired, some appearing uncomfortable and many appearing angry. The man who caught my eye was an elderly, frazzled, thin man toward the back of the line, who looked exceptionally uncomfortable. As I occasionally glanced through the flimsy curtain in between my own Dermatology patients, this older gentleman, obviously in pain, sometimes held his hands over his belly, sometime over his mouth.

After 30 minutes or so, hands clasped to his mouth, he shuffled to the front of the line, past other waiting patients. As he got to the front, the battle-ax receptionist, a behemoth of a woman, looked up and yelled, "I saw you. You think I'm blind? You get back in the line where you belong. NO ONE gets ahead in MY line!" Unhappy and tottering, still holding his mouth, he returned to the rear. When I glanced over sometime later, he was in transition again, shuffling, mouth covered again by hands. This time he didn't even make it to the front. "I see you! Get back in line! Everyone in my line waits their turn!" She almost bellowed.

It was only a few minutes later, when I saw him unsteadily shuffle forwards again, both hands firmly cupped over the mouth. He looked even paler than before, if that were possible. As he got to the sign-in desk, Old Battle-Ax looked up and as her eyes widened with rage, flecks of blood appearing in her white conjunctiva and as she rose to bellow......

He removed his hands from his mouth and propulsively vomited almost a liter of blood over the just-vacated desk, splashing on the hem of her dress and all over the floor.

I thought the enraged receptionist was going to kill him, but after a second, her shoulders shrugged, and she cried in resignation, "Okay, okay, you're next!"

Chapter 15

Not the Typical Jewish Girlfriend

Joan Leung* was my girlfriend for the first half of medical school. She was a lovely biochemistry graduate student at Einstein and hailed from Boston. Freshman year, we lived in the same dormitory building. Joan was hard to miss; petite, exotic, Asian, and lovely in a building whose other residents were mainly nerdy Jewish medical students or unkempt anti-war student activists with scruffy beards. Joan spoke the most perfect English in a soft melodious voice, without any trace of an accent, neither Chinese nor Bostonian.

I met her one day while she played classical pieces on a piano in the dormitory lounge. I started talking to her about her choices of music and we soon fell into a long easy conversation. Months later, when I asked her how we ended up together (I knew she was quite popular with many of the male students, several of whom had asked her out), she told me that I had seemed quite different to her from the first time we met. As an example, she said that the first time we had chatted, I had talked to her about a normal topic (music), whereas 97 percent of people she encountered told her how much they liked Chinese restaurants and the other 3 percent talked about Chinese laundries, a bygone institution of the times. Even then, she disliked my apparently thick New York accent. Somehow, during our time together, she managed to get me to lose it. Losing a New York accent while living in New York is not an easy thing to do. I'm grateful for that as well.

As our relationship progressed, eventually our families became more of an issue. I think her family was about as excited about me as mine was about her. For Christmas break that first year, with nothing else to do, my friend Don and I took up Joan's offer to visit with her family in the Boston suburbs. We stayed for several days. Her several sisters, all cute and giggly, loved Don and me. As to her more inscrutable parents, who were harder to read, not so much. One of the highlights was a family feast, hosted by her father. His family apparently came from minor Chinese royalty and had fled that country during Mao's Communist Revolution in the 1940s, settling in Boston, where her father now owned what Joan modestly described as the best Chinese restaurant in Massachusetts.

Understandably, the trappings for the feast were all hosted at the family establishment. In a large private room, with 40 or more relatives and friends attending, Don, Joan, and I sat as honored guests at the head table along with our hosts as everyone looked on. As is the custom at traditional Chinese events, the guest has the honor of being served the main courses first as everyone awaits their hopefully laudatory reactions. When the piece de resistance arrived, the entire party looked on expectantly watching Don and I take our first samples of the delicacy: cold jellied pig's knuckles. What a treat for the two Jewish boys. Heck, what a treat for anyone. Yummm. I looked at Don, he at me, as we both bravely placed a knuckle into our mouths...and tried desperately not to spit it out or immediately wretch. Looking at 40 sets of eager eyes, we both learned that it is indeed possible to fake a smile despite an overpowering feeling of nausea.

An even more memorable snapshot of the visit was backing Joan's car out of the driveway. The three of us had driven from New York to Boston in Joan's new sporty little red Renault with manual transmission, a fancy looking car that I knew nothing about. At the time, I was still driving my green and white ex-New

York City taxicab and had never driven anything other than automatic transmission. Joan was pretty good with this little roadster and its five-speed manual. When we arrived at her house, we drove it straight into her family's garage—not an easy trick. The home was located on a steep street, Parker Hill Avenue, and it was necessary to head down a narrow, almost vertical drive into the garage, adjacent to the family kitchen. She had negotiated this with nary a concern. After meeting her family, as the three of us left for a ride and headed for the garage, Joan's father unexpectedly came running out of the house, yelling at Joan in Chinese. Don and I were perplexed, Joan visibly embarrassed.

We quickly figured out why he was upset. Despite Joan's expertise in driving her car, despite the ease with which she had descended the driveway, her father now did not trust her to back out the steep drive. He insisted on doing this himself. So, while the three of us dutifully climbed out of the car, Don and I joking, Joan seething and turning many shades of crimson, Mr. Leung proceeded to get into her car. Then, while turning his head to the rear to look as he attempted to back out, he somehow found himself in drive, not reverse—and accelerated forward into the front wall of the garage. Searching desperately for the brake, he instead hit the accelerator, and by the time he had stopped, the car was nestled halfway through the wall into his kitchen.

As he got out of the car, cursing quietly in Chinese, Don looked at him and said, "Gee, Mr. Leung. I sure bet you're glad Joan didn't do that!"

My own parents were little better. My car had essentially died at the beginning of medical school. I had no money to make the necessary repairs. In truth, with some loans and a small scholarship, I was paying my own way through medical school. I had resolved not to ask my parents for any money towards tuition or lodging. However, I would have appreciated some help with the car so that I could enjoy my occasional time off. Early on in freshman year, my mother spoke for the both of them.

"Your father and I have talked it over. We think it's important that you spend your time in medical school studying, not socializing. So we've decided you really don't need a car the first year." Well, thanks very much, folks.

Several months later, now that Joan and I were dating, the conversations with my parents took on a very different tone. My mother would now call and say things like, "Have you got your car fixed yet? Your father and I can't understand why you don't have a car. We think it's important that you get out and meet people. "

Even more impressive were the conversations that took place after Joan and I decided to move together into my room at the dorm. The dorm was indeed an impressive structure. Seven stories tall, with an elevator that frequently didn't work (another story there), I resided on the top floor in a room that was 14 feet long but scarcely seven feet wide. If you fell down, you wanted to do it lengthwise.

Our furniture consisted of a narrow single bed, a small desk, a tiny refrigerator and some hooks for clothing. Somehow, given its tiny size, it managed to feel even smaller than it was. Handsomely appointed in cinderblock painted an institutional green, and with blue-painted fruit crates serving to hold my clothes and books, the room wasn't as cheerful as this description.

Joan lived three stories below and when we decided to room together, she kept her own room for storage and studies. There was no way to adequately have two people fully contained in this tiny area. At $25 a month rent for each of us, money was no object.

When the phone rang, Joan answered since it was closer to her side of the narrow bed. The time was after 11 P.M. on a Saturday evening. My mother was on the other end, and Joan chatted pleasantly with her for a moment before handing me the phone.

My mother was nice enough for several seconds, until she got to the point. "Your father and I are a little concerned about you. We're worried that you don't seem to have much of a social life. While your studies are important, we think you should be getting out more. Have you met any nice women yet?" I thought to myself: well, not really, Mom, unless you count the one who just answered my phone near midnight and was lying semi-dressed next to me on a two-foot-wide bed. Aside from her, hardly anyone. My mom continued: "We're going to send you a check next week so you can get that car fixed. We've been telling you to do that for a while."

I did get the car fixed and one of the first things we did was to drive to Queens and have Joan actually meet my parents. I reasoned that perhaps if they actually met her and got to know her then things might be better. I remember Don laughing loudly and prophetically at the absurdity of this idea when I presented it to him.

My mother, of course, was very gracious as she always was. She was always sweet and charming with people, and Joan was lovely and personable. The first few minutes went surprisingly well. Then my father came downstairs in their small duplex. My father, for whatever reason, could preen himself in the small bathroom, for hours on end. Literally. Three hours was not unusual for him. No one knew what he was doing or why. No one asked.

I've never forgotten his first words as he came down, looked at my very cute Chinese girlfriend. He pleasantly exclaimed, "So, Joan, I see you're of the Japanese persuasion."

Well, at least he hadn't hit her with the Chinese Restaurant line. I'll give him that. Joan and I were together for two years until drifting apart. I'll always remember her fondly, despite the jellied pig's knuckles.

Chapter 16

Home at Last

Unwittingly, as a senior medical student, I arrived at the site of my birth. Albert Einstein College of Medicine was located in the Bronx, the borough in which I was born. While Bronx-born, within a few months, my parents quickly whisked me away to Queens, where we lived in a new garden apartment development built right after the war and meant to attract returning veterans. Over the years, my mother told me that I had been born at an institution named The Bronx Hospital, one I had never seen afterwards. Now, having returned to that borough for medical school, and with several years of medical school behind me, surprisingly I had never heard mention of that particular hospital.

As a senior who had decided to specialize in Pediatrics, I opted to take advantage of some of the excellent pediatric assets that Einstein possessed. One of them was a pair of pediatric gastroenterologists, Murray Davidson and Merv Silverberg, who had written the then-definitive textbook of Pediatric Gastroenterology. They were located at a large hospital I'd not yet visited named Bronx-Lebanon, several miles from the Einstein campus. Apparently this hospital had little else to offer, or maybe it was the neighborhood. You see, the Bronx was rife with lousy neighborhoods—a fellow student doing a surgical rotation at another hospital had recently been stabbed in the back while leaving the hospital after his shift. Thus, despite their esteemed status as respected authors, I had not met any other students who had taken a rotation with these noted physicians.

I used a map of the Bronx to drive to the hospital on the first morning of my six-week GI rotation. Not surprisingly for New York, parking was a major problem. After 20 minutes of fruitless searching, I was happy to find a spot "only" four blocks away. The neighborhood was entirely Puerto Rican and nearly all the signs were in Spanish. I felt a little anxious but also a sense of keen anticipation as I walked to the hospital.

All anxiety disappeared as I strolled into the hospital, glanced up at the large sign in the lobby, and read the words "The Bronx Hospital, a Division of Bronx-Lebanon." Whoa! While I had long heard of Bronx-Lebanon, I had no idea that it was apparently a conglomerate of two formerly separate hospitals, Bronx Hospital, the hospital of my birth, and Lebanon Hospital. I was home! There was something that felt really good standing in the place I was born.

The day got even better as I went up to meet the physicians in charge of my rotation. Dr. Davidson, somewhat of a legend in the field of Pediatric Gastroenterology, was older and soft-spoken. Dr. Silverberg, significantly younger and doing more of the clinical work in the department at that point, was extremely friendly and an excellent teacher. He would later go on to be the Chairman of Pediatrics at another major New York institution. The two greeted me royally and I realized shortly that I was indeed the first medical student to spend time with them in several years. It was a great fit—they liked to teach and I liked to learn. What could be better? To top it off, all the ancillary staff was as friendly as could be. Unlike the main teaching hospitals on the Einstein campus, perpetually teeming with medical students, these folks were only too happy to follow the lead of the chiefs and to make me feel like a visiting dignitary.

At the end of a long and happy day, I whistled as I walked back towards my shit-mobile, er... car. A couple of words about this vehicle. As you've presumably gathered, I was not exactly a rich medical student. My parents had little money; my father was quite bright, had started to become a stockbroker before World War II, got side-tracked and found that he could make a reasonable income owning a taxi. He always delved in the stock market (eventually doing fairly well for himself and even better for some unappreciative relatives) but did not go back to brokering until age 65, after most people had retired. We squeaked by on his earnings as a cab driver, vacationing once a year at Schleiffer's Bungalow Colony in Budd Lake, N.J., whether we needed to or not. We ate out about every four months in The Chinese Restaurant. (I think every Jewish family in New York back then had a Chinese Restaurant—hopefully most of them could afford to go other places as well, but not us.)

My family's financial status was reflected in my cars as well. My father, the expert, took it upon himself to secure me cars without my having a word in the process. My first vehicle was an old Dodge, ex-taxicab, fire engine red (yes, on more than one occasion I was mistaken for a fire marshal's car) and with 170,000 miles on it, already on its second engine. And, for the benefit of anyone younger than me—which at this stage, is almost everyone—let me say that in those days, cars were not designed to last 100,000 miles. To make matters worse, if you looked at the doors, you could see where the old taxi rates (only 25 cents for the first quarter mile!) had been incompletely painted over. This auto was not exactly a chick magnet, as they say.

However, it was far better than the car that I drove that day to Bronx-Lebanon, and to which I was now happily returning. This vehicle, a real head-turner (but not in a good way), was also an old Dodge ex-taxicab, this one on its THIRD engine and with 230,000 miles and painted half-green and half-white. On the hood, one could clearly see the outlines of the four holes that previously held the medallion shield, matched by another set on the roof from the old illuminated TAXI sign. I usually had to suppress an urge to regurgitate when I got into this vehicle. I distinctly remember one of my dates, as I picked her up for the first time, who decided that walking a mile to the movies would be an excellent choice despite the rainy cold of the evening.

But nothing was going to ruin my mood after my first day in this most happy rotation, or so I thought. Whistling and smiling and greeting people, I rounded the corner a quarter mile from the hospital. While I vaguely noted that the car looked a little low to the ground, it really wasn't until I got quite close that this registered—it was a *lot* lower! When I finally got close enough to look at it, I quickly found that someone had slashed all four tires in multiple places. No way this baby was going anywhere. My mood changed in an instant. Joy replaced by despair. There was no scenario in which this poor medical student was going to afford four new tires. Here I was, in a pretty dangerous-looking neighborhood as the evening rapidly darkened. (It didn't take long on this rotation to discover why I had been the only medical student in a protracted period.)

Three short but burly Puerto Rican gentlemen sidled over to me from a storefront a couple of doors away. "Eh, señor, you maybe want to buy four used tires for $11?" I just looked at them. Even for New York in 1972, this was chutzpah. It also was quite a bargain.

I glanced over to the store they had come from. While the signage was in Spanish, I was able to make out that it was an institution I had never heard of before, a USED tire store. I answered, "You fellas must be psychic. How did you possibly know I might be in the market for four used tires?"

After, I talked them down to $9.50, which I proudly note, included installation (but not alignment), I waited while they changed all four tires in a 20-minute period, with much of the neighborhood laughing and joking watching the shit-mobile and its idiot driver with the short white coat and black medical bag.

And then I drove off, the proud new owner of four brand new used tires for $9.50! The first one didn't go flat until I was almost home and the second one lasted almost a week.

Somehow, the reality of finding my roots had not lived up to my expectations.

Chapter 17

Who is Alice?

It was 1976, a tumultuous time for the country and for me as well. As a senior medical student, I had just started my surgical rotation and now, on the second day on the service, I was set for my first night on call. Prior to this, I had rarely been in an operating room and then only as an observer, never an active participant in an actual surgery. Now I was stationed at Morrisania, a dilapidated public hospital in a very bad section of the worst borough in New York, the Bronx.

Late that evening, a critically wounded gunshot victim arrived. He was shot in the back with a rifle and rapidly bleeding out. His crime: on a hot summer evening, he had driven into the tenement neighborhood not far from the hospital and leaned on his horn to summon his girlfriend. Someone had yelled at him to lay off the horn, but he apparently continued to honk loudly. It was the kind of activity on a sweltering evening that might make someone want to shoot him just to shut him up. And, seeing that this was New York in the seventies, a hot evening with a hot populace, someone did just that, and with a rifle no less and from a third-story window. The bullet hit him right in the small of the back.

The ambulance and stretcher that brought him into the Emergency Room barely paused there. Large bore IVs were inserted in both arms, blood was sent for type and cross match, and fluids were poured in as fast as they could be in an attempt to keep the patient alive long enough to make it to the Operating Room. With his extensive bleeding and already low blood pressure, he was unlikely to make it at all. The young man would stand no chance if he were not operated on immediately to control the bleeding.

It was late at night, and the place was frantic although there were only a few of us involved in this little drama. There was the surgery Attending physician, the head honcho; a second-year surgical resident, a surgical intern, an anesthesiologist and myself on the physician side, and the all-important scrub nurse at the head of the operating table. The scene was pure pandemonium. As soon as the Attending cut into the patient's abdomen, the field was totally obscured with blood. It was almost impossible to see anything in the ever-swirling crimson pool. The surgeon and the senior resident probed, the intern and I both straining with retractors (surgical instruments designed to forcefully hold a wound open) to keep the surgical field visible (exhausting work, as I was to discover) as well as providing constant suction for the bleeding, which continued at a frightening rate. By this time, the treating staff were pumping units of blood into both arms with the IVs wide open. Would it possibly be enough?

Through all of this, the experienced scrub nurse was handing out instruments as fast as the chief surgeon could call them out. The scrub nurse is a very important part of the surgical team, particularly in an emergency situation like this. In front of her sit two trays with seemingly hundreds of instruments, including multiple varieties of clamps, hemostats, scalpels, retractors, and others. Although many instruments have similar appearance, all have slightly different functions. As a surgeon looks, probes, cuts, clamps, dries bleeding points, sews, he rapidly calls for these instruments, sometimes 15 times a minute or more, and expects them to be accurately and promptly handed to him instantly. The nurse must keep them sterile, returned to their places so they can be found again a few seconds later. In a life and death situation like this, time is critical, and the scrub nurse must be alert and ready with the right instrument at the right time. All the instruments have names or shortened nicknames and as soon as the surgeon calls out "Kelly" or "mosquito" or "Allis." An experienced scrub nurse like this one will frequently have the correct instrument in her hands, often anticipating the operator's need even before his call.

This case was not proceeding well. The surgeons were frustrated. They had found one small artery that had been severed and they re-attached it, but the bleeding barely slowed. We had still not identified the main source and vision remained nightmarish with the eddying blood.

A short time into the procedure, just before midnight, a gowned figure entered the OR, whispered something to the scrub nurse's ear, and left. It was nothing out of the ordinary and none of the surgical team paid any attention to it. Five minutes later, at the stroke of the hour, the scrub nurse pointed up at the clock and, amidst the chaos, announced: "I'm leaving. My shift is over. My supervisor just informed me that my replacement called in sick so there's no one to take my place. I'm sorry."

As I said earlier, this was a tumultuous period in American society. The Vietnam War had been ranging for years; the country was deeply divided; and it was a time of Black awareness with Black Panthers, Symbionese Liberation Army and other movements. In medicine, for the first time ever, house staff physicians had protested about conditions and nurses, unable to strike, had taken job actions, calling in sick or sticking precisely to their appointed hours.

Sad as it was to say, the nurse was technically right. Theoretically, nurses had shifts. In practicality, everyone knew that a shift was an almost metaphysical concept. In medicine, you stayed until you could leave. Particularly back then, house staff physicians might work an average of 85–90 hours a week and more than 100 hours was not unusual. You stayed until the mission was complete. The same was expected of the nursing and paramedical staff. But now we had a slowdown. For the first time that anyone could remember, nurses were walking out on the sweep of a second hand. I often wondered: could people who had chosen to go into the medical calling really live with themselves at a time like this?

The attending surgeon became apoplectic, bellowing at the retreating figure of the scrub nurse as she calmly walked from the room. He yelled she would never work again: threatening her body, heck, threatening her life. All to no avail. Slowly and deliberately she marched from the surgical suite. In a few seconds, she was gone. I stood in total shock, almost unable to breathe.

But there was no time to ponder. We had a patient who was dying before our eyes, blood continuing to pour into his abdominal cavity faster that we could keep up. The surgeon, so red in the face that I feared he would have a stroke, turned to me and yelled, "Lotner, get over there. You're the scrub nurse!"

Whoa! What was this? I was the lowly medical student and it was my very first night on call. I only had seen a few procedures in my entire life, and at the time, I had been far more interested in the surgery itself than in the name of the multiple instruments. I started to protest but he curtly cut me off. The patient was dying and there was literally no one else. I moved into position over the confusing tray of instruments, my back to the OR door.

The surgeon turned in my direction, seemingly looking past me and screamed, "Alice!" Oh, thank God, I thought. Another nurse must have come in behind me and was going to take over the scrub nurse's role! I took a quick glance over my shoulder and... No "Alice," no anyone. The Chief surgeon screamed "Alice" again, this time his pinpoint eyes focused clearly on me, and I struggled to guess which of the many instruments was the "Alice" clamp.

It didn't go any better with the next 50 or 60 instruments that I had to hand out before we gave up totally on the 27-year-old patient who had just died on the table. I knew my incompetently slow performance at finding the required instruments in a timely fashion had contributed to his demise.

After he had calmed down a little, the Attending told me that the patient was probably unsalvageable from the beginning. He said I shouldn't feel too badly, it wasn't really my fault. The renal artery had been severed and the wound was too serious, the bleeding so profuse that with the inability to immediately identify the source, the patient surely would have died even with the world's best scrub nurse in the room. He walked from the room, his words not really comforting me. The surgical residents, closer to my age, spent more time in their attempts at consolation. Under any circumstances, it is devastating to lose a patient. However, as a student so early in my surgical experience, I was almost inconsolable. It would take a long time for me to believe they were right and for me to be able to forgive myself.

It didn't take me nearly as long to learn that the clamp was named "Allis," not "Alice." I should have known that a medical instrument from a century earlier had not been named after the attractive nurse my imagination had envisioned.

Chapter 18

A Critical Choice

A week later, on the same surgical service at Morrisania, a young man was brought in with a serious gunshot wound to the chest. It was the middle of the night. While most of the hospital was relatively quiet, the Emergency Room was swamped. My small surgical team, with a different attending, a senior resident, an intern and I as the student, hurried the patient to the operating suite. The limited story initially available to us was garbled. But we made out that just before a liquor store was to close at midnight, this patient had tried to rob it and the clerk had shot him. The bullet struck him in the right side of his chest. He was now unconscious and in critical shape.

In what seemed to me to be amazingly rapid time, we had the young man (he looked in his early twenties) on a table, two large bore IVs in place. Blood was pouring in one, life-saving fluids in the other, and his chest cavity was surgically opened. The team madly worked on the young man who was in dire shape. The chest cavity filled with fluid and blood, the trachea intubated but even so, maintaining oxygen and blood pressure was difficult.

In the midst of this chaos, the charge nurse entered the OR and quietly informed us that we had another patient, equally gravely ill. He would require immediate attention. This second patient was unlikely to survive much longer without immediate surgical intervention. At 1 A.M., that meant us: the only surgeons in the hospital at that hour.

The story now unfolded a bit more: this new fellow was a clerk in a liquor store. Two thugs had entered the store to rob it, but before even giving the clerk a chance to open the cash register, had viciously shot him twice, once in the chest and once in the abdomen. Before the clerk went down, he managed to pull a handgun and got off one shot, amazingly hitting one of the assailants in the chest. Another customer witnessed the incident while hiding behind a shelf. The clerk was now unconscious and fading fast. We were currently operating on the robber/shooter.

An immediate choice was required. I know what I would have chosen, as I stared at our current patient with a newfound revulsion. Instead of viewing the fellow as a hapless young robber, he was in fact a thug who had viciously tried to murder the helpless clerk, giving him no chance before opening fire. I wanted to give up on this guy and attend to the real victim here, the clerk who they had just brought in. To my surprise, the Attending surgeon chose otherwise, and I was struck by his words. Seemingly a hardassed, no-nonsense guy who I expected to be law-and-order, he stated that our role was that of physicians, not police, not judge nor jury. As physicians, we were to treat our patients as they came and not to be playing God or choosing favorites. While we would have to live with ourselves if the clerk being transported up died for a lack of attention, our duty as doctors would not allow us to abandon the critically ill patient on the table in front of us.

The Attending sent the surgical intern in to see if he could stabilize the new patient, pending completion of our care on the current one. However, we all knew it probably would not be enough. Feverishly, but seemingly morosely, the rest of us went back to the work at hand.

The intern returned a short time later. He had not been able to save the clerk. Our own patient died a few minutes later. As a physician, I knew I should have been upset about losing any patient, including this young shooter.

But I wasn't.

Chapter 19

This Won't Hurt a Bit

When I look back, medical school was not only challenging and stressful, but at times, it was downright weird and sometimes outright bizarre. Looking back, things happened that most "normal people" would consider outside the usual patterns of life. Things like attending the autopsy of an elderly woman, watching her internal organs removed via a vaginal route, and then an hour later, having a date for dinner. Of the stranger things I recall, one of the more outrageous experience was getting my wisdom teeth extracted by a fellow medical student. Well, it's a little more complicated than that.

When we started our first year at Einstein, the majority of students were just out of college, age 21–22. There were several who were a few years older, having worked in paramedical fields for a while or just taken some time to decide on their career path. Then there was Norm Trieger, who was in his late forties as a first-year student.

He had a unique situation: he was Dr. Norman Trieger, DDS, the head of Oral Surgery at Montefiore Hospital. While almost all students entered medical school with the goal of becoming a physician, Norm decided to attend medical school for a very different reason: hospital politics and more importantly, hospital money. Apparently, of all the departments at Montefiore, a vast, sprawling, and well-respected institution, Norm's Oral Surgery Department received the lowest proportion of funding. He was firmly convinced that of the 20-plus department chairman, his lack of stature as the only one without the magical Medical Doctor designation caused this inequity. Our ages and maturity levels (translate: my immaturity) prevented us in spending much time together early in medical school. Then, by happenstance, we found ourselves on the same surgical rotation nearly three years later. That clerkship, not surprisingly, was at the same Montefiore Hospital where Norm was a Chairman.

AECOM had a vast empire that included hospitals sprawled across the Bronx. On the Campus was Jacobi Hospital, a very big and busy municipal hospital; Van Etten, no longer there, but at the time, the last TB hospital in New York; and the Einstein College Hospital, a boutique-like private hospital. The medical school also staffed several additional municipal hospitals haphazardly located in some of the worst areas of the Bronx, including Lincoln Hospital (where a medical student was stabbed one time after his shift was over), Morrisania, where I had done the first half of this surgical rotation, Bronx-Lebanon, and others of similar infamy.

At these municipal hospitals, where things would get down and dirty and the patient load often overwhelming, the medical students got the greatest exposure to trauma, emergencies, weird diseases, and the ilk. Then there was Montefiore, sort of the crown jewel, and an empire unto itself. Montefiore was a big private hospital, not frenzied like the city hospitals, but large, busy and much more nicely appointed. Here, the student would not only see plenty of action and much of interest, but would be more comfortable and more likely to relate to the patients. Years later, the two systems were to merge into Montefiore-Albert Einstein Medical Center of today, with Montefiore in the lead.

A week into the second half of my surgical rotation, and now at the Montefiore complex, I sat in the Doctor's lounge with Norm awaiting the start of a new case. We had gotten to know each other considerably better in the several days on this clerkship than in the previous three years combined. Earning my great respect, Norm was acting as a medical student during the day and then in late afternoons or evenings, would run back and supervise his department. The life of a normal medical student was crazy; Norm's schedule had to be totally overwhelming and he had been keeping up this schizophrenic routine for almost four years. It bordered on the unbelievable.

Since Norm was an Oral Surgeon, I decided to ask him a question. I had recently had my routine dental exam and was pleased that I had no cavities, much more common 50 years ago than today. But my dentist had told me that X-rays showed that I had impacted wisdom teeth. Although they weren't bothering me at the moment, he advised early removal as the procedure was much easier and less painful at my age of 25 than it would be if deferred far into the future when the impactions would invariably start causing pain. The dentist had provided me the name of a surgeon he respected, but who had proved geographically inconvenient and difficult for me to see with my hectic schedule. Subsequently, two months had elapsed, and I still had not yet been able to set up a consultation. Now sitting here together, I asked Norm if he knew of any good oral surgeons closer at hand.

To my surprise (and I certainly wasn't seeking or expecting this), he answered that he would do it himself! If, and this was a big IF, we had a slow day in the last few weeks of our rotation together. In that unlikely occurrence, he would grab one of his residents, bring me to his departmental suite, administer intravenous relaxants and analgesics and, as Nike ads would say later, "just do it." The plan sounded so simple, and being short on both money and time, so much better! Who wouldn't want to have a fellow medical student operating on them? When I told Norm I wasn't looking to impose, he told me that it was far from an imposition. He shared with me that he was the chairman of the best Oral Surgery Department in the borough and resented that his largely-unneeded medical schooling had dramatically limited his time for surgery. Indeed, he would love the opportunity and who could possibly be better qualified?

He was probably right, and I filed this away under my list of improbabilities since the chance of a "slow day" on this rotation appeared almost nil. I had just about forgotten our discussion when, two weeks later, Norm looked at me, busily absorbed in a crossword puzzle in the OR locker room and asked if I was ready. It took me a minute to catch his meaning—I had forgotten his offer. But a raging storm outside had led to many cancellations in the afternoon's surgical clinic. Almost miraculously, we had some free time for him to extract my wisdom teeth.

I will say, the procedure itself went beautifully. But I remember precious little of the actual encounter. The three areas that do I recall had to do with the anesthesia/analgesia, the few hours after the procedure and, most amazingly, my internship interview the next morning.

With the assistance of a very nice (and very surprised) resident from his department, Norm gave me local anesthetic and IV Valium and proceeded to go about his business. IV Valium, which I had never had before (or since), proved to be a very pleasant experience. I felt woozy, happy and unconcerned. It was a relaxant; it most definitely was not an anesthetic. All I can remember of the procedure is that I was relaxing in a pleasant stupor while the pair went about their business. Periodically, Norm would tell me that he was going to hit me with a hammer to shatter the embedded molar to render it extractable. Momentarily, it would hurt like hell when he did, but a few seconds later I would be almost giddy. We went on like this for a while, me wincing in pain with each strike of the hammer, and then not even realizing the pain a few seconds later. It was a combo of laughter and tears.

After he finished (we did two of the four molars that were impacted and he told me he we would do the remaining teeth on another slow day—that was 1973 and I think I should be getting around to those other teeth any year now), he told me that my mouth was likely to be tremendously painful that evening and into the next day. It was important to get ahead of the pain. For strong pain relief, he gave me a few methadone pills. Methadone is a synthetic narcotic. During an era of heroin addiction in the 1960s and 1970s, it was (incorrectly) deemed that methadone was less likely to be addictive than heroin or morphine, and methadone clinics were used in generally futile attempts to wean addicted individuals from their primary drugs. Unfortunately, methadone itself turned out to be addictive as well. When I expressed surprise about his choice, Norm responded that methadone was a strong opiate with excellent analgesic qualities. Since the hospital had a methadone clinic for treating addicts, they had a few pills he would just dispense to me.

I went off that evening happy as a clam (methadone tended to have that effect). After a couple of hours, I found myself almost ecstatic and in no pain. Now, while it is hard to conceive for today's youth, there were no cell phones, no internet and no computers in this era, and rates for routine calls could be quite high. Thus, for a poor student like myself, barely squeaking by with my schooling and living expenses, even long-distance phone calls proved an expensive luxury that had to be rationed. Consequently, I had lost touch with almost all my college friends as I had become immersed over years in the medical school gestalt.

But not this night. I was so happy, seemingly floating through space with almost a feeling of elation, that I had an uncontrollable desire to talk. And talk I did, including to a bunch of people I hadn't spoken to in a very long time. I spent the next two hours phoning almost anyone I could think of. I called all my old fraternity brothers, several of whom I had not contacted in over three years, as well as high school chums, and a few distant relatives.

The conversations were long and one-sided. I was so happy that words tumbled out in verbal torrents, according to more than one friend. There was only one problem (well, frankly there were many problems) with this scenario. I had just had my wisdom teeth out, had had major trauma to my mouth, and had gauze packing in place. Apparently, while I was joyful and almost explosively verbose, no one could understand what I was saying! Years later, two of my friends denied ever having conversation with me since college. When I told them I distinctly remembered calling them after my oral surgery, they both told me that they remembered the calls but could not for the life of them figure out who they were talking to or why some idiot was calling and screaming at them.

And to top it off, when I received the phone bill a few weeks later, that one night's long-distance calls cost me more than my rent for the month. All that to sound like a happy moron! As weird as the evening had been, it was only the prelude to the larger mini-tragedy to unfold the next morning, the morning of my Pediatric internship interview at the prestigious Mount Sinai Medical School. A more judicious person might not have scheduled oral surgery 15 hours before such an important meeting. However, I was not judicious, and to be perfectly honest about it, the surgery had not exactly been scheduled.

I awakened that morning feeling surprisingly comfortable, showered, shaved and preened, and carefully laid out my only good suit. It was a three-piece gray pinstripe, appropriately serious for important somber occasions (funerals or medical interviews) and reserved for moments like this. As I looked in the mirror, thinking I had achieved the appropriate gravitas, I had one more decision to make. To methadone or not to methadone—that was the question. On one hand, the last thing I wanted was to experience the severe pain I had been forewarned of, potentially to arise during an important interview. That would have been a disaster. The flipside was that I was feeling pretty good, and did not want to be "spaced" like the previous evening. Then a remembrance from Pharmacology class of 18 months earlier kept replaying itself in my brain. The physiologic antagonist of the side effects of narcotics is pain, our professor had repetitively drilled into us. Translation: narcotics are to be prescribed for severe pain; narcotics have lots of nasty side effects; in the presence of pain, the patient was much less likely to experience the side effects. The opposite was true: in the absence of pain, side effects were much more apt to appear. I was not experiencing pain at that moment but decided it highly likely to reoccur shortly as the dose of the last night wore off further. Prophylactically, taking the methadone seemed the more judicious choice.

About 45 minutes into the subway ride to Mount Sinai, I caught my reflection in the window (Gee, I looked damned good in that suit!). I found myself contemplating the situation and deciding it was pretty funny. I also remembered reading about narcotics the previous year during my Pharmacology course. One thing that I had always found peculiar in the long list of adverse reactions listed in the Pharm textbook: towards the top of that prodigious column was listed NAUSEA; VOMITING; NAUSEA AND VOMITING. How peculiar. Didn't vomiting and nausea always go together? Did people suddenly start retching without feeling nauseous? Did they really have to list Nausea and Vomiting separately as well as together?

A few seconds later, I had my answer. I remember thinking to myself, "Gee, that's funny." Within a second, I opened my mouth and commenced vomiting all over my suit pants, shoes, and the subway floor. Wow, vomiting with no nausea. I literally had not felt that coming. It was quite disgusting as I tried vainly to use my copy of the New York Times in a futile attempt to at least partially clean myself. Embarrassed and totally disgusted, I thought how strange the experience was and hoped I never experienced anything like that again. That hope was dashed less than a minute later—once again I opened my mouth and inundated the lower half of my trousers and shoes in a torrent of vomitus. Ashamed, and more horrified, I looked up and surveyed the other passengers. No one bothered to look up at me or meet my gaze.

Only in New York can a well-dressed fellow heave all over himself on the subway with no one glancing, commenting or offering assistance. Oh, yeah, it's just another suit retching on the

D-Train. Yup, happens all the time. We had arrived at the Mount Sinai exit at this point, and as I exited the train, I noticed no other passengers willing to stand near my door. Then, I did something I had never previously done as a life-long New Yorker. I dared to enter the bathroom in a subway station. I had of course heard of patrons brave enough to have used these bathrooms but had never actually met anyone who admitted to such a foolhardy act. It was as bad as I had feared it to be. But I had no choice. Using water and toilet paper (paper towels would have been too much to expect), I judiciously tried to wash down my pant legs and took off the shoes, putting them into the sink to clean. Considering the circumstances, I hoped I had succeeded but I had my doubts.

I was one of eight Pediatric intern applicants at Mount Sinai that morning, there for orientation, tours and interviews. I noticed on tour that the two young Pediatric residents who led us did so while assiduously avoiding standing in my vicinity. When the group moved, which we did frequently, I noted that I was often by myself. Later, when I had one-on-one interviews with some of the more senior physicians in the department, I noted with chagrin that they stood and roamed the room as I sat in my assigned chair, and that the discussions tended to be far briefer with me with me than any of the other applicants. Not a good sign.

Two months later, we had the matching program for internships. The students ranked each program they had interviewed with, from their first choice down to their last. The institution did the same with all the candidates. Ultimately, on Match Day, a computer paired up intern prospects and institutions and matched them. I ranked Children's Hospital of Philadelphia, a great hospital, as my first choice and was delighted to match there. I had ranked Mount Sinai last and I suspected they had put me in the same position. Or perhaps—they hadn't even bothered to rank me at all!?

Chapter 20

"I Quit!" Well, Sort Of

Late in my fourth year of medical school, I had just started my externship. To those unfamiliar with the term, an extern is akin to an intern but without the title, experience or the (meager) pay. That may have been stated a little facetiously. The intern has completed medical school and is a salaried licensed physician, licensed to work in a teaching hospital. While he is supervised by a resident, the intern is able to write his own orders on patients and can legally write prescriptions. In contrast, the extern is still a student and unlicensed, so he or she must have all orders and prescriptions co-signed. Even worse, an extern isn't paid for services. In theory, the extern's patient load is lighter, the number of admissions permitted in any given period is fewer than for the intern, and the resident must more closely monitor an extern's work on patients. It is a stressful but valuable period for the student, often the first time in which the student has charge of their own patients.

My rotation was at the Albert Einstein College Hospital, the jewel of the medical school campus. The Einstein complex held several facilities, including municipal hospitals as well as the College Hospital. The municipal hospitals, Jacobi or the more distant Morrisania, were trauma centers and had busy emergency rooms. Poor sick patients without physicians and frequently with complex, terribly controlled illnesses could show up at any time and often did, sometimes seemingly in coordinated mass groups.

Conversely, the College Hospital was where staff physicians in the Einstein area would send their own private patients ill enough to require admission. These tended to be somewhat more educated and healthier in general. Admissions were often elective and theoretically fewer required emergency hospitalizations. In theory, this should make for an easier rotation. However, I was to shortly find out, in medicine, there is often a big difference between theory and reality.

The two-month period began quietly enough. An excellent resident in Internal Medicine, Dr. John Greene, led our team. He supervised another extern and me, as well as two true interns. The hospital was busier than anticipated. I started with about 14 patients, more than an extern was to be handling. They restricted my New Patients (NPs) to three a day. (In retrospect, this was actually a fairly heavy load to begin with. In many teaching hospitals of present day, an actual intern might not have as many patients.)

It would have been better to start slowly; the new doctor-to-be had too much to learn, including the terminology of medicine as well as the very thought patterns of the physician, to be very effective initially. Remember, this was an era preceding Google, cell phones, even the internet, and the quantity of material to be learned and memorized was immense. Even the routine act of admitting a patient was initially overwhelming. The neophyte, being unsure of what in history or exam was important and what could be reasonably omitted, was trained to ask everything and examine everything. Then copious notes had to be handwritten longhand, orders entered, blood tests drawn, samples transported to the labs. At the onset, inefficient at all these steps, admitting the NP might easily take two to three hours, a procedure that would later be cut by more than half after months or years of being an effective physician.

Although the first day of externship was mildly unnerving—

there was a great difference between assisting someone else in the care of patients and actually being responsible for those patients yourself—it progressed without major trauma. The next day was to be my first on call, where the young doctor, or in my case, student-doctor, would remain in the hospital with a somewhat skeletal crew. I would be taking care of whatever NPs arrived and tending to any problems with the current roster of patients, not only my own but those of any other member of my team. Nights on call could be frightening. To complicate the situation, we had started this rotation on a Friday. My first night on call was Saturday and at this particular hospital, staff would be on call through the entire weekend until leaving on Monday evening, roughly 60 hours later. Hopefully, this would include some periods of sleep.

Early Saturday was busy and exciting but very manageable. I remember feeling for a while that things might not be as terrifying as I had anticipated. I wish they had remained that way. I only had one admission during the day; the patient neither terribly complicated nor terribly ill. Although I was slow and some work on other patients began piling up, it was not yet a major concern. It was about seven that evening when the wheels started to come off. A patient presented through the ER with diabetic ketoacidosis, a complicated patient in semi-critical condition, more challenging than I would have preferred at this infant stage of my career. Under normal circumstances, they would have tried to give this patient to the actual intern, not the novice extern. However, Saturdays were not normal. We had just admitted another even sicker patient. Luckily, with much help from my resident, Dr. Greene, who was likewise on call that weekend, I was able to pretty much get the patient's care started, IVs going, insulin, and other medications prescribed. However, my beeper went off as I was writing my note. It was the ER, and I had another admission, this time with a gastrointestinal bleed. Again, a very ill patient in need of a good deal of immediate care. I knew there were things I still needed to do to on my diabetic patient; they would have to wait until this patient was stabilized, again with Dr. Greene providing invaluable assistance. I was feeling just a little panicky about that time as the evening latened.

The one thought in my mind that helped prevent me from completely unhinging was knowing that, as an extern, I was limited to three NPs a day. While the last two had been pretty ill, I was at my quota and safe for the night. Almost simultaneously with this comforting thought, the beeper went off again. Responding to the call, it was Dr. Greene from the ER. He apologized profusely but told me that there was another patient being admitted, and the other intern was off taking care of his own catastrophe. "I know it's not supposed to be working this way, Lotner, but it's yours and I'll give you some help." I was still working on NP number three and luckily, this new one wasn't too ill and could wait. An hour later, number five showed up and it wasn't too much longer before I was advised of number six.

By this point, I had almost completely decompensated. Although no one seemed in imminent danger, I felt like the little Dutch boy, holding my fingers in far too many dikes. While I had written orders on all and started IV's, I had many half-filled histories (including patient number four with almost nothing written down), whose stories and problems all seemed to blur together now. I could see work piled up hours in advance. The unseen NPs, the unfinished NPs, tests that still remained on the more established patients. Blood work needed. IVs to start. My head seemed about to explode...It was four in the morning—if only I could put my head down for a minute. Things were a little quieter now; I was more in the writing stage. Oh, to just rest my eyes. They were dry so I took out my contacts for a minute as I continued to write up a history. Terribly myopic, I could see up close so I was able to write and now my eyes felt so much better. I did not have a backup pair of glasses with me. I kept writing.......

BEEEP! BEEEEP! The blare of my beeper and the shrill overhead PA awakened me less than ten minutes later. I realized I had fallen over asleep, drooling on a patient's chart. The announcement: There was a Code Blue, a cardiac arrest, in the ICU one floor below. Contactless and semi-blind, I stumbled towards the stairwell and the unit. Normally an extern would have nothing to do with ICU patients, but all bets were off during a code. I arrived in just a few seconds, discombobulated and panicky. I also realized at this ungodly hour of nearly five in the morning, with few staff around or awake, that help might not be so quick to arrive. Codes were life and death events, every second crucial. I had participated in a few codes but had never run one on my own. Now I was overtired, overwrought and confused. I also couldn't clearly see more than a few feet in front of me. I prayed someone more senior was there.

My prayers were answered when I saw what appeared to be another physician already on the scene. He was artificially breathing the patient using an Ambu-Bag. I began CPR chest percussions. Usually the senior person would be running the code. I didn't know who this other guy was in scrubs and I couldn't read his name tag. But I had no doubts that he had to be more senior than me, an extern on the service for only 48 hours. Yet he was strangely silent and grunted when I barked at him for instructions. The nurses had given some medications. We knew other physicians would be coming but at 5:00 in the morning, it might take longer to get there than usual.

I was acutely aware we needed to be giving more medications and looked expectantly at the other doc. But he still didn't call out any orders. Figuring it was his place, I said to him, "Are you going to call this or am I?" He incoherently mumbled something, but never called any directions. Finally, heart in my mouth and with far too much time having elapsed, I yelled at a nurse to push more epinephrine and some additional medications, each time looking expectantly at the other strangely silent physician. Things were not going well, and we were getting no response from the patient. In what seemed to be a half hour but in reality was likely only a minute or two, Dr. Greene and another resident groggily ran in, and quickly assessing the situation, took over. It was too late. The patient, an elderly woman with intractable heart failure, had never made any progress during the code and was pronounced shortly afterwards.

Dr. Greene came up to me afterwards while I sat huddled against the wall. He consoled me on what had been a tough night. He asked me why so few medications had been called at the point when he had first arrived. I explained that I assumed the other physician was senior and since he was there first, I thought it was his place to be in charge. John looked at me and asked about the other physician. I pointed in the direction of the other doctor. Dr. Greene choked a little and explained that the "Doc" was the respiratory technician who just happened to be wearing scrubs and wasn't a doctor at all. In fact, he spoke little English. I was the only doctor (or student doctor, really) in the room; it had been my code to run. At that point I didn't think I could have felt worse than I was already feeling, but now I somehow sunk considerably lower. The realization that the patient had an unsalvageable condition and that a few seconds would have been unlikely to produce a different outcome offered me only limited solace.

John told me to get some sleep, but I explained I had a lot to do. At 5:15 A.M., I showed up at the room of patient four to get a history that should have been obtained eight hours earlier. Naturally, I awoke him from the distant Netherlands. He was a frail 90-year-old, who for reasons somewhat incomprehensible to both him and me, was admitted from the ER for a workup for moderate anemia. At that hour, he seemed to be as unhappy to be there as I was to be seeing him. A few minutes into his history, desperately trying to make it through my memorized list of questions, I asked him if he ever had chest pains. Awaiting a response, I blanked out. I woke up a few seconds later, having drifted off myself and realized I had missed his answer. Not wanting to look even more stupid, I tried to rephrase the question. "Do you ever have any pains in the chest?" Again, I awakened seconds later in the same situation: I had dozed and had no idea of his reply. Trying not to look like a total idiot, I re-phrased again,

"Do you ever have pains around the area of your heart?" This time, as my eyelids grew heavy, I felt a bony hand clasp tightly around my wrist. "Look, Sonny, I'm as tired as you. Why don't you tell me what the hell you want me to say and I'll say it!"

I tried to take Dr. Greene's advice and get some sleep, but I was so anxious that I felt as if my body was being bombarded by a series of electrical shocks. I had a panicked mind. As I lay, wide-eyed, in the on-call room, I thought of the recently deceased woman in the ICU. I then thought of all my other patients. The beeper went off a few minutes later. It was 7 A.M. and I had my first admission of the morning.

I was exhausted by the late afternoon, panicked and stumbling around like a zombie. If I wasn't crying, I was close. I knew I had sick patients to see. The thought of it made me start to hyperventilate. I felt I had so many things to do that I didn't know where to attack first.

The episode that broke me concerned my own patient, Mrs. Schmidt, an elderly woman on my service who had been seemingly stable on Friday and now her blood pressure had suddenly started to drop. It was just one more patient that had to be dealt with and I literally didn't know what to do first. Sitting there morosely, Dr. Greene approached me. "Lotner, go home." What? Was he serious? "Lotner, go home. Get out of here."

It was 5 P.M. on Sunday. I was not scheduled to be off duty until the next evening.

I protested that there were so many sick patients, so many things I had to do, notes I had to write, Mrs. Schmidt that I had to work up. He looked at me coolly and answered, "You're not helping anyone at this point. If you stick around, you'll be even worse tomorrow. I'll write your notes, I'll see the patients, I'll draw the blood. Now go get some sleep—here's a sleeping pill— and come back and be ready to give me some help tomorrow."

I slept for twelve hours straight.

At lunch the next day, Dr. Saul Morrow called me into his office. He was the attending physician in charge of the entire teaching program at the College Hospital. Dr. Morrow, then in his fifties, was a learned, thoughtful, well-respected physician, the kind of doctor admired by others. I had interviewed with him earlier and admired both his knowledge and demeanor.

He started off by saying he had heard that I had a rough time over the weekend and quietly asked me to describe what had happened. After I finished my story, he grew thoughtful for a few minutes. He then went on to tell me that while the circumstances were tough and the patient count exceeded what was recommended; medicine was a calling that required more. The physician was ultimately responsible. In real life, the physician did what had to be done. In an emergency, there is no limit on the number of patients you might have to see. If a physician cracked, like I had, it was actually in Dr. Morrow's discretion to drop them from the program. Instead, he thought that I had the makings of a good physician and that the circumstances had gotten the best of me. He asked me to take a good look at myself, make both of us proud, and not to lose it again. He was encouraging and helpful.

I made it through the next ten weeks with flying colors. I got very good grades on the rotation, although, in my mind, with a giant asterisk. It sometimes humbles me to think how close my career came to an end before it really started. I am eternally grateful to Dr. (Superman) Greene and Dr. Morrow.

Chapter 21

Mrs. Miller

As my externship continued on, I was several weeks into this essentially unpaid internship. The travails of the first weekend now long behind me, I managed to get through most days, if not with confidence, at least with some degree of proficiency and without the constant dread of the world crashing around me. I actually felt comfortable NOT asking every question; I could write at least a brief holding history until I had more time to expand on it more fully. To improve matters, I was getting pretty darn good at starting IVs. The externship proved a great time for learning. In a sense, everything was new to me. There was a vast difference between reading about a disease and actually diagnosing and treating it in a real patient for whom I was responsible. Diseases and treatments, which would seem routine in a few months, were all still new at this point.

Mrs. R. Miller was a little different for me than many of the other patients I encountered in my first few weeks on the ward. She was an 85-year-old Jewish woman with insulin-dependent diabetes and sadly, with a malignant cancer which had metastasized to many parts of her body. Her chart was excruciatingly heavy. She had what was semi-facetiously termed an ominous chart-to-body-weight ratio, considered a very bad medical indicator in those days where an extremely heavy chart was indicative of a seriously ill patient with far too many difficult hospitalizations. Review showed that in just the last eight months alone, she had been repetitively hospitalized for numerous problems related to her cancer: sepsis (a severe systemic body infection), diabetic ketoacidosis, hypercalcemia (severely high calcium), anemia from acute gastrointestinal bleeding, sepsis again, and several more. She was like a walking textbook outlining the complications of medicine, her problems involving all organ systems. She had so many medical illnesses and so many variations of them that, depending on what she presented with at any particular moment, a young physician could learn a tremendous amount of the fundamentals of medicine in the care of this single patient.

She presented this time with fevers, chills, pains, and unstable diabetes. I can no longer remember all the details. It was complicated. After spending an inordinate period of time on her history and exam (H&E), I discussed her at length with Dr. Greene, my resident and mentor. John was very bright, caring and thorough; as previously noted, he proved to be a big aid in my training.

Early in her stay, I was fascinated reading her chart. I reviewed, in detail, how doctors approached her problems and complicated care. But after a few days, as I spent more time getting to know her, I found myself challenged in a much more fundamental way. I couldn't understand the point of her continued care. Clearly, we had no magical bullets for her. Ultimately, each of her frequent and way-too-close-together hospitalizations just treated the current emergency, doing nothing for her long-term well-being. She had a terminal condition, a cancer that had spread to much of her body, that left her racked in pain and that had long since stopped responding to the few chemotherapeutic agents available at the time. She was now suffering. What was the purpose we were serving in keeping her alive and miserable? In response to my questions, Dr. Greene pointed out that the family wanted everything possible done to save their mother. Furthermore, he (correctly) added, there was much to be learned as a physician in treating her various maladies, which would be important developmental knowledge and skills for me as a young physician.

While rationally I understood all this, I still remained bothered. I understood the intellectual and medical challenges in her treatment, and I understood the family's desires (guilt?) in preserving life. But something was missing here—the patient. I had spent two hours taking my H&E and knew I was dealing with a tired soul and a good woman who was at the end of a long life. While her life had been a generally happy one, she now was exhausted, in pain, overwhelmed, and knew to her core that that there was no prospect of recovery. She just wanted to pass in peace.

I had a chance to observe her family up close over the three weeks that I cared for Mrs. Miller. She had two daughters, pleasant enough and caring women in their late fifties, who were present almost daily. While they loved their mother, they could not deal with her imminent demise and would never willingly discuss anything meaningful. They insisted to her that she would improve, that something would change. When she would try to talk to them of her pain or concerns, of her wish to just go, they would have none of it. Instead, they would try to unrealistically reassure her and would switch to banalities of things that held little interest for her in her diminished state.

Sadly, much worse than these daughters was Mrs. Miller's only son. While he also appeared with some frequency, he could barely talk to or look at his mother. His visits always seemed obligatory. He would curtly say "Hi, Mom," then walk around the room, dismiss any concerns of his mother, and talk brusquely to the staff. He spent even more time repetitively informing me that he owned several of the Bronx's best haberdasheries than he would spend discussing his mother. I had a chance to observe his obnoxious behavior on many an occasion. My general impression was that a lovely woman deserved much better than such a shmuck of a son.

My role with Mrs. Miller evolved into one that was different than I had with most of my patients at this very early stage of my medical career. Yes, I tried to take care of her elevated calcium, and her diabetes and her sepsis, and prescribed pain medications when needed. But my heart was not really in it. At the end of each day, I would go and sit with her and we would just talk, sometimes finding myself holding her fragile hand. She would tell me about some of the joys of her life in happier times and outline her current sorrows, pains and fears. She would talk to me about how hard it was for her to talk to her family and the sadness and false bravado that they showed that would not let them hear what she wanted and needed to say. And she would tell me how, despite her fears, she was ready to die and just hoped it would happen quickly and painlessly.

We became good friends in that short time, and I felt closer to this elderly woman than I did to many of my own relatives. While her story was sad and I could offer no salvation, I felt more human in the process than I did in the technical aspects of the medicine. Her daughters took me aside on several occasions (I would frequently be sitting with their mother at the end of my day, about the time they would come to visit) and thanked me for the kindness I had shown their mother. While I was almost certainly the least experienced "doctor" who had cared for her in her frenetic last few months, they told me I was their mother's favorite and did more to help her than all the other doctors combined.

Toward the end, it was clear to all that the end was rapidly approaching, and it was just a question of days or hours. When Mrs. Miller passed away after nearly three weeks in the hospital, I sat down with the family to break the news and to discuss things. The family wanted to thank me for "the extraordinary kindness" I had shown their mother and again, how at the end, I had been the only one able to talk to her.

Several days passed and I was handed a message to call her son. When I did, he wanted to thank me again for the compassion I had demonstrated and I accepted his gratitude. Then he added, "You know, Doc, I own what are the best high-end men's stores in the borough. I'd really like to do something nice for you. If you'll come down to the store, I have something I'd really like to give you."

I knew I shouldn't. Oh, there was nothing wrong with taking a gift. I was a terribly poor medical student, eking by on a little bit of scholarship, a few loans, no money from my parents, and a few bucks from working at some odd jobs around the school complex. I had almost no nice clothes and survived on a wardrobe rich in hospital scrubs that frequently served me in the outside world as well. Accordingly, there was good reason to be grateful for some nice clothes. But the guy was such a jerk—what was he going to give me? Plus, I was working over 90 hours a week, had almost no awake time off, had no car, and knew that buses and subways to the address he gave me would likely require at least two hours of precious time.

Still, he insisted. Against my better judgment (maybe it had been the stress of his mother's difficult last weeks that had brought out the worst in him), I relented and agreed to visit his store on my one day off. It actually took longer to get there than I had thought. The store itself was indeed quite impressive with rows of beautiful suits, jackets, pants, all of them seemingly far more elegant than anything I owned.

I asked the clerk for Mr. Miller, who was to meet me at the store at that hour. The young man apologized, telling me that the boss had a pressing appointment but had left a package for me when I happened to arrive. The clerk added that Mr. Miller, somewhat out of character, had several nice things to say about me. With that, from behind the counter, he handed me a handsomely wrapped package. That was it. In less than a minute, I was out the door and back to a long subway ride home. On the train, I decided to open the package and see what treasures awaited. And there it was: a gaudy pink dress shirt.

A PINK shirt! This was a time that no men wore pink. That bastard of a son had probably gone through his entire inventory to find the single item in his beautiful store that had the least chance of selling! And I had used my few hours of precious free time for this.

Mrs. Miller, I'm sorry. You deserved better.

Looking back through the lens of almost half a century, I find myself reflecting on patients like Mrs. Miller. I was blessed with a long medical career, one in which I helped many people and made more than my fair share of challenging or previously missed diagnoses. I was able to take great satisfaction in improving the life of many long-term asthmatic patients, who had previously suffered from years of poor control. Yet, in some ways, it was with the Mrs. Millers, patients whom I had not helped as much medically but instead had connected on a deep and intimate level, offering them some solace or peace that they were otherwise lacking, that, in looking back, I would feel the most like a true physician.

Chapter 22

When I Almost Quit Medicine...Again

At the beginning of my externship two months earlier, my first thoughts of quitting medicine stemmed from my own fear of incompetence and feeling overwhelmed. But the second time I almost quit was entirely different, a function of my disgust with medicine itself. At the time, my externship was in its later stages. In contrast to the very tentative medical neophyte of several weeks earlier, I had increased my familiarity and even developed some basic confidence in myself and my medical abilities. I wasn't all that great by any means, but I could work up a patient more quickly and assuredly and was better at formulating treatment plans. In addition, I acquired a nascent trust in my ability to manage medical problems. Still with plenty of bad moments, but there was a striking difference over these three short months. So the scenario was quite different the second time I started harboring doubts of my path in medicine.

My new admission, Mark, was a relatively healthy appearing 46-year-old businessman, a more typical College Hospital NP than the critically ill ones I had encountered early on. Mark arrived with a single discrete problem—severe pain in the back of his right calf and a previous history of having DVTs (deep vein thrombosis) and a pulmonary embolism. DVTs are clots in the veins, most commonly by far involving veins in the back of the calf, and often characterized by certain areas of major discomfort which can be intensified by the squeezing of the calf.

The danger with DVTs lie not in the leg itself, but in the very real possibility of part of the clot breaking away and lodging in the lung, a so-called pulmonary embolism (PE). Mark had already experienced one several years previously. PEs were serious, and depending on the size and location, frequently proved fatal. This was not a problem to be taken lightly. Mark had started with his DVTs years earlier, significantly younger than most patients particularly given his degree of fitness. Because of the frequency of his problems and the ensuing PE, several years previously, doctors had performed what was then a relatively new procedure on him, the placement of a trap in the vena cava. This was essentially a piece of mesh placed into the largest vein returning blood to the heart from the body. The trap remained in place to snare any clots that might arise in the future before they could travel to the lungs. Similarly, he had been placed on oral anti-coagulants and had been well for five years prior to the onset of this current episode one day earlier. (In later years, a patient like Mark might be evaluated for a clotting disorder or other malady as the cause of his multiple DVTs; this was not a consideration in 1973.)

Mark's personal physician had decided that admission was required for emergency treatment of what was presumed to be yet another DVT. While the mechanical trap would hopefully catch any thrombus that broke away, his doctor wished to minimize risk and ordered heparin treatment initiated, a powerful anticoagulant administered intravenously, and which required close titration and monitoring. I took my relatively complete history and physical exam (both notably more efficient and purposeful than they would have been several weeks earlier) and entered the routine orders required of every admission, including a chest X-ray.

While Mark's case initially sounded straightforward (in a patient with known history of repetitive DVTs, sudden onset of calf pain would certainly suggest another episode of DVT), I was somewhat bothered by this presumptive diagnosis. Although I had never encountered a DVT patient in my brief medical career, there were certain facts that did not ring true and might suggest other possibilities. The patient indeed had severe pain in his leg, but it began in his thigh before moving to the lower leg, a progression he had never experienced before. Indeed, merely touching the side of his thigh was agonizing to the point that even the weight of the sheet to the area was excruciating, unusual in DVTs that did not typically affect that area of the leg. When I further pursued the characteristics of the pain, which his personal physician had apparently not raised in any great detail, Mark noted that the pain was worse than he had ever remembered. Squeezing his calf, which characteristically produced exquisite pain in DVT, proved no worse than squeezing any other part of his leg. Moreover, he had already been taking oral coumadin, an anticoagulant used to prevent this type of problem and had not experienced a recurrence in the several years since this medication had been initiated. The drug should be protecting against DVTs.

Despite my concerns that the diagnosis might be incorrect, after conversation with his outside attending physician, the doctor in charge of the case, we started intravenous heparin to replace his oral coumadin. Along with everything else I was doing, I also checked the patient's X-ray, which appeared clear to my eye.

Then things fell apart.

Several hours after admission, Mark broke out in a severe dermatomal rash on his leg. It was typical of shingles. Shingles, or varicella-zoster, is a virus frequently acquired early in life that can sit dormant in nerve roots for many years until making its presence known decades later in the form of nerve inflammation. This is accompanied by rash and pain that can be quite severe. The rashes are quite characteristic in that they are limited to a single dermatome, the area enervated by a particular nerve root. If the dermatome involved happens to be in a patient's leg, the pain and rash will have a very distinctive distribution, mirroring the path of the nerve from the spinal canal spiraling downwards to the lower leg. While the rash appearance can be distinctive, it is this peculiar distribution of the rash and pain following the nerve's path that is essentially diagnostic in and of itself. Also, while some patients with milder cases have less dramatic pain, many will experience a pain that is apparently truly excruciating and difficult to alleviate. Diagnosis could be very difficult if the pain preceded the rash, as was the case here, but any mystery is removed once the rash appears.

Around this time, I also learned to my considerable surprise that the radiologist read Mark's admission chest X-ray as suspicious. Apparently, there was a shadow in his lung field that had escaped my detection. When time permitted, several hours later, I ran down to review the films with the radiologist. He pointed to an area in the right lung field. But even with being directed to the specific area, I remained unable to see the shadow. The radiologist suggested we schedule a tomogram, a relatively new procedure at the time that involved considerable radiation exposure and was quite expensive, to better define the lesion that remained stubbornly invisible to me. Despite trying, I wished I could see the spot.

I spoke to Dr. Greene and proposed we send the patient home since Mark did not have DVT but instead had shingles, a condition that could be very painful, but not one warranting hospitalization. He agreed with my assessment but told me protocol demanded approval from the patient's admitting personal physician. However, when I reached him, this doctor insisted we keep the patient until we were sure nothing else was going on. I could tell he was playing a game of CYA—Cover Your Ass—and did not want to look stupid in front of the patient. I understood what he was doing but in truth, the shingles diagnosis was not obvious prior to the appearance of the rash, so there was little reason for him to be embarrassed. He also insisted that in view of the X-ray, even before the tomogram, I place a PPD test (used to detect tuberculosis) on the patient's forearm, an injection of material that will elicit redness and firmness 48 hours later if the patient has possible tuberculosis. I told his doctor that in my history taking, I had learned Mark had received a BCG immunization years earlier, a technique more commonly used in Europe particularly in earlier years to prevent tuberculosis than at the current time (and interestingly, as I am reviewing this in 2020, a technique occasionally recommended for conferring non-specific immunity in the time of COVID-19). One problem with BCG use is that it usually results in false positive responses to this sort of TB testing. While not familiar with it myself, I had heard that these reactions could be quite large in some cases and that in general, PPD tests should be avoided in patients who had previously received BCG. When I mentioned this to the attending, he seemed embarrassed that he didn't know about the BCG and insisted I proceed to place the PPD, nonetheless. It was his patient and he was the boss.

That was the background. Now, let's review the tragedies that befell Mark over the next three days that left me pondering my medical career:

1. Despite the patient clearly having shingles, not DVT, the attending doctor would not let me discontinue the unnecessary IV with the heparin and switch back to his oral coumadin.

2. While TB tests often take 48 to 72 hours to start to show a response, because of his past BCG immunization, Mark—not totally unexpectedly—began within 24 hours to have a relatively large reaction on his right forearm, with fairly marked redness, swelling, and later, with some pain.

3. His IV infiltrated that night (i.e., came out of the vein, discharging fluid into the local surrounding area: a common problem then, now somewhat less frequent of an issue with more modern plastic IV catheters currently in use. The staff that restarted the IV that night placed the new one in the same right arm that was beginning to blow up, not an issue unless the IV should infiltrate again, as they were wont to do).

4. While we waited for the attending to agree to discharge the patient, who clearly did not require hospitalization, the new IV infiltrated the same area as his positive test, markedly compounding the pain, induration (hardness), and swelling in the patient's forearm. By the next day, this had swollen to dangerous proportions and the patient was in agony. It was not clear how much of this uncomfortable mass of fluid under pressure was inflammation from the huge PPD reaction, from the IV, or possibly even bleeding since he was on anticoagulants. All that mattered was that it was very uncomfortable and that the patient was actually in some danger as a result.

5. At that time, the radiologist had finally obtained the tomogram. I huddled with the radiologist to review the study. Instead of the dreaded possibility of lung cancer, the patient had...nothing. The radiologist could not find anything amiss on this more advanced test. He called in his chief and together we all reviewed the original films that had led to the need for tomograms. The senior physician now read them as normal, just as I had done originally. The tomogram, with all its expense and considerable radiation exposure, had been unnecessary in the first place. More importantly, there had really been no reason to place the TB test, more dangerous in this particular patient.

6. The forearm was now so swollen that the pulses in his wrist were becoming weaker. That meant he might be developing what is termed a compartmental syndrome, requiring a surgical consult. A compartmental syndrome is a condition in which swelling in an extremity becomes extensive and confined by anatomical barriers, potentially com-

promising blood flow, may require immediate intervention with a long surgical incision to relieve the pressure. The surgeons were extremely concerned, both by the arm but also at the prospect of operating on a patient who was being actively anti-coagulated, making control of surgical bleeding much more difficult. They decided to postpone a decision until morning unless Mark further deteriorated and required immediate intervention.

I mentally reviewed the three-day hospitalization. Mark, who I had developed a close rapport with during this time, was admitted for a condition he did not have. While initially a reasonable consideration, a few more questions (in this case by me, as a medical student) revealed the original diagnosis unlikely and the hospitalization probably not required. In any event, when the true diagnosis of shingles became evident, the patient should have been allowed to return home. It was only because of physician embarrassment on the part of his attending that he remained. Similarly, it was only to appear to be doing something that kept the patient's IV remaining in place, an IV that was only to administer a medication definitely no longer required in view of the correction of his diagnosis.

Compounding this, an over-reading of his X-ray led to additional unnecessary testing. This then led to the placement of a TB test, a procedure usually benign, but which probably should not have been done in this particular patient with his prior BCG immunization. Now it was the combination of an unneeded test and an unneeded IV that led a relatively healthy younger individual to a situation that might require potentially dangerous surgery. And all this from physician error or misplaced hubris.

I spent a long time that evening examining myself in a mental mirror. I decided I would seriously reevaluate my career in medicine if Mark required surgery the next day. My intent was for healing people, not harming them. Even though I had not been the culprit here, I was overwhelmed with the potential that physician mistakes or misplaced ego could cause such potentially dire consequences for a patient.

Thankfully, Mark's arm swelling considerably improved by the next morning and he was out of any danger. He would not require surgery. We removed his IV and he was now allowed to return home, a decision that should have been made days earlier. Mark was still bothered by his very painful shingles, but could nurse his discomfort with medications in more comforting surroundings at home. Before he left, Mark profusely thanked me for all the care and kindness I showed during his stay. While I accepted his gratitude, I was never sure if he understood just how dangerous and unnecessary the many tribulations of his stay had been.

As he departed, I waved goodbye. Inwardly, I felt like crying.

Chapter 23

Don't Give that Insulin!

Stress. Exhaustion. Fatigue. Anxiety. Panic. Sometimes I look back upon the early days of my actual medical career and wonder how I survived it. The same goes for any other house staff member of my generation and by description, even more so for those of earlier years. As I've enumerated, the hours were inhumanely long and the stress levels almost insanely high. This was particularly true in those earlier days, when the trainee was not just learning the facts of medicine but also developing the ability to think like a doctor.

Learning medicine has often been likened to taking a math class which is being taught in Greek, while trying to learn Greek at the same time. You're learning gigabytes of facts at the beginning, but you have not yet developed the framework to organize this information around. It is only later that a student/young physician develops the ability to "think like a doctor," to have that framework to organize the pertinent facts, to have the knowledge become second nature at one's fingertips.

Now, in fairness, the world of technology has made the system light years better over the nearly 50 years since I started my career. Consider the advent of computers and smart phones at hand, making it instantly possible to look up findings of obscure diseases, lists of differential diagnoses (i.e., the list of all diseases that have rash, abdominal pain and fever) or of medications with doses based on patient's weight and renal function, as examples. Prior to these technological advances like the Internet and Google, the trainee had to attempt to memorize all this and more.

The hours were brutal, too. There was no way to sugarcoat it. A day's work might include arriving by 6 A.M. and not leaving until seven that same evening. If on call, instead of leaving in the evening, the extern or resident would stay all night and not leave until he put in a full shift the next day. It was not unusual to be in the hospital for 36 hours consecutively and when on call, get less than three hours sleep (and not infrequently, no sleep at all) while being confronted by repetitive life and death decisions. I've heard this former training schedule described as a pathway to Post-Traumatic Stress Disorder more than once in recent years. Indeed, the connection seems appropriate.

By the end of my externship, while I was considerably more comfortable than the rank beginner of a few months earlier, that did not mean I had any less work or any more sleep. I may have been more effective and a little more confident, but that did not prevent me from walking around in a semi-stupor on very busy nights.

The day had been trying and I was on call that evening with several late admissions. Finally, around 3 A.M., things had quieted to the point that I might actually try to catch a bit of shut-eye. I had attempted to lie down once earlier in the evening but had not even hit the pillow before my beeper had summoned me to the emergency room for another admission. Now I lay my head down to sleep... and I was called about a medication adjustment on a patient I covered. I was totally exhausted by the time I lay down again but was so tense that I doubted sleep to be possible. But slowly.....

The phone rang in the on-call room. I was dead to the world. I wearily answered it. Donna, the night nurse informed me that Mrs. Gold, an elderly woman with diabetes, had a blood glucose that had skyrocketed. Through my mental fog, I instructed the nurse to give the diabetic woman a stat dose of insulin. I started to drift off again before we were even off the phone. I could feel my eyes closing, I dreamed I was on a boat, rocking gently with the swells... and .... SAT BOLT UPRIGHT AND ALMOST SCREAMED! What had I done? That patient didn't have diabetes. I could only pray that the nurse had not given the insulin yet. If too late, I feared what might happen to the patient.

I frantically, called the floor and got the nurse on the phone. "Donna, please tell me you haven't given that dose of insulin on Mrs. Gold. I was fast asleep when you called and must have hallucinated. Please tell me you haven't given it yet or I think I may have killed the patient." I was so scared that I'm not even sure I was coherent. The nurse was also excited as she answered, but in a different way. "Please, calm down, Dr. Lotner! I have no idea what you're talking about. I haven't spoken to you in the last two hours and I didn't call you about anyone's blood sugar and you didn't tell me to give insulin to anyone. And who's Mrs. Gold anyway? We don't have a patient here with that name tonight!"

I had hallucinated the whole thing in my sleep. As I write this 47 years after the fact, I can still feel my heart pounding and the beads of sweat gathering above my lip.

Chapter 24

Internship

Externships behind me, I had made it to Children's Hospital of Philadelphia, the great pediatric hospital associated with the University of Pennsylvania Medical School to start my internship. At the time, CHOP, as it is known to the general public, was and still is considered one of the finest pediatric hospitals in the world. Firmly convinced that I wanted to go into Pediatrics, I considered myself to be very fortunate to have "matched" at such a prestigious institution. I was to spend four years in Philadelphia, first as an intern, then two years as a Pediatric resident with the final year in Pediatric Allergy, Asthma and Immunology fellowship.

I loved my time in Philly. It was a hard decision to leave New York. I was 25 and considered myself a New Yorker to the core. But after just a few days in Philadelphia, a big city in its own right, I wondered why I had lived so long in New York. Philly seemed to have a lot of the amenities but without all the crime, the grime or the constant hectic pace of the Big Apple. (While I loved the time in Philadelphia, in retrospect, I'm amazed how little I really got to know it. I was in the middle of four years of training so intense that I rarely had time to explore the outside world. Many years later, when our son Dan was applying to the University of Pennsylvania for college, we accompanied him on a tour of the Penn campus. There was a sprawling, open grassy area in the middle of the campus. I asked the guide when the college had put this in, and he informed me it dated back to the 1700s and the founding of the college—by Benjamin Franklin, of course. I had never managed to see this large and beautiful area in over four years during my training on the Penn campus.)

My training days were to be a time of transition for CHOP, as well as for me. The physical building housing The Children's Hospital when I arrived for internship in 1973 was almost a hundred years old, seated a mile from the Penn campus in a dreary and rundown part of town. The structure creaked and leaked and was to be replaced a year later by a brand-new beautiful glass structure at the edge of the Penn campus. The move would come at the very end of my internship year. It was in the new structure that I would spend my last three years in the city. The modern building was to be a wonderful improvement, but the old building had a certain charm of its own, including conference rooms on the roof that we would use (particularly on the oncology wards), to meet with patients or parents, sometimes even having to walk through rain or snow to get there.

I loved my internship, a sentiment rarely expressed by medical personnel in those days. Old docs, like myself, weren't "pampered" like today's young physicians-in-training. (My son, a doctor a generation later, would vehemently disagree with the use of the term "pampered.") This was one of the same complaints leveled against my cohort by the generation of doctors before me. And while I'll agree that older group had it even rougher than mine, our life wasn't easy as house staff (interns and residents). We would be on-call every third night, every other night on some rotations. This meant that following a "normal work shift," usually 12 hours long, the young physician would get to spend every third night in the hospital tending to any of the patients who needed immediate attention (usually many of them) and admitting anyone who came in from the emergency room, too ill to leave.

Sleep was a precious commodity, usually two to three hours a night if you were lucky. During my worst rotation from a physical viewpoint, the Neonatal ICU, a six-week stint, of my 14 nights on call, I had a total of six hours sleep for the entire rotation! And then, at the end of that night on call, the intern or resident would still not get to leave. He or she still faced that next "normal" work shift from 7 A.M. to 6 P.M. before being able to depart. No wonder we were exhausted almost all year.

As an intern, I was paid $8,700 a year for the privilege of spending 60 percent of my waking hours working in the hospital, being rewarded with meal after meal of soggy, bland, tasteless hospital food, of being constantly tired and stressed, of getting little to no exercise. This was far less than most of my friends in considerably less rigorous careers. And, if translated into today's dollars, that still worked out to being…very poor!

Somehow, despite the stress and hours, my house staff days were amongst the happiest of my life. A lot of this had to do with the process of building of confidence and self-worth that had started a few months earlier as an extern, as well as the camaraderie found in working so closely with a group of similarly stressed people. I grew up a lot during those years. I had previously known I was bright, but there was a tremendous difference between book knowledge, which had always come naturally to me, and being an actual practicing physician, treating sick patients.

While my training started out, as it does for many doctors, with concerns of adequacy and competency (asking questions like: can I really take care of someone with a life-threatening illness? Can I make decisions rapidly and confidently under the most trying of circumstances? Can I handle the responsibility of having some-one's life in my hands in a critical situation? Can I live with a pa-tient dying while under my care?), I began to realize after several months that I was actually pretty good at this medicine stuff. I went from being a fumbling klutz to someone who could start an IV easily on a three-pound preemie or thread an umbilical cathe-ter or put in a chest tube. While I didn't make every diagnosis, I became skilled at sizing up situations quickly and logically, formulating a treatment plan and taking care of the critically ill. The realization that I could do this gave me a feeling of confidence that I had never experienced before and a feeling of worthiness that I also had not known previously. Lack of sleep and a couple of years of poverty were small price to pay for this experience.

Chapter 25

Assault, No Battery

It was my first week of internship in July of 1973. I had just survived my second night on call and was very tired. Now at 7:00 P.M., I started to walk the several blocks to where I had parked my old clunker of a car. I was exhausted and couldn't wait to get home. As mentioned above, CHOP (Children's Hospital) was set in a crumbling tenement neighborhood in central Philly, in a decrepit building, preparing to move to the University of Pennsylvania campus a year later. There wasn't much to like in the surrounding neighborhood although, considering the long hours, many of the house staff rented nearby apartments. But not me.

I had paid close attention at orientation a few weeks earlier, when Dr. Carlos Rodriguez, the Chief Resident, had briefed the new interns on the important stuff, like how to physically survive working 80–100+ hours a week, where to live, and where to eat. Having no money, I paid particularly close attention to the part about where to live. I was intrigued when Dr. Rodriguez talked about considering the benefits of living across the river in New Jersey, where you could get bigger, newer apartments for half the rent. So, one weekend I drove down from my last medical school rotation in New York to look for an apartment. I quickly decided he was right; Philly apartments would stretch my very limited budget.

In my price range, I could find a marginal small flat in a transitional area near the hospital, none of which seemed particularly nice. However, driving 30 minutes, a beautiful big two-bedroom with lush lawns and endless blue skies was quite affordable even on an intern's ridiculously small salary. I once calculated that working 90 hours a week, which was on the moderate side, we made about $1.67 an hour. Although there was no minimum wage back then, that was lower than my jobs had paid when bagging groceries in high school. I didn't care that all the other interns I had spoken to opted to live close by the hospital; I would be smarter and avoid the local rat traps.

Oh, stupid me. I had failed to adequately consider those 90+ hour weeks or the challenge of long drives home following all-nighters on call tending to the sick. I frequently dozed on those drives, surviving two minor accidents, having fallen asleep at the wheel and drifting off the road, luckily with little damage. I also didn't think that the 30-minute drive on a weekend might turn into 60–75 minutes at rush hour. And I surely didn't factor in that Rodriguez had three kids and a wife and was living in an apartment complex where everyone else seemed to have three kids and a wife. A single guy with an intern's horrendous schedule probably wouldn't have a single date during an entire year living in a bedroom community in Lindenwold, New Jersey.

I most definitely did not factor in parking around the hospital, where one could drive endlessly and aimlessly for half an hour looking for a legal spot. That is, unless you were willing to drive south a few blocks into never, never land (a no-no also covered by Dr. Rodriguez in his introductory talks), where you would probably find a spot but with no guarantee that your car would be there upon your return. That was the area that I now found myself coming back to fetch my car that July night so early in my internship. When I had arrived at the hospital the day before, unable to find a spot in the "good area," I eventually made my way further south and came across a spot in short order and luckily, set right under a streetlamp. I was not particularly upset about the neighborhood. I had survived two years in college, living in a fraternity house in Harlem, one of the very few white students willing to live near the CCNY campus. This area was surely no worse.

Approaching my car (yes, the veritable chick magnet of an earlier tale, the green and white ex-NYC taxicab with fare rates still visible on the doors, barely camouflaged by the last paint job), I smiled to see the car was present and waiting for me. As I approached, I mentally noted that the angle of the hood seemed a bit funny but paid it no mind. However, when I started the car...nada, nothing, the rather deafening sounds of silence. As I morosely exited the car to see what was wrong, I noted that the hood was already slightly ajar. When I lifted it, there was an empty space where the battery should have been. I couldn't believe it. Someone actually had the gall and stupidity to steal a battery out of an ex-cab with 270,000 miles on it!

Cursing, muttering, I walked the six blocks to a service station and found a nice guy who drove me back with a new battery (that I could barely afford), which he installed for me. The next morning, waiting for house staff rounds to start, I started telling the other interns about my tale of woe, and then went into a diatribe about the idiots in the neighborhood who were so dumb that they would take my old, almost-dead battery from my veritable jalopy. What jerks! How dumb could you get!?

I hadn't realized that while I was talking, the aforementioned Dr. Rodriguez, the Chief Resident, had walked in behind me. He tapped me on the shoulder and then said in a very loud voice, "Lotner, you're the one who's dumb if you think they wanted your OLD battery. They wanted your NEW battery!

"They know the car; they know you're on call every third night and the car will be there and they know your car will have a brand-new battery when you leave it out there tomorrow night! Get a hood lock before then!"

I had no idea what a hood lock was (a small but sturdy chain-like device with a lock that needed to be opened with a key, without which the hood could not be lifted more than three inches) and had one installed at the same service station the next evening.

Two evenings later, after my next night on call, I returned to find my car with the hood opened three inches—but no farther— and my shining new battery still in place.

Thank you, Dr. Rodriguez, wherever you are. And I never dissed the local residents again when it came to street smarts.

Chapter 26

Too Close to Home

I was two months into my baby-ward rotation, taking care of children too old for the nursery but below age three. It was my third rotation as an intern. The year started out with me, like most of my colleagues, feeling tentative, anxious and unsure of ourselves. But somehow, over the next several months, we transformed into a group of much more confident and competent young doctors. I was taking care of roughly 20 young children and would be responsible for the pediatric medical experience of two new medical students starting with me that morning. They'd follow me around and learn under my tutelage, the same position I had myself been in two years earlier with Dr. Aiges.

During the several weeks students would spend with me, I preferred they listen more in the earliest weeks, observing how I took my histories, performed physicals, and made assessments. As their familiarity increased, they would be assigned more and more responsibilities. But it was important during the initial part of the rotation, before they were allowed more freedom, that they learn about the important parts of the pediatric history and exam, which had considerably different emphases than those for adult patients.. With a new group of students such as the ones today, they would be in listening mode as the proctorship began and my history-taking tended to be just a little more thorough than it might otherwise be.

That particular morning, trailed by the two eager new students, I entered the examination room to interview and examine our first admission, a 14-month-old with a seizure disorder. This would be the first pediatric patient these third-year medical students had ever examined. Ultimately, it would be one that they (and I) would probably never forget.

Entering the room, we met what at first glance appeared to be an extremely striking couple, the mother half-turned, with a baby nestled against her chest. Initially, the parents seemed indeed a handsome pair. A well-to-do young couple from the upscale Main Line suburbs, they were the kind of couple with whom I was easily able to identify (assuming, of course, that I would at some point find a wife and start a family). The husband was quite handsome and the mother, well, frankly stunning. A slightly closer look however gave a somewhat different impression, as both looked more than a little haggard and stressed: the mother's makeup askew, hastily applied and stress lines obvious. When she turned, I could finally see the baby—and sadly, instead of the beautiful infant that should accompany such a good-looking couple, was an infant who would qualify as an ignominious medical term, a gork.

Gork is one of those absolutely atrocious but useful medical terms, never used in front of patients, but capable of quickly conveying a picture. Such terms saved a lot of time and helped to relieve the anxiety of the medical staff. Someone once told me that the term "gork" originated as an acronym for God Only Really Knows. But the term later came to reference a patient with irreversible loss of brain functions. In common parlance, a vegetable. It could cover patients with severe trauma in permanent coma maintained on a ventilator, or with expanded usage, such as for this baby, a patient with almost no cerebral functioning and one unlikely to ever improve. The baby lay in his mother's arms, eyes unfocused, drooling, all limbs rigidly locked in place and with contractures at strange angles, emitting a series of piercing, high-pitched shrieks.

A tale of horror unfolded as the family answered my questions and shared the history. I no longer accurately remember many details of the exchange, but the story generally went along the following lines: The parents were two young professionals, recently married and thrilled in anticipation of their first child. Pregnancy had been uneventful until eventually something had gone egregiously wrong in the delivery room. There was an unexpected breech delivery, too much use of forceps, inability to extract the baby vaginally, a loss of blood, a mad rush to an operating room for a C-section on the infant who was initially not breathing, an inability to resuscitate the baby after the procedure, and then, just before efforts were to be called off, Baby Jimmy had miraculously (tragically?) started to breathe.

A long NICU admission followed with chronic seizures and multiple other complications. When finally allowed to go home after several months, the parents were accompanied by an infant with no signs of significant higher brain function, one who had frequent seizures, could not eat, did not follow sounds, and showed no signs of recognition. He could only feed through an indwelling tube inserted through the nose. During seizures or with aspiration of meals, the child often suffered cardiorespiratory arrest and the parents had long since been taught resuscitative measures to be initiated until paramedics could arrive.

The baby had been admitted and readmitted to the hospital at least 15 times over the last year, sometimes after paramedics were called during one of these arrests. Other hospital stays were for medication adjustment when seizures became more severe than usual, or for pneumonias suffered from aspirating stomach contents with feedings. Because of this, the parents constantly remained at home, their personal and recreational lives long since vanished. I gently asked if they ever got any relief; a night out. The mother teared up, then answered that they had only tried once, several months earlier.

Their neighbors (and best friends) had constantly prodded them that they, the parents, needed a break. The neighbors had been there often enough through Jimmy's seizures to know how to suction him or deal with problems. It was only at the insistence of these friends that the parents had anxiously taken a short evening, two hours for a nice dinner with a glass of wine. They joked and partially relaxed. When they returned home, smiling but anxious, their worst fears had materialized—an ambulance was outside their house, about to depart for the hospital. Jimmy had aspirated, arrested after suctioning. The friends, unable to get him breathing for a couple of minutes, called 911, finally getting a response with the resumption of a ragged breathing pattern just before the arrival of the paramedics. Although the child survived, the friends, trembling, were besides themselves, crying and apologizing, and it was clear that they would never be able to tend to Jimmy in the future. Several months had passed and neither the friends nor anyone else had offered to assist again.

The child was on the neurologic service and this admission, like so many others, had followed an arrest, CPR initiated by the parents and continued by the paramedics. His current unresponsive state was his normal one, not occasioned by the earlier arrest. There had been no developmental milestones met and the family had been warned not to expect anything more in the future, short of a miracle.

As I somehow continued on with the history, trying not to cry myself, I looked at my students in the background, the male choking back tears, the female sobbing softly. I probably would have deferred further questioning had I been alone. But with new medical students, I felt compelled to push further. I asked about the parents themselves and what must have been absolutely horrible changes and stresses in their lives. The answers were even more shattering than I could have anticipated. The mother, of course, had quit her job, giving up what had once seemed a promising career. The father's career in a prestigious financial institution was jeopardized by his frequently necessitated absences. Both had started smoking and put on weight, unable to sleep. They were using Valium and the mother was on other sedatives as well. Both cried frequently, nerves frayed. While they tried to be a team, tensions were high, and they frequently fought and yelled at each other. They sometimes screamed at their own parents and anyone else who tried to give advice. Recounting this, the mother briefly broke down sobbing and had to leave the room. I used the opportunity to take the father aside for a few minutes (most of the history had come from his wife). He told me he worried he could not personally continue this course much longer and feared he might have to leave the home. He choked up as he said this.

When everyone was back in the room and we were all relatively quiet, I finally asked how the parents would feel if there were a time Jimmy arrested and could not be resuscitated. The mother fidgeted and cried, the father nodded and softly answered that it would probably be better. Had they themselves ever thought about not resuscitating the child? Mother sobbed more loudly and finally murmured that while she knew that he would never develop into anything, and she hated her life and thought her marriage might fall apart if they continued this way, every day hoping (and hating herself for hoping) that Jimmy would die, she could NEVER live with herself if she did not try to resuscitate him. As she said this, my new female student ineffectively stifled a shriek and ran, sobbing, from the room.

When I collected myself, I soberly went on. I understood that inaction at home was out of the question for them, but how would they feel if Jimmy were to arrest during the hospitalization and not be resuscitated? The parents tearfully looked at each other for some long moments, almost unable to speak. It was the young mother who finally responded. "Doctor, I think we would pray for that. We can't NOT treat him at home, but we would pray for that."

I asked if they would want me to write a DNR (Do Not Resuscitate) order, something I had never asked a family before. They both shook their heads in the affirmative, and cried softly, holding each other. When the parents, students and I all stopped our tears, I wrote the first and only DNR order of my medical career.

The next morning, Dr. T, the Neurology attending in charge of Jimmy's long-term care as well as in the hospital, hauled me into a conference room. There I received the loudest, longest, and harshest lambasting of my medical career before his two neurology residents, my supervising resident, the other interns and my students. He correctly asserted that the patient was on his service and it was not my place to write such an order without consulting him (he was totally right in that regard). Moreover (as a strict Catholic, which he didn't add but I was well aware), he believed in the sanctity of life and it was not the place of Man (or doctor), to ever write such an order and none would ever be written on any patient under his care. The chastisement went on, long and loud. It was the greatest whiplashing of my medical journey.

Looking back 45 years later, I would have made the same decision I made that day. Jimmy's hospitalization lasted two days, was uneventful, and the family somberly departed. I never saw them again and know nothing of the child or the family's fate.

Chapter 27

Now That's a Cough

It was 3:00 A.M. on a wintry Philadelphia night. I was the intern in the ER, currently seeing an eight-year-old boy and a very frustrated, very unhappy mother. It was the midst of the virus/flu/bronchitis season and half of Philadelphia was sick with one thing or another. This kid had a bad cough and it was driving the mother batty. He apparently had been coughing for almost three weeks and she had given him "everything" to no avail. This particular evening, having listened to him barking both in and out of bed, awake or asleep, she had decided to bring him in in the middle of the night since "We weren't gonna' get no sleep anyhow." They had been in our Emergency Room a week earlier. The child was no better.

I asked her to describe the cough, but she was clearly tired and angry and past the stage where she was about to offer any help. All she knew was this cough was bad and she wasn't happy. I persisted: "Was it wet, or dry?" Just bad. "In his throat or chest?" Eye roll. "Fever? Sore throat? Wheeze?" Eye rolls and foot tapping. "All I know is it's the worst damned cough in the whole damned world. I ain't never heard such a cough! It's terrible and I ain't never heard a cough so bad."

There was a lot of bronchitis in the community and it was lasting a long time, as I well knew. The whole ER staff, definitely including myself, had caught various things from the hordes of sick kids who had been piling in endlessly for weeks. They say that a pediatrician in a new town is likely to catch many respiratory infections during their first year and that axiom certainly held by me. I had been sick almost the entire winter, including needing a ventilating tube inserted in my ear in the operating room when an unresponsive ear infection had lasted well over a month.

Currently, my own bronchitis was particularly severe, my cough now in its sixth week. While we were all ill, the other staff members were particularly worried about me since my cough was so harsh and persistent. At three times during that period, my co-workers had insisted I have a chest X-ray before letting me continue on with my shift. Like this kid, I'd had no response to "everything," in my case including several cough suppressants, codeine, and antibiotics. I knew how he felt.

Still, before ordering an X-ray and some tests, I wanted a little more information. The mother looked no more cooperative. I said to her, "Let me ask you, does his cough sound like this?"

Mildly anxiously I forced myself to cough once, knowing the bouts that maneuver could sometimes trigger. Sure enough, after the first forced cough, I felt the all-too familiar irritation in my throat, and I coughed in a paroxysm, much more intensely. I could feel the cough settling more deeply into my chest, a feeling I knew only too well after all these weeks. As the spasm worsened and I could no longer catch my breath, my knees started to buckle and I was then down on them, trying to catch my breath between coughs. It started to abate after a minute, but the spell resumed just when I thought it might end. Now even more intense, this time with me fully down to the floor, coughing and trying to grab a breath. By the time I looked up, my eyes were tearing freely, and I knew from experience I was probably almost blue. I hunched over for a minute, gasping, finally beginning to catch my breath. I pulled myself back up. The mother looked at me, rising from the floor.

"Yeah, it's just like that...but his ain't nearly that bad."

Chapter 28

Pediatric Clinic, Part I

It was Tuesday afternoon, a dreaded time. I headed for my General Pediatric Clinic. I was a hotshot pediatric resident at Children's Hospital of Philadelphia and was rotating through the ICU that month. Throughout our residency, it was mandatory to attend my despised General Pediatric Clinic no matter what else was going on over the course of an assigned afternoon. Why dreaded or despised? As we would discover later in our medical careers, pediatric clinic would prove much closer to real life general pediatric practice than our life-or-death hospital experiences. But at the time, it was hard to leave the desperately ill patients on the wards to tend to daily trivialities like well-baby check-ups or immunization administrations. The contrast between the severely ill and the mundane could not have been starker. My entire clinic would be spent thinking of the sicker ICU patients who cried for my immediate attention.

That afternoon, as I ran late as usual to Clinic, with my mind totally engrossed in the very sick six-year-old I had just admitted with pneumonia complicating his severe asthma, my first appointment was with a new family, 14-year-old Janine and her parents, Delores and Fred. The parents' (or should I say the mother's) concern was that Janine weighed far too much. I looked at the three people in front of me. The patient, Janine, was 5 foot 5, weighed about 220 pounds, and spent her time studiously counting cracks in the ceiling during the interview. She was a clone of her mother. Delores, the talker in the group, was about five-three, weighed about 250 and was a human chatterbox, who never stopped talking. On the other hand, father Fred, who I felt a certain kinship with, was about six-two, probably clocked in about 138 and sat hunched over in his chair, seemingly fascinated by some pattern in the linoleum flooring. If the women resembled overripe cantaloupes, Fred was the proverbial string bean. He looked to be in almost physical pain, having been so obviously forced by his wife to attend the visit. He never said a word.

Delores droned on and on, needing no prompting, talking about Janine's history, starting seemingly in utero and proceeding in painfully minute detail through early childhood and only after a seemingly interminable period, even reaching current years. Agonizingly, she left nothing out of her saga. Meanwhile, everyone else fidgeted in our own ways. Initially polite and letting Delores continue to talk, I then unsuccessfully tried to cut her off. Father Fred continued to fidget as she droned on, staring at the floor and tapping his shoe. Finally, my mind clearly on my ICU patients, I interrupted. "Tell me, Delores, do you have any thoughts as to why Janine is so heavy?"

Delores suddenly became very serious, her face taking on a demeanor usually reserved for someone about to say something very profound. She pronounced, "Yes, Doctor, we really think it's her GLANDS."

At this, Fred, previously silent and uninvolved, suddenly could contain himself no more. Propelling himself from his chair, he jumped up, extending to his full height, spun towards his wife and yelled, "Oh, shut up Delores, you know she eats too f**king much!!!"

Couldn't have said it any better myself, Fred.

****

Most of my patients in my General Pediatric Clinic were relatively poor people from the surrounding community, the majority very nice but medically unsophisticated and with the most basic pediatric needs. Jennifer and her parents stood out conspicuously in this group. They were a suburban family from Philadelphia's prestigious Main Line suburbs, clearly intelligent, quite well-educated, well-dressed, well-mannered. They were usually the only white family that I would see in an afternoon of Clinic.

I had first taken care of Jennifer two years earlier at age 12 when she had been admitted after a prolonged illness had turned out related to a chronic kidney problem, conspicuously missed by her personal pediatrician. Her course had been a somewhat complicated one and considerable follow-up had been required. I had seen her back frequently, often consulting the hospital's renal specialists.

Normally, we would see a patient like this for her specific issue while her outside pediatrician would continue to see her for on-going general care. However, the family took a liking to me, and despite the high regard that their private physician was usually accorded in the local community, asked if I would consider following her as a regular pediatric patient. I was more than happy to do that. Since I had diagnosed her illness and she was now doing well, I could sense the respect they had for me on anything they asked about. I had to admit it felt pretty good. Here was an obviously sophisticated family that had evaluated things and esteemed me more than their own well-thought of pediatrician. Every time they came in, and thoughtfully listened to whatever I said, I did feel a certain little ego boost that felt, as Larry David might say years later, "Pretty good. Pretty, pretty good."

At her last visit, age 14, Jenny's kidney disease had been very stable. Now she was brought in for a different reason, the parents frustrated regarding some acting out issues not unusual in adolescence. They were hoping for some thoughtful guidance.

As I've made clear, my thinking about myself had changed

markedly over the previous two years, having transformed from uncertain medical student into a fairly confident and competent intern. I'm not saying I was necessarily the best intern or resident—I had friends who I deemed even better. But even then, I was pretty damned good. It may have been the first time in my life that I really felt confident in myself. You got a kid who needed critical care? I can do that. You got a 1,000-gram (two-pound) preemie who needed an umbilical line? I can do that. You got a kid who no one else can find an IV? I'm your guy.

You got a sophisticated suburban family that I can identify with and a 14-year-old girl who's acting out? No idea. I mean, like, none. But I had read my texts and I was a people person and I had learned with my newfound doctor's confidence that I could usually bullshit pretty well. So I regurgitated some suggestions from one of the respected pediatric texts about handling such problems, hoping I sounded at least somewhat authoritative. I almost thought it actually sounded pretty good.

As they usually did when I gave them information, the parents carefully considered everything I said. These people loved me! The father, a teacher, always nodded thoughtfully while pro-cessing. Finally, he looked at me and said, "You don't have any kids, do you, Doc?"

Thus another false god crashes to earth. But I learned from that experience. A few years later, when doing my second Fellowship in Allergy and Immunology at National Jewish Hospital in Denver, I moonlighted at a Pediatric ER at a major hospital. When parents brought in a 16-year-old girl for a sinus infection, but started questioning me about behavioral issues as well, I told them quite authoritatively that my own daughter was not exhib-iting that type of behavior now. However, I said, this is what I would do if she did. They seemed quite happy with my advice. And I most certainly did not volunteer that my own daughter was six months old at the time!

Chapter 29

Assault, Almost

I had finished a long shift after an on-call night late in my internship, and I was walking the six blocks to the High-Speed Line railroad to Lindenwold, New Jersey. As usual, my old car was in the shop. So once again, I was taking public transportation to get back home from the hospital. To add to the joys of working all night long, followed by a full next day at the hospital, I now would endure the long walk to the station, face a 45-minute train ride, then either hitch a ride or walk two miles back to my apartment complex from the station. I found it amazing as to how many people refused to stop for a guy in scrubs, a white coat, and with a black medical bag.

On this particular evening, the sky already darkened in Philly as I walked toward the station. Three young teens approached me, and as they passed all pulled pocketknives and closed in around me. One of them hissed: "Give me your wallet! Quick, if you don't want us to cut you!"

I looked into three young black faces, about 14 years old or so. I only had $11.00 in my wallet. It was 1974, a long time before I would own a credit card. I wasn't in total shock, as I had been held up a couple of times years earlier while living in Harlem in college. I was not about to resist. Slowly I reached into my back pocket and pulled out my wallet and started to raise it high.

Suddenly, as I extended my arm, one of the kids, yelled, "Oh, shit! That's my Doc!" Instantaneously, the three young thieves glanced quickly at each other—and then suddenly turned and ran off into the darkening night.

And I stood there, my hand with wallet still held high in front of me, thinking, "What the F...?" I had no idea who he was.

There were some benefits to General Pediatric Clinic after all.

Chapter 30

Just Don't Touch His Ear

The child looked like Little Lord Fauntleroy. Edward and his mother stood out from all the other patients and families waiting in the Emergency Room. Bedlam was the rule. CHOP still rested in that century-old building, two miles from the Penn Campus in a ghetto neighborhood (we would be moving to our almost completed new Glass Palace in just a few months). The place was pure chaos. Most of the patients were poor and frequently unwashed African Americans or Hispanics, with a healthy spattering of poor whites mixed in. Most people did not have their own physicians and would come to the ER, frequently to wait three or more hours to be seen for trivial problems such as rashes that had been present for several weeks or a fever that had "spiked" to 99 degrees. If you combined this mass of humanity with those with true medical emergencies, too few seats in the waiting area, dim lighting, insufficient bathing and poor ventilation, you had a scene presumably arising from Dante's *Inferno*.

Edward and Mother appeared in this maelstrom one afternoon, looking to be directly from the pages of an English novel. They were distinguished by appearance, demeanor and costume. Edward was three years old, nearly four, a perfect little English gentleman. He appeared to be clad like a country squire's child in blue collared shirt and cuffed pants. His blonde hair was carefully parted, in keeping with his overall appearance. He spoke in the educated clipped English accent that Americans have come to so readily associate with taste and breeding. He was paired perfectly with his mother, elegantly dressed in subdued tweed, with a self-assured bearing and possessed of an identical upper-class diction. The two seemingly exuded more class than the entire waiting room collectively.

When I inquired why they were there, Mother responded that Edward was perfectly capable of telling me. And indeed he was, and he did. Although only three, nearly four (as he repetitively pointed out), he told me that he had a long history of ear problems with previous ventilating tubes on several occasions and he was now going to require additional surgery. He answered every question I asked with, "Yes, Sir; No, Sir; Thank you, Sir." That was more "Sirs" than I had heard in my several months of internship in total.

Mother rather precisely added the rest of the history. The family, obviously British, now lived in a wealthy outlying area of Philadelphia, where the father was a respected History professor at a major university. Edward had chronic ear problems from a very early age. After two previous surgeries from a local otolaryngologist, when problems recurred, the family had been referred to Dr. Sylvan Stool, head of ENT at CHOP and one of the most respected founding fathers of pediatric otolaryngology. As was the custom at CHOP, all surgical admissions had to have a brief pediatric note placed on the chart clearing them for surgery. Usually a Pediatric Resident would rotate with Dr. Stool and perform this chore. As no resident was available that week, they had been sent to the ER for a perfunctory exam.

As I started to perform a quick exam, Edward remained the picture of English civility.

"Take some deep breaths, please."

"Of course, Sir."

"Can you lie down?"

"As you wish, Sir."

I complimented his mother on what a perfect little gentleman

Edward was and how refreshing to see such manners in a three-year-old.

"Thank you, Doctor. He really is a very good child although I have to warn you—he does not like having his ears examined." That seemed perfectly reasonable in a child with such intractable ear problems.

I reached the part of exam where I would normally be looking at the ears next, but the child suddenly became very squirmy and obviously agitated. While good physicians prefer to always do their physical examinations in the same order, I decided to defer the ears until last. (When examining a patient, if the physician does not keep an order and instead concentrates only on the complaint, it is far too easy to realize later that some part of the exam has been omitted. As an example, I have diagnosed at least four cases of Hodgkin's Lymphoma in patients who were seeing me for unrelated allergy problems and whose family physicians had missed all important clues.) Thus, most physicians have a routine they prefer to adhere to invariably. When I told Edward we would defer looking at his ears, his demeanor instantly improved again, and the perfect little English squire reappeared. "Of course. Thank you, Sir!"

A few minutes later, I could no longer postpone the inevitable. Otoscopic ear exams are not painful to children, provided the child is still and not moving, either of his own accord, or in a frightened childlike Edward, by being firmly held in place by the physician, parent or staff.

Despite his anxiety of the ear examination, probably not entirely unexpected in a child with this long history, this was the most important part of the physical considering the circumstances and complaints. The child immediately tensed up, squirmed and bawled. This was before I even touched him. I had no chance of holding him down by myself without the assistance of another. His mother suddenly seemed flummoxed by the events and was of no help whatsoever. Cheryl, our incredibly effective nursing supervisor, who a few moments earlier I had noted beaming at the manners of this toddler, came over and started to position him.

Mother called out, "Don't hold him too tightly!" Au contraire, it is the child who is left free to suddenly jolt that can actually injure himself, not the child who is immobilized. With Cheryl's invaluable assistance, we pinned Edward down. For a moment, I thought him to be calmer and no longer frothing at the mouth as he had been seconds earlier. As I started to gently insert the otic speculum, he suddenly yelled out, "GET OFF OF ME, MOTHER F***ER!"

I paused for a moment, not believing my ears. And as the cacophony of sound that usually enveloped the whole ER and waiting room came to a ghostly silence, he could be heard clearly and loudly and with perfect diction yelling out for all to hear: "GET THE F*** OFF OF ME, YOU BLOODY BASTARDS!" Mother said later that he really was sensitive to having his ears examined. I do believe she was correct.

And thus ended my encounter with the young English Lord.

Chapter 31

Lotner, You're a Genius

I was on call on Baby Ward late one night when I got a call from the ER. That usually meant there was an incoming admission. But this time, it was just a question. Several months earlier, when I had rotated through the ER, I had seen a child with chronic abdominal pains of long duration. I had prescribed something for him and it was apparently the only thing that had ever helped. The medication had come with very unusual instructions. Now he had run out of the pills and was back in the ER again. The mother remembered my name, remembered the medicine began with "Plack," remembered the somewhat unusual administration technique, but could not for the life of her, remember the full name of the medication.

The ER intern, my friend Jan, on call in the ER that night, was hoping I might remember what I had prescribed since the chart was not immediately available. No one could figure out what medication it might possibly be. They hadn't wanted to call me at 2 A.M., but when none of the emergency room staff (the intern, resident nor charge nurse) could think of a GI medication with "Plack" in it, they determined it was worth waking me.

It took a moment or two, but I indeed remembered the patient and the treatment and had to suppress a big smile. Since I had never received any follow-up, despite the hour, I was actually quite pleased that I had had been successful in figuring out how to treat a recurring problem. I had seen the child, a nine-year-old boy from the community, who had a two-year history of abdominal pains. He had appeared at the ER at least 15 times during that period, always at night, always crying, but with no distress and with normal abdominal exam. Previous physicians had ordered several tests over time, and all had returned normal. They then had referred the child to the Pediatric Gastroenterology Clinic, where further evaluation had likewise proved unremarkable. However, the child had continued with his periodic pains.

When I saw him for the first time late one night, with the exam confirming he was in no danger and the pain already improving over time, I confidently had told the mother that I knew of a medication that would help during these dreadful attacks. However, she must follow directions exactly. When he awoke upset and whimpering in pain, she must give him one of the blue pills I would prescribe, and slowly drink half of a glass of warm cocoa. Then over the next ten minutes, she would gently rub his tummy in a clockwise direction. It was important that it was clockwise! She would then give him a second pill with the rest of the cocoa, continuing to gently stroke his stomach for another few minutes.

Apparently, this had done the trick (the mother told my co-intern that I was the only one in the hospital smart enough to figure out what was needed!) and they had done very well, with only occasional episodes, always responding to treatment until the medication ran out. Now if they could just get a refill. The medication I had prescribed? PlackyBow, or at least that was the way I had pronounced it to mother. The spelling, P-L-A-C-E-B-O, was a little different and luckily the CHOP pharmacy had this prescribable as white, pink, or blue tablets. I guess I was smart enough to have chosen the blue ones.

So, as I told my friend, in the future, if confronted with a healthy child with mild abdominal pains regularly occurring on nights before school tests, remember it's the BLUE PlackyBow pills and remember to instruct the family to rub the belly CLOCKWISE.

Sometimes, the magic is in the details.

Chapter 32

Sure I know Louie Capistrano

During my residency years, I went out with some interesting women prior to meeting Sandy, the woman I would later marry. The word "interesting," of course, being one of those words that covers a lot of territory, is often used when one is not quite sure what else to say. In retrospect, I would say that these women had one thing in common: at some primal level, I knew they were not marriage material for me. Of them, Laura was amongst the strangest of the strange: a very cute surgical nurse at CHOP, a very good nurse under pressure, but more than a little spacey in other aspects.

Amongst Laura's many stories that fell way beyond my rather straightforward, New York Jewish, college-to-medical school up-bringing was a claim that sometime earlier, she had been the live-in girlfriend of one of my favorite singers, Jim Croce. If that idea hadn't seemed ludicrous enough, Laura insisted that she had spent almost a year living with Croce and his wife together on a farm in some sort of blissful threesome. Furthermore, she maintained that Croce wrote the popular song "Operator" with her in mind after she left. No, definitely not the typical nice-Jewish-girl that I would be looking to bring home to Mom.

Laura had many more tales to tell. I was never sure how many had a basis in truth, or how many had originated in a drug-enhanced imagination. I suspected relatively few were real, but later found out that at least some of the characters she claimed to know actually did exist.

We were lying in bed one night, having dated several times, and Laura questioned why we had not left her apartment and why I seemed to no longer have a car. After our first date a few weeks earlier, she noted that subsequently we would just hang out, never straying beyond walking distance. I explained that my car had died, and I had little money or time to get it repaired. This was one of a series of early cars I owned that fell into the clunker category. This one had been a step up and was actually the first that had not started its existence as a taxicab.

Indeed, I had started out with (relatively) high hopes for this car. It had belonged to my dear cousin Helene and her husband Jack, two of my favorite people, who had served as my substitute parents when, during a gawky and trying adolescence, I had problems with my parents. Jack and Helene had a car they had owned for a few years, a green Dodge, one they had cherished and nurtured, serviced religiously, never had any problems with, and only because they loved me, were willing to part with for a much lower price than they would normally have sought. My luck!

It broke down for the first time three days after it left its original home. Over the next several months, the only thing that I could count on to occur as regularly as my every third nights on call, was the frequency with which this babe broke down. Sometimes, I suspected that I could just look at the car and it would die, presumably of laughter.

On our first date the month before, Carol and I had doubled with my friend and co-resident Gary Fleisher. At the end of the evening, the car failed to start when we left his apartment. Jump-starting with cables proved fruitless. In despair, I had just left the car where it sat. Miraculously for the city of Philadelphia, where every street had alternate side parking which required moving a vehicle daily, Gary's particular apartment complex had a circular parking area with no parking restrictions! To show how dire parking was in Philly back then, because of this legal spot, I almost regarded my broken-down vehicle as a victory. Six weeks later, the car sat untouched and unmoved. I wasn't even thinking about how I would deal with it.

When Laura heard this tale, she asked me how I would feel if my car were to disappear. What did she mean, disappear? She said, "Well, if your car were to just disappear one day then couldn't you just file for insurance?" I asked how my car could possibly disappear, as it couldn't even move? She said, "Well, like if it someone else was to take it maybe?" I looked at her askance, finally getting her drift (this was not in my usual thought patterns). I reluctantly said that wouldn't be too bad because I suspected it was going to cost a fair amount of money (again!) to fix, money I didn't have. In any case, the darned thing was breaking down so frequently that I was thinking I would be better off without owning a car. (By this point in my training, I had moved from New Jersey's hinterlands to an apartment in the city and a car was less essential than before.) As I pondered Laura's ludicrous proposal, I added that I didn't think the car could even be stolen because no one would even be able to start it. This argument, however, did not seem an obstacle to Laura. "Do you want it gone or not?" Well, theoretically, if it were to disappear, that wouldn't be a bad solution. But I sure didn't want to know about it. Laura said that she had some "friends" who just might be able to take care of it, and not to worry, these guys could start anything! And, no, I wouldn't have to be involved. We looked at each other a little weirdly. She said, "Don't worry about it, just tell me where the car is and at some point ,you may hear from a guy named Louie" with a long, unpronounceable Italian last name.

I left, Laura saying that "the boys" wouldn't need a key or any of the things that a more normal person might think of as being helpful in starting a vehicle. Laura and I never went out again. After a week went by without anything happening, I started to forget the entire unholy conversation, much to my relief. I'm not cut out for cops and robbers.

More than a month later, I was harshly awakened by a phone

call at 3 A.M. I had had a rough night on call in the hospital the previous night, was thoroughly exhausted, had fallen into a coma, and was only semi-coherent when awakened by the persistent phone ringing. It took me almost a minute to figure out that it was a cop on the phone. Even then, I couldn't get it together to make out what he was talking about or why he was bothering me. Yeah, I had a car. Yeah, I did but it was sitting a couple of miles away and I couldn't get it going. No, of course, I didn't know anyone named Louie Capistrano or Scaramouche or Montevideo or whatever. What kind of names were these? Then I sat bolt upright. Louie? Louie! Oh, Officer, you caught me off guard at three in the morning. Yeah I know Louie, who was apparently in my car at the moment with a friend, as they unsuccessfully tried to hot-wire it. Yeah, that's right. Louie with the really long last name, the one with the car theft record, yeah he was the friend of a friend of a friend and he was just going to try to help me out and get my car in working order and back to me. And it was probably stupid of me to not have given him a key to get it going. And maybe I should have told him not to try to fix it in the middle of the night.

Damned Louie couldn't get my car going at three in the morning. I considered myself lucky to have stayed out of jail. A month later, I had decided I really did need to buy another car. A radio ad came on from a local Chevy dealership, proclaiming that if you purchased a new Chevy Vega, the dealership would give you $400 on a trade-in, no matter what shape your vehicle was in. I called up and was patched through to a salesman. To get this deal, I inquired if I physically had to get my car into the dealership to take them up on the offer? He thought about it for a minute and said that if the car could be towed in, they could probably work with that.

I had the evening off, walked to the dealer half a mile away, picked out a color for the first car I looked at, and bought my new Chevy Vega. This was the first new car I had ever owned, the first car with under 100,000 miles on it and the first car I had ever purchased without my father's help. I did not bother to find out that the Chevy Vega was widely considered the worst car in America and I certainly didn't know that you were allowed (expected) to bargain with the salesman when they gave you a price. No, I felt like I had pulled a pretty fast one, getting them to pay me for my old Dodge that had somehow morphed into a neighborhood statue.

Damned straight, I know Louie Capistrano!

Chapter 33

The Hat was for Dignity

We were interns and still in the old CHOP, the 100-year-old hospital in the 100-year-old building on Bainbridge Street, a world-famous hospital nestled in the ghetto. It was several months before the hospital building was to close and we would move to our new glass palace on the UPenn Campus.

At 2 A.M., a large Black man entered the hospital and trudged down empty corridors to the Emergency Room. (This was in the days when life was more civil and it was not necessary for hospitals or other buildings to have round-the-clock security.) The somewhat panicked staff noted a very large fellow in his late 50s, estimated to be six-foot-two, 250-plus pounds and somewhat muscular, sporting a derby hat on top, combat boots below—buck naked in between! —and carrying a metal pail half filled with water. The gentleman wished to be seen in the ER: he was having chest pains that started while he was enjoying sex with a woman in a local tenement building across the street.

The nurses were forced to wake my friend, Julian, the intern covering the ER that night and who had just lay down to his first and only sleep of the evening. Sleep, as previously acknowledged, was a scarce and valuable commodity to any intern on call in those days. The ER interns used to average two to three hours a night if they were lucky.

Poor Julian. The staff's sense of panic had begun to sink into him, too. Julian tried to explain, as calmly as possible, that although the patient indeed had a problem and needed to be seen, our Children's Hospital was strictly a pediatric hospital. As such, our hospital only saw patients to a maximum age of 18 and was not equipped to treat someone with a possible heart attack. We would call an ambulance to transport him to Graduate Hospital, three blocks away, and should have him there in just a few minutes.

Against the protests of the staff (although I suspect, much to their relief), the man announced he would just walk the few blocks. Julian feebly tried to stop him, but the patient picked up his half-full pail and was last seen trudging toward the main entrance, clad only in hat and boots—his rear flapping in the wind, the pail swinging. Must have been quite a sight.

I arrived on the scene an hour later, called to the ER to admit a routine patient with an asthma attack. I was the first doctor that Julian had seen since and he animatedly described the scene. While I was not there personally, his description was vivid enough that I can still picture it in my mind more than 45 years later.

As he finished, I turned to him and said, "Julian, I get the hat, sort of—I get the boots, I can kinda get the no clothes, but what the heck was the guy doing with the pail of water?"

Julian assumed a faraway look. "I have no idea, and I've been thinking of nothing else for over an hour. The nurses and I kept looking at the guy and the pail, but he was so damned big, none of us were willing to ask him—and I sure wasn't going to try to stop him!"

Chapter 34

Black Power Meets Jewish Power

It was a strong name.

Shakila. Shakila Smith. The young mother told us it meant "Beautiful" or "Well-formed."

A strong, lovely name—but sadly, a name for a scrawny, sickly infant.

We were on the baby ward (children under age two) early in our internship. The team consisted of a resident and three interns—all of us Jewish, as luck would have it. The baby was about seven months old, had a serious congenital heart condition with a shunt, and had already been hospitalized several times with secondary pneumonias. She was severely undersized for her age.

This was the early 1970s: a time of significant unrest and change in society, the Vietnam Era and an era of rising Black awareness and Black Power. Many African American children were being given African or Muslim names, something not previously seen any with any frequency to speak of. We were seeing many monikers that were new to us—names that, we were told, meant things like "Heart of the Lion" or "Courage."

This baby was not the first Shakila we had seen. And while beautiful, she certainly was not well-formed. She only weighed a few pounds and in those days, was deemed too small and too sickly to be operated on for her heart condition. She would have to get bigger and stronger to tolerate the cardiac surgery that would inevitably be required, and in the interim, she had to be kept alive. Many infants with this condition had repetitive pneumonias, and a high percentage would succumb before reaching a size where they could tolerate surgery.

Sam Fagin, a very sensitive young doctor, was the intern who picked up the child when she was admitted on our second day of a 12-week rotation. As we made rounds sometime later, Paul Fernhoff, the resident, looked at the chart and said, "Dr. Fagin, tell us about Baby Sheh'-ki-lah," pronouncing the name like an old Jewish comic in the Catskills (think of Shecky Greene with a "lah" at the end).

The young mother—a petite, defiant, proud woman—overheard Paul and said rather hostilely, "It's not SHEH'-ki-lah, it's Sha-KEE'-la," pronouncing it with the stronger African intonation.

We stood off in a corner the next morning as we rounded, and Paul said more softly, "Dr. Fagin, anything new on Baby SHEH'-ki-lah?" and from the other end of the room, where she sat rocking the baby, came back, "It's not SHEH'-ki-lah, it's Sha-KEE'-la!"

Medical personnel, particularly in a tertiary care center where patients tend to be very ill and disaster or death may not be far away, frequently developed weird humor to relieve the constant stress. In those days, the schedules were relatively inhumane for the house staff: early in our training, frequently working 36 hours in a row, and making life or death decisions that we did not always feel confident making. To relieve tension, we looked for humor wherever we could find it, and sometimes inappropriately.

And so, during the week the baby stayed with us, we repeated this ritual once or twice daily until it was time for discharge.

Baby Smith and Mother Smith were back just eight days later, with another pneumonia and her heart condition. Sam was again taking care of her, and at the end of the day, we stood outside the room as Paul said, "Dr. Fagin, I see that Baby SHEH'-ki-lah is back." Although we thought we stood safely out of earshot, the retort came from the hunched figure we had not even seen was there: "IT'S SHA-KEE'LA!!!"

The mother usually sat with her back to us. She was a quiet, proud, single, very young woman who barely talked to us unless addressed directly and was clearly always unhappy to be at the hospital. On the other hand, she was always there with her baby, holding her, rocking her, caring for her. It was hard not to feel for her and to respect her.

Again, for the entire several days of admission, the game went on, Paul softly talking of *Baby SHEH'-ki-lah* with the never-distant echo, *Sha-KEE'-la!*

They returned for the third admission a few weeks later.

On rounds, we stood off to the side again and Paul said, "Dr. Fagin, I see baby SHEH'-ki-lah is back."

With a resigned voice came the response from the figure rocking the infant: "It's not SHEH'-ki-lah, it's SUSAN!"

She had had the name legally changed.

Chapter 35

Ah, Chava Beans

I was on call that night for the general pediatric ward, one of three admitting interns. Around 10 P.M., Alan Cohen, the excellent Assistant Chief Resident in charge, called me about my next admission. "I'm saving this one for you but I don't know what time he'll be here," was his cryptic introduction. Usually nighttime admissions came in sick via the emergency room; there wasn't a whole lot of mystery about when they were coming.

He went on, "It all depends on when the plane arrives from Chile."

While CHOP was an internationally recognized pediatric institution, and we had our share of patients traveling a long way for specialized care, this was definitely out of the ordinary.

The patient would be a six-year-old son of an American couple, originally from the Philadelphia area, the father now serving as a highly placed diplomat in our embassy in Santiago. The child had suddenly become very ill with an anemia of potentially life-threatening severity and was now being transferred from Chile to our hospital for diagnosis and treatment. It sounded a little unnerving; under the circumstances, Alan promised that both he and the hematology fellow would be working closely with me.

The plane, anticipated before midnight, did not actually arrive until closer to 2 A.M., affording me the rare luxury of actually reading up on a case before its arrival. It also served to keep me up when I might have had a few precious hours of sleep, but that's a different story. The presentation strongly suggested a class of anemias called hemolytic anemias. Anemias in general are not unusual, but hemolytic anemia is much less common. Anemia is a deficiency of the red blood cells, or frequently, of the hemoglobin they contain: the chemical that helps bind and transport oxygen from the lungs to where it is needed in the body. Far and away, the most common anemia familiar to the public is iron-deficiency anemia, caused by a lack of iron, the element essential for hemoglobin to work effectively. In such a disease state, iron may be low from lack of dietary intake or from excessive loss, seen most frequently in women of menstruating age with inadequate iron supplementation. These types of anemia usually are chronic and mild, and if more severe, might present with fatigue and pallor. Such conditions rarely will present acutely, as this youngster was doing.

The mechanism of hemolytic anemia is quite different: instead of having a problem with inadequate production of effective red blood cells, hemolytic anemia results from the much-too rapid destruction of these same cells. A healthy red blood cell lives for close to four months, and about one percent of them are destroyed in the course of a normal day. With hemolytic anemia, red blood cells undergo drastically accelerated rates of destruction. There are several entirely different mechanisms that may be responsible. In many, the condition will be chronic, with low-grade symptoms over longer periods of time. On the other hand, a patient can be totally well and then encounter something that leads to the destruction of massive numbers of cells, creating an acute crisis that may be serious—even fatal.

Of the various causes, one of the most common of these is G6PD deficiency, a deficiency of one of the enzymes in the red blood cell that protects it from oxidative injury. There are several variants of G6PD; all of them are inherited and X-linked (carried on the X-chromosome and thus seen in their severe forms only in males). Different varieties tend to be seen in different populations, including African Americans, Nigerians, Kurdish Jews, and in peoples of Mediterranean origin. Despite the name being relatively unknown to the public, G6PD problems are not totally unusual and may affect a few hundred thousand Americans. Some variants of G6PD may present with chronic anemias but others may be known only through acute crises, where a particular agent—frequently a drug, but sometimes a food—can trigger a severe episode.

Our patient and family finally arrived, the child nice but clearly ill, exhausted and frightened. He was pale, jaundiced, and squirming with back pain. The anxious parents were frantic and terrified. We already knew from the basic blood tests in Ecuador that he was severely anemic and there was nothing in his appearance contradicting the hypothesis of an acute hemolytic crisis.

In short order, lab tests were drawn, blood was cross-matched and transfused, IV fluids and medications started, and the next morning, the child underwent a bone marrow test. The transfusion worked wonders; soon, his hemoglobin rose, his pains subsided, and after a few hours of rest, he was a different child.

Laboratory tests rapidly confirmed that this was indeed a hemolytic form of anemia, and in another day or two, further tests confirmed that of the multiple types of hemolytic anemia, the child had a G6PD deficiency of the Mediterranean variety, the most common variant in white patients. This illness often presents for the first time in boys of his age, and, as the name would indicate, in families of Mediterranean extraction (all of his grandparents were of Italian descent).

Now that diagnosis was established, it became of paramount importance to ascertain what had triggered the acute episode. In this variant of the condition, the patient is usually entirely well until exposed to a certain triggering agent, which may not be the same for all patients. Further exposures could again lead to life-threatening episodes, making it absolutely crucial to identify the trigger. The process can be like a detective game. This child had no known exposure to any causative drugs (anti-malarial agents tend to top the list of likely suspects). Hemolysis could be triggered by chemicals, certain dyes, or even mothballs. Careful history-taking and repeated questioning of his doting and observant parents failed to reveal a likely candidate from this list. This brought us to the category of foods, which along with drugs, were the most likely causative agents. Of various foods, one of the most commonly implicated culprits is fava beans, a staple often eaten in Mediterranean countries. (At this stage of my life, I had no idea what a fava bean was except for having read about them as a cause of G6PD crises a few years earlier in a medical text; I could not personally have picked out a fava bean from a lineup of kidney beans, string beans, garbanzos or pintos.)

So, the hematology fellow repeatedly asked about fava beans. The parents tried to rack their brains, certain they had never knowingly eaten anything with that name. The best the mother could come up with was that, while in Chile, she had gone the week earlier to a farmer's market and bought something called chava beans. Unfamiliar with this, she had specifically asked the farmer if they were fava beans, a name she had at least heard of. He had vigorously shaken his head "no," and had slowly repeated, "Chava beans. Chava!" She was quite sure of the name.

As the diagnosis had become clearer over the first two days of hospitalization and the patient out of danger, the only mystery remained to pinpoint the trigger with more certainty. This was of more than academic interest; in G6PD Mediterranean, not all patients will respond to the long list of all the known potential causes and we needed to identify this child's specific cause in order to prevent potentially catastrophic recurrences for this family in the future. The best idea was the mysterious chava beans that the mother had bought; we had no idea what this was but strongly suspected, given the similarity of the names, that it was probably the Chilean equivalent of fava beans. Still, it would be nice to know, not to be left guessing.

As the weekend approached, the hematologist had an idea.

Sunday morning, my day off, the hematologist, the mother and I made a field trip to South Philly's sprawling Italian market. We wandered around for a while among the biggest display of fruits and vegetables I had ever seen. (The Italian market, one of the landmarks for which Philadelphia was known, was one of those many highpoints of the city that my crazy schedule had not allowed me the time to visit.) After a seemingly fruitless search, the mother looked excitedly to a cart across the narrow street, her eyes wide, and screamed as she ran, "Look, Chava beans!" She joyfully raised a handful as the hematologist and I stared at the sign above: FAVA BEANS.

We had our answer. No more fava beans (or "chava beans") for our youngster. The family took some vacation time back home before transferring to a different embassy for their next assignment. The last I heard several months later, the child continued to do well, with no recurrences, no fava beans, and no adventures with unknown foods.

Chapter 36

A Boy Named Beverly

I'll never forget Dr. Beverly Rainey. During my internship year rotation, Beverly Rainey was my resident on Pediatric Oncology—a notoriously difficult service. He was an excellent physician who taught me a great deal and was caring and thoughtful with patients and families. But none of this was apparent to me when I first arrived on the Oncology ward.

I can't say I enjoyed Oncology. Most pediatricians have upbeat personalities and many pediatric specialties generally have happy outcomes. Oncology was not one of them, especially back in the early 70s. While we were starting to develop effective chemotherapy for certain acute leukemias, the most common pediatric cancer, it was not as effective as today and many other cancers had abysmally poor prognoses. The Oncology ward was one on which the young physician could learn a tremendous amount of medicine (the patients all had compromised immune systems—either from their disease, the chemotherapy, or both—that led to normally rare infections being seen with great regularity), but it was not a happy service and many children died.

Compounding the dismal nature of the Oncology floor were the equally dismal physical surroundings. I've already described that we were in the last days of CHOP's century plus in an old building. (We were shortly to be moving to our new gleaming glass cathedral on the Penn Campus—in fact, this was nearly my last service before the move.) Oncology occupied the very top floor of the rickety edifice. The rooms were too few, too small, and in a general state of disrepair. Making matters even worse was the lack of a reasonable venue to hold private discussions, more of a necessity on that ward than others. An old service shed in the middle of the roof had been outfitted as a small and inadequate conference room. It had to be accessed by walking outside and across the rooftop, often braving the elements of a cold Pennsylvania evening. It was here that we had our teaching conferences and it was here that we brought parents to hold what often could be heart-wrenching discussions.

We had an admission of a new patient early in my first week. Jonathon was a very sweet and intelligent seven-year-old who had been referred in by his Main Line pediatrician for evaluation of a terribly abnormal blood count and suspected leukemia, although the parents had not been informed of this suspicion. The child had been ill for two weeks, running fevers, pale, nauseated, extremely lethargic, and had not responded to antibiotics that had been prescribed for a possible infection. As he worsened, lab work showed a dramatically elevated white blood cell count, deep anemia, and markedly decreased platelets, a picture almost perfectly diagnostic for leukemia. He had been sent to CHOP for admission, evaluation, and treatment. With my assistance, Dr. Rainey had performed a bone marrow test. The results returned a few hours later with numerous lymphoblasts, a finding diagnostic of ALL (acute lymphocytic leukemia), the most common pediatric cancer. Thankfully, recent years had seen the development of relatively good chemotherapy to treat this terrible ailment. A few years earlier, ALL had been a horrible and almost uniformly fatal diagnosis for a child; while it was still a very serious disorder with significant mortality, a considerable number of children were now being cured. Still, cure was by no means certain, and the words "cancer" or "leukemia" could drive terror into patients and families.

I had only been on the service for a few days; I had not had a new ALL patient before and it was my place to listen as Dr. Rainey explained the results and the condition to the parents. Understandably, they were emotionally distraught. As traumatic as this would be under any circumstance, the mannerisms of the oncology resident had to initially give them even more pause.

The parents were clearly Main Line, the elite region of the Philadelphia suburbs. They were upper class, posing a stark contrast to the families that more commonly came through our emergency room. They also were markedly intelligent. The father was a professor at Haverford College, one of the elite nearby universities, and the mother worked as an administrator at another educational institution. Both were conservatively and elegantly dressed, the father fittingly in a tweed jacket and tie, the mother in a dark wool dress. Their diction and manner were equally elegant.

Dr. Beverly Rainey, in contradistinction, looked like somewhat of a country hick, and with good reason. He hailed from the hills of rural North Carolina and had the drawling accent of the deep South. He spoke slowly and with a twang, his speech perhaps half the typical pace of the typical residents of hectic Northeastern cities. Enhancing this country image was his physical appearance. Bev was a large man, who wore an ill-fitting short-sleeved white shirt, seemingly a size too small, with a necktie that always ended several inches above his belt. His horn-rimmed glasses were not only entirely unstylish, but always sat askew. As we led this elegant couple outside in the dark, across the roof through the cold February rain, and into our dreadful little meeting hut, I could almost read the thoughts behind the parents' furtive glances to each other. *This is the famed pediatric hospital? What kind of a place are we in? This is the brilliant oncologist whose hands now hold our child's life?*

We sat down at a small table. As the parents fidgeted anxiously, Bev pulled out a small container of homemade soup and asked if they minded if he ate while we talked, having missed dinner due to Jonathon's prolonged work-up. The parents exchanged more glances with each other. In a voice straight from the old Andy Griffin Show, Bev started talking, impossibly slowly, in the deepest drawl I had ever heard outside of the movies. He began, "I'm afraid young Jonathon has leukemia. Now, leukemia is like weeds in a garden. The bone marrow is the garden, the leukemia cells are the weeds, and little Jonathon, well, right now, he's got a lot of weeds in his garden." I looked at the educated parents and thought they were going to emotionally decompensate. My own level of anxiety had jumped up along with theirs.

Bev kept talking through spoonfuls of soup, explaining things in his own unique way. Gradually, the longer he talked, a funny thing happened. Despite its folksy charm, his speech became a little more precise, his command of the subject more obvious. The parents' initial hysteria at this dreaded diagnosis started to abate, just a little, as Dr. Rainey enumerated everything we would be doing, both diagnostically and therapeutically: the anticipated course, the potential side effects, and the reasons for certain agents over others. While his speech was strewn with quaint homilies, there was no doubt that this was a man in command of a great deal of knowledge and in control of the situation. Somehow, his corny analogies made a complicated and scary issue seem somewhat less so.

When we left the roof-side shack 45 minutes later, the parents were noticeably calmer (as was I).

Jonathon's course went very well. By the time he left the hospital, he was well on his way to remission. I could only wish that all my Oncology patients had done as well.

Dr. Rainey certainly stood out as a unique character in the Penn scene. While CHOP was one of the most respected pediatric institutions in the country (always seemingly ranked in the top two or three children's hospitals nationally), the staff, not surprisingly, largely hailed from the Northeast. Beverly was from the rural South, and while he came from a family of physicians, he had the rural mannerisms not normally associated with the Northeast. His countryside background belied his intellect. Trained at Duke Medical School, Bev had a first-class mind and was an excellent oncologist with a broad swath of knowledge and a compassionate manner that was truly needed in this difficult specialty. I won't pretend that I enjoyed my time upon the cancer ward—too many nights I found myself crying on that abandoned rooftop after the death of another child—but I learned a great deal.

While I could forgive him the goofy manner and the unsophisticated appearance, as we became friends, one day I couldn't resist the urge to ask him the origins of his name. I kept thinking of Johnny Cash singing "A Boy Named Sue." Bev told me the story. His grandfather, a physician, had been named Beverly and so gave his son, Bev's father, the same moniker (Beverly II later became a respected orthopedic surgeon). In turn, his father bestowed the name on his own son, and so there we were: Beverly III, the respected oncologist. I asked if he liked the name.

"Heck, No!, Gary. I detest it." He told me the story many years earlier of his first day in second grade. The teacher, an imposing older woman, had called each child's name in alphabetical order, asking each to stand up so she could put names and faces together. Towards the end, when she reached his name, the teacher called "Beverly Rainey." As Bev arose, the teacher gave him a stern look and loudly asked him to sit back down and not be silly. In a deeper bellow, she once again called, "Beverly Rainey," and dutifully, he stood once more. This time she bellowed, "Not you, Mr. Clown! Now, sit down and we'll see about a visit to the principal later!" He said the embarrassment this episode caused him had not subsided until halfway through the school year.

Since his wife was expecting in several months, I asked him if he was going to keep the family tradition going. "Darn, no, Gary. I don't know yet what we're going to call him, but it sure as hoot won't be Beverly!" I was on another service the next year when I learned of the birth of little Beverly Rainey IV.

A corny name—a corny speech—an excellent physician.

Chapter 37

The Empress's New Clothes

I was a resident in my second year of pediatric training, working in the ER on a cold, wintry Philly night. At the end of my internship year, the hospital had moved two miles from its run-down, crumbling building on Bainbridge Street to our beautiful new structure on the edge of the Penn Campus, where we could have had a more integrated relationship as the pediatric hospital at the University of Pennsylvania.

The physical changes for the ER in particular were impressive. Instead of a tiny area with limited seating and only a few exam rooms, separated by flimsy curtains, we now had a vast waiting area, much better to accommodate the usual two to three-hour backup, great treatment facilities, and a line of 14 exam rooms with doors in front and back. When it was a new patient's turn to be seen, the nurses would take a waiting child and their family into the rear area behind the exam rooms. The child would be weighed and temperature-checked, then led into an exam room. The nurse would switch on a light by the front door, signaling to the interns that a patient was ready to be seen, and in which order.

We were a teaching hospital and we were thorough, doing relatively complete exams on almost every child—in part because it was the right procedure, but also because kids from the surrounding areas tended to have terrible medical care. Some had never even had a thorough exam before coming to our hospital. Particularly in winter, as this was, it would often take the parent a long time to undress the child. In our crowded ER with critically ill patients, waiting for patients to undress led to the loss of valuable time. Accordingly, the nurses would instruct the mothers to have their children undressed before the doctor arrived, down to their underwear and, in the case of children under two, would tell the mother to have the child completely undressed to their diaper.

After 18 months as an intern and resident, I thought I had seen everything, but was woefully unprepared when I walked into the room and found an infant sitting in her mother's arms, clad only in a diaper, while the mother herself sat there totally naked. I probably gawked at Mom. While the young woman looked to be someone who didn't embarrass easily, she was clearly uncomfortable. She said, "The nurse said we should get undressed, but I could leave the diaper on. But I wasn't wearing a diaper!" I should say not.

All I could come up with in response was, "What else is wrong?"

I rushed out of the room mumbling that I thought I had seen enough (more than enough!) I told her everyone could get dressed and I would return shortly after checking on another patient before coming back to complete my history.

Looking back over the years, I can still picture the mother sitting there. I have no idea what was wrong with the child.

Chapter 38

A Long Year

It was toward the end of internship year and we had all been working long hours. This morning found me in unusually good spirits: I arrived at the hospital cafeteria at 6 A.M., hoping to get a quick bite before starting my scutwork prior to rounds, already in anticipation of my "Free" night. To clarify this, I need to describe the typical schedule of an intern back then. The rigor was demanding, to say the least.

Everything went in three-day cycles, and the days were indeed long. Although I've talked of this before, let me expound just a bit. We were expected to be on our respective wards by 7 A.M. to begin rounds with our team (composed of a junior resident, three interns, and several medical students). During Team Rounds, all patients were seen by and discussed within the team. The new patients (NPs) of the previous night were presented and examined, the supervising resident listening to the intern's assessment and plans and then (hopefully) providing helpful guidance. This might last 30 to 60 minutes—rarely longer—as there was too much urgent work to attend to.

Over the next hour or so, the interns and students would rapidly try to see their patients more extensively, write orders to set plans in motion, and then perform the dreaded scutwork. "Scutwork" consisted of the tedious tasks of drawing blood, starting IVs, running samples to the labs, viewing X-rays, etc. To call scutwork time-consuming doesn't do it justice. (Thankfully for interning physicians of today's generation, most of these tasks now are performed by ancillary medical personnel, and almost all hospitals have IV and blood-drawing teams.)

This work process was next interrupted by Attending Rounds. "Attendings" were the senior physicians of the hospital. Each month, a new attending would be assigned to a particular ward. Many were specialists with knowledge to impart in specific areas. They would tour again with the team, hearing about interesting patients, making suggestions, and teaching where they saw fit. While their advice was frequently appreciated, the time spent often wasn't. Interns had so much physical work to be done, too many sick children to attend to, and so little time available that any activity that infringed on work schedules was often regarded as a significant imposition.

When the attending departed, there were various teaching conferences almost daily, attendance generally being mandatory. Subsequently, the interns were free for the next few hours—or at least free in the sense of being able to do their work—which left them to tend to their current patients, conduct physical examinations, talk to parents, complete the scutwork they had been unable to finish earlier, call consults to discuss patients, schedule appointments for X-rays—and in some cases, physically haul the patient down for said X-rays. All this was just regarding their *current* patients. Between existing patient work, the intern would be receiving and working up NPs (some elective, some emergencies), and new patients required much more time. An intern typically anticipated three or four NPs a day, each requiring at least an hour of focused time.

The days were obviously long. While officially starting by 7 A.M., most staff tried coming in earlier to get a running start. There was no set leaving time. Five o'clock was theoretically possible; six o'clock more reasonable; later, not unusual. Days ran in three cycles, which could be summarized as: On Call, Sleep, and Free. The On-Call night is familiar to most readers—two thirds of the staff would leave around 6 P.M., signing out all of their patients to the care of the on-call intern, who would suddenly find himself in charge of 60 patients, hopefully stable, but rarely so. This intern was also now responsible for any NPs admitted on an emergency basis over the next 12–14 hours, a number that might vary from two to six per night, occasionally more. Often these patients were quite ill, and there was not as much backup staff at night to assist. The On-Call night was long, rough and stressful. While a lucky physician might see three to four hours of sleep on certain rotations, no sleep was a was more common scenario. I believe I probably averaged about two and a half hours of sleep each On-Call night during my internship year.

At the end of this much-too trying cycle, the second night (which I've termed Sleep) would begin. Although exhausted from the night before, the young doctor still had to work until six or so before signing his patients out. This was the time to go home and try to get some sleep.

The third night of the cycle (the one I've designated as Free) was eagerly anticipated. While the day was no different than the previous two in the cycle (always with way too much work and way too much stress), on this night, the intern who had slept the night before might actually have a few hours to live outside the hospital: to have a date, to be with family, or to tend to life's normal demands. It wasn't much, and in reality, it was often used just to in a vain attempt to cut into the chronic sleep deficit—but the Free night was the closest the house staff physician was going to have for relaxation and a little semblance of normal life throughout an entire two-year period.

This particular April morning, feeling refreshed from my Sleep night, I entered the cafeteria and spotted a good friend. Dan Dubner was a fellow intern, and we had bonded during two earlier rotations together. (Two years later, when he had transferred to a program in Seattle, Sandy and I would spend a considerable part of our financially strapped honeymoon camped out on a futon in the Dubner's basement.) Dan was a quiet, thoughtful guy, and tended to worry even more than most of our generally neurotic and anxious group. I hadn't seen him for several weeks and had lost track of which ward he was on. This particular morning, he looked terrible—haggard, scruffy, bleary-eyed.

I was feeling pretty chipper and was actually looking forward to a rare date that evening. I could tell Dan was not in the same mood as I cheerfully greeted him, "Dan, how are you doing? You look like crap."

He replied, "I can't help it. I'm just really depressed this morning. It's terrible."

I wasn't quite sure if he was just coming from a night on call with no sleep, the most likely situation, or starting a day where he would be on call and already dreading the night. "Rough night on call last night?'

"No, I wasn't on call."

"Oh, busy ward and you're upset about being on call tonight?" I couldn't imagine getting that worked up about what had become routine ten months ago.

"No, I'm not on tonight."

I looked at him. "Wait a second," I said incredulously. "Weren't here last night? Not on call tonight? You're upset and…it's your free night?"

He looked down solemnly. "Yeah, I'm just really anxious about being on call again tomorrow night."

Tomorrow night? That's a rough way to be thinking on your good nights—especially when you have two years of that three-night cycle still in front of you.

No one ever said internship was going to be easy.

Chapter 39

My Worst Night

Although my career eventually evolved into Allergy/Asthma/
Immunology, I knew from the start that I wanted to go into
Pediatrics, having always considered myself a big kid at heart. As
is the case with many professions, certain personalities migrated
to particular medical specialties. While some, such as neurology,
seemed to attract more than its fair share of physicians who were
serious, precise and with little humor (a broad generalization),
pediatricians were generally upbeat, happier, somewhat looser
folks. They were a pleasant and enjoyable group overall.

Another major attraction of pediatrics was that, for the most
part, young patients tended to get better. While this is hopefully
true in all branches of medicine, some areas (particularly with
older patients) had specialties with few positive long-term outcomes, even more so years ago than today. Kids tended to be more
resilient—if you saw them through the acute crisis that led to their
hospitalizations, most did well. Of course, there were exceptions.
During my training back in the 70s, the two areas that were the
most somber were the already discussed Oncology ward and the
Neonatal ICU (NICU).

I was in my second year of pediatric residency and found
myself two weeks into my time in the NICU. The rotation was
living up to its reputation as a grueling one; indeed, it was the

only service at CHOP where the house staff were not allowed to serve until their internship year had been completed. The hours were exceptionally long, the opportunities for sleep during an on-call night almost non-existent, and the numbers of critically ill infants staggering. In sharp contrast to most rotations where I had experienced few deaths, an infant died almost every other night during that six-week NICU period.

There were several reasons for this high mortality rate. The vast majority of our babies were premature, and significantly so. We weren't treating almost full-term infants (i.e., 36 weeks instead of the normal 40). NICU physicians were dealing with 28–30 weekers—some 26 weekers, some even younger. Many of these infants weren't destined to live, particularly before technology would prove able to push the envelope even further in the future. A fair number of babies admitted to the NICU were 1,200–1,300 grams (about three pounds), and it was not unusual for some to be significantly smaller. In addition, quite a few had critical and incurable congenital problems, sometimes incompatible with life, which may have caused their premature delivery, such as a severe underdevelopment of the heart chambers. There was no treatment for such a condition at the time, but the staff might spend many long and trying hours in the care of such an infant before the true and untreatable nature of the problem would become known.

In addition, we were a tertiary care hospital: any hospital in the greater Delaware Valley would send their sickest infants to us. We had a huge catchment area and frequently found ourselves receiving a transfer of a moribund two-pound infant after an hour ambulance ride from an outlying hospital, the hapless neonate often succumbing during the ride or shortly thereafter.

Further complicating this situation and our trend of seeing a progressively greater number of horribly ill or hopeless transfers was a court decision a year or so earlier: the Edelin decision. This case involved a physician in Massachusetts who performed an abortion in mid-pregnancy at the request of the mother. The actual technique of the abortion had encountered difficulty, and when Dr.

Edelin completed the procedure using a less established method, a very aggressive prosecutor, using novel legal arguments prosecuted him for manslaughter. To the amazement of almost all observers, Dr. Edelin was found guilty and placed on a year of probation although it was noted that his "crime" could have resulted in a sentence of many years. Not surprisingly, this appalling decision rapidly sent a chill through the entire medical world, particularly in specialties such as obstetrics and neonatal care.

In short order, no one felt safe in refusing treatment to any fetus, no matter the size or viability. Before the Edelin decision, a baby born at 22 or 24 weeks—far too small to expect to live, at least by 1974 medical practices—would have been placed in a quiet area until its heart naturally stopped beating after a few moments. Many of these infants were now subjected to arduous and hopeless treatment. Some would die quickly, some would receive long and incredibly expensive care before expiring, and a small percentage would somehow live after months of care (but usually with severe retardation, blindness, or other multiple, horrible, permanent medical and developmental complications). A very few would survive relatively unscathed, and while the ultra-religious would proclaim the miracle of this, the cost to society was high in terms of emotions, dollars, care hours, and permanently altered parental lives. In the Philadelphia area, many of these babies were now being shipped to the few tertiary centers. CHOP got more than its fair share.

All this translated to a NICU service in which many infants died and where the pediatric staff, a generally upbeat lot, saw more deaths than they did at any other point in their training. The effects could be devastating.

My worst night started inauspiciously. One of the tiny preemies with severe respiratory distress syndrome (RDS, an underdevelopment of the lungs so often seen in very immature infants) had been experiencing a severe and complicated course for several weeks. The baby had taken a marked turn for the worse over the past few days and had been signed out to me at 6 P.M. by my co-resident as near-terminal with sepsis. Sadly, but not unexpectedly, the infant passed away almost as soon as the other residents had left for the evening. Not my fault and not a surprise, but it still made for a bad evening. Almost simultaneously with this event, an 850g fetus (at less than two pounds, it was hard to call it a baby) was transferred in from a distant hospital. While it was certainly going to die, I now had to spend much time and resources doing delicate procedures, such as placing umbilical catheters, before it expired two hours later. During this time, a new gravely ill preemie, somewhat larger, was admitted and I spent several hours in treatment and diagnosis until diagnostic studies finally revealed it had hypoplastic (underdeveloped) left heart syndrome: a severe, relatively uncommon, fatal condition that I alluded to above. Amazingly and awfully, this was my third death in just a few hours. In my eighteen months in the hospital, I had never experienced the loss of even two, let alone three, patients in a single night.

I was emotionally drained, close to tears but there was little time to reflect. Another new admission had presented and that now occupied me, again for a period of several hours. This preemie was a little larger than the last, with severe breathing and oxygenation problems. Depressed, I worked feverishly with catheters, tubing and ventilators, other intravenous lines, diagnostic procedures, getting nowhere and enveloped in an increasing sense of dread. I had presumed the infant to be a typical RDS baby, which could be severe and fatal, but most of them responded at least somewhat. Sadly, this one did not. Finally, despite all efforts, the baby went into cardiac arrest. As a nurse and I initiated CPR and emergency measures, to my horror, another nurse screamed from the other end of NICU. Another baby, a preemie with a complicated course (now two months old and thriving, stable the past few weeks) had suddenly decompensated and was in severe distress. What was I to do? Continue with the new infant who would surely be dead in a minute without constant treatment but whose path was looking increasingly grim, or abandon him and tend more established patient who was decompensating just a few feet away but might have a better chance at survival? It was 4 A.M. and there was only one of me, with no immediate backup on hand. What a horrible decision to face: my own version of Sophie's Choice. I couldn't abandon one to certain death, so I feverishly continued on our new arrival, hoping our old-timer could hang in for a few minutes with nurses doing the best they could. Sadly, I could not resuscitate the newcomer; in even greater horror, by the time I freed myself, the baby across the room had also expired.

Five dead infants in less than 12 hours. To make things even worse, if that were possible, came the knowledge that I had made the wrong choice (although I could not have known it in the moment). The baby that I spent so much time with and had assumed was an RDS baby turned out to be another infant with hypoplastic left heart syndrome, the rare condition, incompatible with life (at least back then) and had in fact stood no chance. And the older baby, that I had not had time to examine when the nurse screamed, had a routine pneumothorax (a leak from a lung that leads to air being trapped in the chest cavity under pressure, thus preventing the lungs from expanding), a serious but common problem in the NICU and one that easily could have been treated quickly with insertion of a chest tube.

Five babies in 12 hours! My world collapsed around me. I sat in a rocker in corner of the NICU, head in hands, weeping softly. Soon a somber nurse (the entire staff was similarly shell-shocked) called to me that a baby's intravenous line had infiltrated and I was needed to restart it. I rocked a couple of times, looked up gloomily, and replied, "I refuse to touch another baby tonight. Anyone I come near dies." There was little salvation in the knowledge that none of the infants had been savable with the glaring exception of the last one.

The night ended like so many before, and so many to come. I rocked a few more times, and then got up to do my job.

Chapter 40

NICU Benefits: No Smoking?

The NICU was by far my most difficult rotation, both physically and emotionally. It proved to be perhaps the most trying period of my medical career. Weirdly, however, it did prove to have one major benefit: in a semi-perverse way, it was responsible for me finally being able to quit cigarettes for good.

I had never been a heavy smoker, having started my senior year in college and continuing through medical school and into my years as a resident. Always smoking less than a pack a day, I nonetheless couldn't quit. I had enjoyed it for a year, had been relatively neutral the next, and had spent the last four years trying vainly to stop.

Once during a radiology lecture, back when smoking indoors was commonplace—including hospital classrooms—a radiologist held up a film with a large "cannonball," the signature appearance of advanced smoking-induced lung cancer. Finding myself very nervous in front of this frightful image, I instinctively pulled out a cigarette and lit up in the back of the room. The radiologist turned in my direction, then angrily put down the film and glared. "Ladies and gentlemen, this is not the desired result of my showing THIS X-ray!" (For those too young to know anything of the 1970s, smoking was not only permissible in most hospitals, but cigarettes were often sold in cigarette machines prominently placed in the lobbies. Such was the case at Einstein in my medical schooling, and now at CHOP during my pediatric training.)

My preceding shift in the NICU had been exhausting. It was a Saturday, which meant that unlike normal weekdays, where a full complement of staff is present until early evening, the entire 24-hour period was covered by one doctor. As the infants don't know this and are just as sick, there was a constant stream of desperately ill babies to tend to. While none had died, the physical toll on me had been high. The possibility of sleep had never even entered my mind. When I desperately needed a smoke at 2 A.M., during the few minutes between crises, I discovered I was out of cigarettes and did not have the time to run down to the lobby machine. Surviving the night, I was finally able to sign out at 9:30 the next morning and took the nearly deserted bus back to my apartment, 15 minutes away. I was awakened two hours later by the friendly bus driver completing his third loop around the city. "I know where you live, Doc." I had been on his bus before. "You were sleeping so soundly, I figured you needed it and let you go for a while, but my shift is ending soon." I thanked him and reached in my pocket for a cigarette as I walked the last few yards home, finding only the empty pack from the day before.

Twenty minutes later, I jumped into bed for a quick nap and awoke at 5:30 A.M. the next morning, almost 18 hours later, the time permanently set on my alarm. As I reached for a non-existent cigarette, I realized I had now gone 36 hours between smokes, the longest I had ever been able to last in my many attempts at quitting. I had made it through what was probably the hardest portion of smoking cessation. I realized with that unexpected head start, I just might be able to give up the evil weed.

That was 1975. Forty-five years later and I've never had another cigarette.

It was an unlikely and unanticipated benefit of my arduous and overwhelming NICU rotation but one that was much appreciated, nonetheless.

Photo #1: Gary and his brother Larry. His brother's congenital illness would affect his decision to enter medicine (1965) (Chapter 1)

Photo #2: Gary as a pediatric resident physician, Philadelphia (1975) (Chapter 31)

Photo #3: Gary and Sandy at their wedding,
with Gary's parents, Claire and David Lotner
(1976) (Chapter 47)

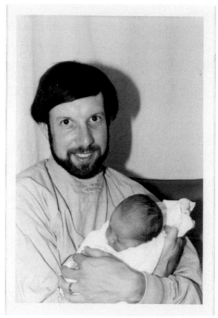

Photo #4: Gary with Baby Jessica, who happily
was not born early (1977) (Chapter 51)

Photo #5: Sandy and Jessica, age three months, who suffered a series of
mysterious illnesses requiring ICU admissions (Chapter 52)

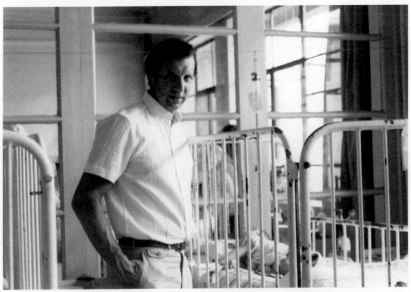

Photo #6: Gary, at pediatric hospital in China (1980) (Chapter 55)

Photo #7: Sandy with three-year-old Jessica. Cute but not politically correct (1980) (Chapter 56)

Photo #8: Danny, age four. Thank goodness he could run (1984) (Chapter 58)

Photo #9: Gary and Sandy with Jessica and Dan, France (1994) (Chapter 68)

Photo #10: Grandma Norma Cuttler,
possibly looking for birthday
presents (Chapter 70)

Photo #11: Gary and Sandy (2006) (Chapter 73)

Photo #12: Jessica and Andy Lala, Bella and Jacob (2020) (Chapter 79)

Photo #13: Monique and Daniel Lotner, with Zach, Anya and baby
Eli (2020) (Chapter 79)

Photo #14: Staying at home (2020) (Chapter 79)

Chapter 41

Not What They Taught in Harvard

It is frequently said that there is as much art as science in medicine and it was certainly true that there was much of clinical medicine that came from experience, not from textbooks. This point was sometimes driven home in strange ways.

My seemingly interminable year of internship was over, and I was just beginning as a junior pediatric resident, which meant that on most rotations, I would be supervising rather than directly caring for individual patients. It was the first week in July and I was in the emergency room supervising a new group of interns on their first rotation. They were bright and eager and generally impressive for this early in their pediatric careers. While it was the beginning of their training, Harvard-trained Joanne Y. was clearly one of the brightest and most competent of the group.

She asked me if I would check on a child with her, as she was perturbed about his apparent lack of response to treatment. Just eight months old, the child had been seen for an ear infection three nights earlier by one of the outgoing interns. The child had been placed on amoxicillin, the treatment of choice and usually effective. After what should have been plenty of time to respond, the infant was clearly worse. Not only was he continuing to run moderate fevers, but his ear had turned into an ungodly mess that Dr. Y. had never encountered in her pediatric experiences as a medical student. While it was not unusual that an antibiotic might be ineffective and need to be changed, she was at a total loss in determining what was going on with an ear that could only be described as ugly—and goopy. In fact, she wasn't even sure that she was viewing the ear drum with her otoscope; all she could see was a pink, foamy discharge filling the ear canal. Dr. Y. worried that the tympanic membrane had ruptured and this might be a weird infected discharge.

We met the concerned single mother in the exam room. She was anxious and clearly very young, holding a crying, distressed infant. After a quick general exam, I looked into the ear as best as I could. The canal was messy, gluey, pink—one of the ugliest ears I had seen, which was saying something as I had been peering in multiple ear canals each day for two years. I had only seen one ear that looked like this before.

Completing my exam, Dr. Y. anxiously turned to me and asked me my thoughts. Before answering, I turned to the concerned young mother and asked her how much amoxicillin she had been giving the baby. She replied that she had been told to give a teaspoon three times a day. And then I asked how much she had actually succeeded in getting in.

"Well, they said a teaspoon three times a day. But after a couple of drops, the rest just comes pouring out of his ear."

I turned to the embarrassed intern. "And that, Dr. Y., is what an ear looks like when treated with the amoxicillin placed in the ear instead of in the mouth!"

There are some things they don't teach at Harvard.

Chapter 42

Bicycles are Nice

The young mother was eleven.

Yes, you heard me correctly. THE MOTHER WAS 11 YEARS OLD.

During my residency, we were encouraged to moonlight at Philadelphia General Hospital (PGH), the adult hospital on the University of Pennsylvania campus located within easy walking distance from CHOP. The hospital had a busy labor department and nursery but was left without a dedicated pediatric staff. Consequently, CHOP residents were either required or recommended to moonlight in order to provide nursery coverage. When on call at PGH, the moonlighting pediatric residents would be notified in advance of any particular high-risk deliveries so we could prepare for the worst.

Although the University of Pennsylvania is an amazing institution, both at the undergraduate and graduate levels, it resided in a relatively impoverished section of the city. As with most big-city municipal hospitals, the patient population was typically poor, lacking in education, and often without ongoing medical care. The women using the labor and delivery services were no different. Most of the mothers were unwed and many had been unsupervised during their pregnancies. Alcoholism, drug usage, and smoking were all too common and many of the women were young. Very young. When I first started doing some shifts at PGH, I was surprised to see how many 15- and 16-year-olds were having babies. Over the next several months, it was the influx of 14- and 13-year-old girls delivering that shocked me. The babies of all these mothers were at high risk.

While I was distressed to see how many young teens had babies without even a second thought (indeed, in some of the poorest communities, having a child seemed to confer a certain status), I gradually found myself becoming inured to the sight of yet another young mother.

Not so for this one. As was routine, the on-call pediatrician had to check on all the babies born to any high-risk pregnancies. We did not usually need to have prolonged conversations with the mothers if there were no problems with the neonates. However, when the nurses informed me that the mother of the baby I found myself examining was only 11 years old, I was in disbelief. I decided I needed to talk with her when time permitted.

Several hours later, after several mini-crises had subsided and I had a few minutes, I wandered onto the delivery floor and stuck my head into her room. The young mother held her baby in one hand and a large teddy bear in the other. No visitors were present.

I started talking to the young woman—just a child, really—as I would any other mother, congratulating her (if that was the correct word here) on having a healthy baby and asking her some questions. Physically, she looked to be 14, not 11. When I first chatted, I acted as if motherhood conferred maturity, as if she must be older than her chronological years. She was not. She was definitely a pre-teen in her thoughts and her mannerisms. She was a sweet young girl, who smiled and talked excitedly in a sing-song manner. Within moments of conversation, any ideas that I might get some meaningful clues or insights vanished: this was a very young girl whose baby was the next step up from her teddy bear. My level of conversing dropped to the tone I would use with any child in this age group.

After a few minutes, I had exhausted almost all conversation. I finally turned once again and said, "Janeen, when you found out you were going to have a baby, did you ever think that you were only a little girl yourself? Why did you decide to have the baby?"

Her face lit up. She looked up at me eagerly and gave me a beaming smile. "For the bicycle!"

"The bicycle?" I asked. I was confused.

"My mommy told me if I had the baby and gave it to her, she would give me a bicycle. When I go home, she's going to have a new bicycle waiting for me. I never had my own bicycle before." Her grin was even bigger now.

It didn't seem like a fair trade, a bicycle for a baby. I hope at least that she got a ten-speed.

Chapter 43

What's in a Name?

It was a cold wintry night, and as was always the case, the Emergency Room waiting area was spilling over with patients. Waiting time was running almost three hours. As was usual for backups like this, we had a triage system in place to make sure the true emergencies, children who truly needed to be seen quickly, were identified. Sometimes they could be lost among all the kids with rashes, snotty noses, and families who had decided that 10 P.M. would be the perfect time for their child to be seen for constipation that had been present for six weeks.

As the assistant chief resident on call that evening, it was my job to be Dr. Triage. After a child was brought to the ER and signed in by a clerk, a nurse would get a temp and weight, write up a chief complaint, and add the chart to a pile for the triage doctor. (In truth, our ER nurses were great, experienced, and at least as good at the doctors at assessing which kids needed our immediate attention.) As senior resident, I would be in charge of the ER for the night, supervising the interns and residents, assisting in diagnosis and procedures, and occasionally seeing patients to speed things up. Every 20–30 minutes or so, I would be grabbing that pile of charts that had been added, going out into the mass of humanity, calling the name of a child, and asking a question or two. In truth, my chief goal was just eyeballing the child to make sure they were not going to be harmed by what would certainly be hours of waiting.

The name on the next chart in my hand was Ronttie Robinson. While the first name looked peculiar, this was an era of increasingly imaginative names with odd sounds and unusual spellings. I strolled out into a sea of mainly Black and Hispanic faces and called out for Ronttie Robinson. There were no takers and so I yelled louder, *Ronttie Robinson* and while nearly 40 groups of kids, mothers, friends, siblings, and others looking to stay warm all turned to me, no one answered. Since no one seemed to have died or appeared to be in serious distress, I figured Ronttie Robinson was probably in the restroom.

Ten minutes later, I picked up the new charts to screen and, naturally, the same chart was on top. I yelled out once more, *Ronttie Robinson,* and then again even louder when no answer followed, pronouncing it very carefully: RON-TEE ROB-IN-SON. Everyone turned, but again, no answer. I returned the chart.

Moments later, an elderly black woman, hunched over and limping, came up to the desk where I sat, looked at me and said, "Who you call? Can I see?" I showed her the name on the chart: Ronttie Robinson. She peered through thick glasses and said, "My granddaughter is Ronette Robinson. That's her." I was embarrassed for her and said the clerk must have misheard or misspelled the name and it didn't look like Ron-ette but like Ron-tce. She said, "How she spell it?" I told her the clerk had written R-O-N-T-T-I-E. She said, "Yeah, that's right, R-O-N-T-T-I-E, Ronette. Ain't that how ya spell it?"

Even more embarrassed for this nice elderly woman, very poor, missing most teeth, but obviously caring, I tried to be gentle. "Well, that's not the most common way to spell Ronette but I don't see any reason why you couldn't spell it that way."

She looked up at me and said, "I don't read so good. I thought maybe I spelled it wrong."

"No, ma'am, I'm sure you got it right. I'm going to put your granddaughter's chart in the pile to be seen and we'll see her in just a few minutes."

I left the chart in the To Be Seen pile and thought how difficult it must be to exist in a world where you couldn't read and didn't understand.

Thirty minutes later, a nurse picked up the chart and bellowed into a sea of dark faces, "RONTTIE ROBINSON!"

I tried not to laugh. Inside, I almost cried.

Chapter 44

A Cast of Thousands

July 3 of my third year of training marked my first night on call as assistant chief resident, the position where I was basically the highest on-call authority for the general hospital. Of course, there were many attending physicians higher than me and each service would have someone in charge, but most of the higher authorities would be gone at night. If no one else were available in a pinch, immediate decisions would fall to me. The July 3 date was important, since July was the month where all the staff would change. The interns were new and only a few days removed from medical school status, some making decisions on patients for the first time. Above them, the junior residents who supervised the interns were only a few days beyond their own internships, and the junior fellows on various specialty services were also brand new. (Thus, in specialties such as gastroenterology or urology, the physicians covering those services had three days earlier been residents in general pediatrics or general surgery and had limited specific knowledge of the specialties they were now covering.)

It was around 7:00 P.M. and I was making rounds, checking out how things were in the Emergency Department on the first floor. This was about the time that most of the staff would have finished working and would have just left for the day. CHOP, like most teaching hospitals, had an on-call system that might vary by specialty, but generally involved being on call every third night for most of us. This meant that interns and residents for major departments such as pediatrics (or internal medicine at an adult hospital) and surgery were always in attendance 24 hours a day, in contrast to most community hospitals that have to call in physicians as needed. Suddenly, from both my pager and the overhead PA system, a Code Blue was called from a surgical unit on the sixth floor. I took off running.

I had participated in countless cardiac arrests (Codes) over the past two years like most senior residents. While Codes are by definition life-or-death situations, incredibly tense with split-second decisions to be made and not always successful, by the time of senior residency, most physicians have participated in enough that there is a certain degree of familiarity and proficiency in these critical situations. (As a much more experienced doctor 45 years later, I am far enough removed from this type of situation that I would have not be nearly as adept in running a Code as a house staff member near the end of her internship year.) As I ran from the ER and headed up the several flights of stairs—no time to wait for elevators—I realized this would be the first time that I was the absolute senior person in charge of a Code. And while later in the year, I would feel very comfortable in the abilities of the more junior staff who would have arrived before me, that confidence certainly was not there that first week in July.

After running six flights (at that time, I was actually able to do that!) and rushing breathlessly down a corridor, I was met by a scene of confusion—but not for a reason I might have anticipated. While nurses and other staff stood around, administering oxygen and meds, some just looking confused, two doctors were engaged in a shouting match. The problem: the patient, a child of about six, had apparently undergone major hip surgery that afternoon and now sported one of the largest casts I had ever seen, starting from the knee and extending upwards over the abdomen and ending high on his chest. The argument: the junior pediatric resident (an excellent physician who had been one of the interns I supervised a few months earlier) screamed that the cast needed to be removed because chest compressions were impossible for this patient who was now in cardiac arrest. Meanwhile, the other physician, unfamiliar to me, was the new orthopedic resident, obviously new to his service, who insisted that there was enough room to try to work around the cast. The procedure had apparently been a long and complicated one, and hours had been spent on the cast's construction. The entire surgery might be jeopardized if the cast was cut away.

I sized up the situation immediately and pulled the orthopod aside. I felt sorry for him, I really did: first few days on service, probably feeling very overwhelmed, and probably thinking he's going to get his head handed to him by the attending who had performed the operation if the surgery was screwed up. Technically, he may even have outranked me in a sense. Children's had such an incredibly strong Surgery Department (headed by C. Everett Koop, who later became one of the country's best-known surgeon generals) that the surgical department pretty much had final say over any surgical patient.

Yet the decision was an obvious one and no seconds could be wasted. I looked at the harried orthopedist and firmly but gently said, "Look. You can either have a live kid with a broken cast that you may take hell for, or you can have a dead kid with a beautiful cast."

The cast was rapidly cut, the CPR successful, and the child revived. When I checked back a couple of days later, they had indeed needed to spend considerable time in remaking a cast, but no additional surgery had been required.

A week or so passed before my paths crossed with the orthopedic resident in the cafeteria. He started to apologize, saying that it was his first night on call, he had lost his cool, and wasn't thinking straight. "I really don't know what I was thinking about then." I stopped him and told him that we'd all been there at some point, too new or too inexperienced or too overwhelmed to make the right decision, and that's why we had backup, and hopefully we all learned from these situations.

And we had gotten lucky this time because the patient survived.

Chapter 45

Hero or Goat?

That same night, early in July, another episode occurred. July, as anyone who knows academic medicine is aware, is the month of change. All interns start on July 1; on June 30, they had been senior medical students. The past year's interns are now junior residents; some juniors become seniors and some start new careers as either fellows in a specialty or go on to general pediatric practice. The one thing that is certain at a major academic institution is that early July is the time of greatest change; without a doubt, this 31-day span contains more novices taking up new roles than any other time period.

Which meant that when the four-year-old with a malignant brain tumor on the Oncology ward passed away, no one present at the hospital that evening really knew him. Although he had apparently been there for several months, the interns that evening were brand new. None of the remaining staff familiar with the child would be available until the next morning.

Someone had to tell the parents. The brand-new intern, just three days out of medical school, was clearly going to have trouble. It is troublesome for almost any physician to deal with death and even more so for pediatricians, given the age of the patients and the general demeanor of the specialty. Oncology, at least in the 70s, was somewhat unique, as it was one of very few pediatric subspecialties with frequent deaths. While pediatric cancer is still troublesome and with significantly higher mortality than we would prefer, it was much more difficult then. An intern starting with oncology as a first rotation might be anticipated to have difficulty dealing with the emotionality of the situation.

So, on this particular evening, I was the most appropriate person to sit down with parents of a child I had never met, tell them of his death, and try to comfort them. Years later, I remember reviewing the chart, calling the parents in, and having a discussion. I was generally very good with people—one of my strong suits in medicine—and I hazily remembered a very nice but clearly grieving and bewildered young couple. I do not remember the specifics of the conversation, though I recall having spent quite a period of time with them.

Several months later, as I waited for an elevator in the main atrium of the hospital, a young couple stood near me. The pretty and beaming woman, clearly pregnant, looked at me and said, "You're Dr. Lotner. Right?" When I confirmed that I was, she asked me if I remembered them. Unfortunately, I didn't, which was not unusual. I saw a lot of children in the hospital and spent considerably less time with the parents—and as a senior resident, it would have been the intern's role to handle the majority of communication with families.

She told me that they were the parents of Joey, the four-year-old cancer patient who had passed away so early in July, and they wanted to thank me for my kindness to them that evening. Although they understood that I personally had not known their child, and the circumstances were so tragic, they both felt that I had gone out of my way to show compassion and to ease their pain—and in a small way, I had helped make a terrible situation just a little bit more bearable. They had been back to the hospital several times for counseling and always hoped they would run into me, to have a chance to express their gratitude.

The couple standing in front of me bore little resemblance to the distraught pair that I vaguely recalled from months earlier.

How could they? That night, they had been dragged from bed to learn their child had died, their emotions worn on their sleeves. Now, while the father was a bit more reserved, the mother in particular was composed, almost glowing—seemingly to me, basking in the early months of pregnancy.

I was very pleased with their kind words. It's great to feel as though you've done a good job on a medical level; it's even more rewarding to be appreciated on a human level. It is one of the great joys of medicine, the human connection.

Rather embarrassedly, I thanked them for their kindness and said I was pleased if my actions that night had been able to give them any comfort in the face of tragedy. I further told them that while no one could ever replace their child, their beloved Joey, I could see they were creating new life and wished them much happiness in starting a new family in the future.

That was my downfall.

The father, until then so thankful, looked at me and almost spat. "She's not pregnant! The last few months have been hell and we cried all the time. Jan just sat around for weeks and ate, and she's just putting on weight. And you're talking about starting a new family!" He grabbed her and pulled her away.

I stood there shell-shocked. It had taken approximately 30 seconds for me to go from an emotional glow and self-satisfaction to an unbelievable low. It truly counted as one of my most excruciating moments in medicine. How could I be so stupid? How could I just assume that she was pregnant? I wanted to shoot myself.

The next morning, I answered a page for an outside phone call. It was Jan, the young mother from the day before.

"Dr. Lotner, I'm so sorry about yesterday. After Joey, Paul has had such a hard time with this that I didn't want to tell him until I was totally sure that everything was okay. I've known for several weeks that I'm pregnant but was afraid to tell him. I know I should have done it earlier.

"You were great. Thank you again!"

Chapter 46

The Eyes Have It; or, Love at First Sight

As my medical career progressed, I was becoming more and more comfortable as a young doctor and as a relatively happy young adult. One thing that was missing was a loving partner to share this with, and it was around that time that Sandy came into my life. I'm often asked how we met. Not surprisingly, there's a story there.

As a medical resident, I lived in a then-regentrifying historic area of Philadelphia, the pretentiously named Society Hill. A historic area with some of the country's more famous and oldest institutions (including Independence Hall and the Liberty Bell), it had previously fallen into urban disrepair. Now, in the mid-70s, the neighborhood was undergoing a rebirth. I was renting an adequate but totally nondescript one-bedroom walk-up on Pine Street. From there, in my few spare hours as a medical resident, I would watch happily young yuppie couples coming and going as I trudged along, sometimes spending hours in exciting activities such as reading medical journals while seated in a historic church cemetery, perched atop the gravestone of the country's first naval secretary or—thrill of thrills—perhaps nestled near the cold granite marker for a signer of the Declaration of Independence.

While my building was rather ordinary, across the street was a beautiful newer brownstone that had recently been constructed.

Community scuttlebutt held that it had been built by a young couple and that the structure had won an award the year before for the best interior design in the Delaware Valley. After several months I met the building's owner, Phil, out walking his dog, and in making conversation, noted how lovely his home appeared. He proudly invited me in for a tour and I was indeed impressed — not only with the beautiful design, but with the exquisite furnishings. (In contrast, my own apartment was largely furnished with old fruit crates that had been painted either bright orange or bright blue to spiff up the place. Even with my recently raised salary of $9,500 a year, my decorating options were limited.)

To my surprise, a few minutes into the tour, Phil invited me to move in as his roommate. I was honored, awed and surprised. He explained that while the house was indeed exquisite, it was also very expensive. Soon after completion, he found himself in the midst of a messy divorce that was leaving him short on servicing what was a very steep mortgage. Any income from a renter to defray the cost would be welcomed. What an opportunity! My very average apartment with linoleum floors and Formica counters (did I mention orange fruit crate furniture?) compared to a beautiful home with hardwoods and atria and skylights? I impetuously jumped at the opportunity save one significant impediment — I had just signed a year extension on my lease across the street with 11 months to go and knew my landlord would not let me leave. Phil offered an immediate solution. He carpooled daily with a very nice young woman from Philadelphia to his job in Princeton, New Jersey. She lived by the Penn campus I knew so well and was looking to move to a more upscale part of town like Society Hill. He was certain she would just love to sublet my apartment. This being the era before cell phones or home computers or email, he would not be able to reach her at that moment, but if I liked the idea (I did!), he would send her over the next Tuesday evening.

I left his little Shangri-La, hovering over the ground, excited about my forthcoming move into luxury — until reason set in. The problem? While Phil's city manor was indeed beautiful, the bedroom itself that would be mine was miniscule, a seeming afterthought in an otherwise lovely house, perhaps a third the size of my current bedroom. There was no way I could stay in there very long. Forget about studying or even watching TV (assuming one would fit alongside my bed): I wasn't even sure my feet would fit in the room when the door was closed.

The more I thought about it over the next couple of days, the more I knew it wouldn't work. Great idea, but it was not going to be a great reality. I went across the street—twice—to tell Phil that I couldn't move in with him and to please cancel the now-unwanted visit from the unnamed woman who was coming over in a few days. Unfortunately, Phil wasn't home, I had no last name for him, no phone number, and then got involved with my 36-hour shifts at the hospital, and....

I had totally forgotten the appointment the next Tuesday evening, staggering home after a hellacious evening on call, when the doorbell rang. Who could it be? Oh, crud, and I remembered. When I opened the door, there stood a very attractive young woman who introduced herself as Sandy and who was there to look at (and hellbent on renting) my apartment. I apologized profusely that I would not be moving but was unaware how to reach her to cancel the visit, and (did I mention that she was very cute?) not to be an altogether cad, offered to take her out to the trendy little coffee shop down the block for a quick drink.

So, there we sat and I found out very quickly that Sandy was not only my age but intelligent, Jewish, confident and vivacious, and boy, this was pretty good, and I was getting happier about this serendipitous evening save one problem—her drooping eyelid. Or was it both eyelids?

Now, to a "normal" person (that is, non-medical), there's not too much to be made of a somewhat sagging eyelid.

But I was not "normal," and a drooping eyelid was a medical condition called ptosis. Ptosis could be a big deal (according to my medical texts and training) and it made a big difference whether one or both eyelids were involved. While I was a pediatric resident—not an adult internist—and while neurology was not my strong suit, I'd sum up the differential diagnoses of ptosis that I remembered very simplistically as this: both eyes, you had some serious or nasty problems such as significant thyroid disease or neurological problems like myasthenia gravis, serious but treatable; but if only one eye was involved, the first thought was, *Where's the brain tumor?*

I had one rule for dating back then: don't get involved with a woman who's terminally ill or dying. After medical school and during my training at one of the more rigorous academic hospitals in the country, I spent all day taking care of sick and dying patients—and the last thing I was going to do was get involved with a woman with a serious chronic illness that would involve my tending to her in a long downhill spiral. Was this being nice? Heck, no. Real? Yeah, pretty much.

And so I sat there in this little bistro filled with dark wood, ferns, and exceedingly dim lights. And those low lights? Well, that didn't make it any easier as I gazed into Sandy's pretty eyes and tried to determine whether it was one eye or both that were drooping. Now, I'm a pretty good talker. I can sit there and carry on a pretty lively conversation, sometimes even if distracted. Thus, while semi-squinting in the darkened interior, I made pleasant conversation but my thoughts were: *one eye or two?* I had pretty much decided if it was both eyes—well, I'd ask her out again. But if it was the dreaded "one eye," she might be cute, but I wasn't going to get involved. I spent the next hour staring at her eyes in the dim light and continuing to talk.

My conversation, which never let up, went along the lines of: "So, Sandy, how are you finding the time to be doing graduate studies at the Annenberg School at Penn and working full-time in Princeton?" And while she would answer, I'd be thinking it was just the left eye drooping a bit. And then, while I made a joke or described an interesting case I had just seen, I'd be thinking, *Oh, that's better, It's both eyes.* So it went—a lot of talking, a lot of desperately looking at her eyes.

As the shortened evening progressed (this was a Tuesday evening and I had been up all night), the time rapidly approached, demanding a quick decision on my part: to ask her out or not. After all, there were many fish in the sea, and I was not going to start a relationship with a woman I perceived to be dying.

As the moment arrived, I decided. Sadly, while I couldn't be 100 percent sure, it was only her left eye that was drooping; the woman had a brain tumor in all likelihood and was probably soon to be no more, and as for this fisherman—why, I'd just find another fish. And armed with this insightful logic, I did the only thing I could—I asked her out!

After all of that, why did I take the leap? I believe my thinking was along the lines of: *She's really cute; while I think it's only one eyelid, I can't really be sure in this light,* and *She's really, really cute.* I also kept coming back to the "fish in the sea" analogy. Working 110 hours a week, it had been a long time since I had caught any fish. My track record wasn't so great either: the last woman I had dated (more than a few times, at that) had come up with a scheme to have my car stolen! Yeah, I had been fishing in the Dead Sea.

So my little brain had won out over my medical brain, and Sandy and I went out for a real date a few days later and lo and behold, she showed up, bushy-tailed and BRIGHT EYED. And widely open-eyed. And still very pretty.

When after a very enjoyable evening I casually mentioned, "Gee, Sandy, I couldn't help but notice the other night, that your eye, or eyes, were drooping a little." She thought about it for a couple of seconds and then answered that she might have pulled an all-nighter the prior night for an upcoming test, and she suspected that when she was really overtired, her eyelids had a tendency to droop. I answered something insightful, like "Huh!" which loosely translated meant, "The damned neurology textbook sure didn't list 'Pulled an All-Nighter' as a cause of ptosis."

So that was the end of the ptosis and the drooped eyelids, until a year or so later when we were engaged. Sandy was on the phone with her aunt, and while I could only hear one end of the conversation, the question was obvious: "Of all the guys you were going out with then, when did you know it was going to be Gary?" Her answer was sweet to my ears. "Oh, right from the beginning, Aunt Sheila. On our very first night together, he was so romantic! All he did was gaze into my eyes!"

That's me, folks. Mr. Romantic.

Chapter 47

You're Related?

Like many physicians, I was always good at math and science.

I also had a great bedside manner (if I do say so myself), and over my medical career, took much pride in knowing my patients. For many years, I knew what was going on with the majority of my patients without having to look at their charts. I could instantly recall their diseases, their medications, and their general course. Even more so, I knew what most of them did for a living and what was happening in their families and in their personal lives.

This familiarity ended strangely at the office door. When it came to people I knew in other capacities, as Sandy has pointed out (frequently and repetitively over 43 years of marriage), I am "clueless." She picked up on this trait very early in our relationship. As a resident and fellow at University of Pennsylvania, there were frequent house staff parties for physicians and spouses, and I studiously avoided inviting Sandy to attend any of them. After having skipped several get-togethers, when Sandy inquired if I was ashamed to introduce her, I had to assure her it was just the opposite: I had met the spouses of the other docs multiple times, but still had almost no idea what anyone's name might be and was embarrassed to ask again.

The place I really didn't get it was with family—and in

particular, Sandy's family. Her family was large, teeming with cousins, and in distinct contrast to my much-smaller clan. I had enough trouble remembering my own few relatives, much less Sandy's 12 first cousins, all of whom she was close to and had grown up with; a bevy of second cousins; and a seemingly endless branch of indeterminate cousins. When I would meet them (the first time and any subsequent meetings thereafter), I would have no idea of who was who, and could never remember who was on her mother's side and who was on her father's.

When it came time for our wedding in Albany at the lovely Americana Hotel, charmingly close to the intersection of two interstates (and home of the sign "Congratulations, Sandy and Gary. Welcome Elks!"), my smaller family schlepping up from NYC physically resembled Sandy's much larger kin group.

At the end of the evening, I happily stood on the reception line. "Hi, Gary. I'm Sandy's cousin Marlene and this is my husband Ed. Great to meet you."

Next group. "Gary, welcome to the family. I'm Carol and this is my husband Jack. I'm one of Sandy's first cousins on her mother's side."

"Gary, Cousin Steve here. Great to meet you."

It was a lot of faces, a few of whom I'd met before, coming at me fast and furiously—but whether we'd met previously or not, I was clearly not going to remember them.

The next group walked up and I smiled and nodded at more faces that looked equally unfamiliar. "Gary, great wedding! You're getting a great girl in Sandy."

I warmly clapped the pleasant couple on their backs, gave my biggest smile in return, and answered, "I know! And how are you related to Sandy?"

"Through you!"

Got me again.

It was my father's second cousin and his wife from Rochester. In fairness, I had met them for the first (and only) time a few years earlier on my way to a rigorous internship interview. On the other hand, while I could try to tell myself that under those extenuating circumstances, I should forgive myself, they had put me up in their home for two nights—so any relief was minimal.

Like many physicians, I take comfort in my skills in math and science. I'm still clueless on the rest.

Chapter 48

Are You Sure That's Old Enough?

After my senior year of Pediatric Residency at CHOP, I made a decision that was surprising to many people: I did a fellowship in Pediatric Allergy, Asthma and Immunology. I had always thought I would have a career in General Pediatrics, but late in my training, I decided that the more general practice might not be sufficiently exciting or stimulating (not to mention, it would come with exceptionally long hours and very low pay). I explored pediatric hematology, an area of interest, managed to get accepted into the excellent department at the hospital, but was warned by the director, Dr. Eli Schwartz, that I should only consider the field if I intended a career in academia. I was not enthralled with what I'd seen of the academic life, and so gravitated toward Allergy/ Asthma instead.

I was particularly interested in pediatric asthma (which was a very different disease back then), by far the largest cause of pediatric hospitalizations for any chronic illness. In fact, one study had suggested there were more admissions of asthma than all the other chronic diseases combined. In my year as Assistant Chief Resident, I believe there were only three days of the year that at least one child wasn't admitted for asthma. Some kids were regular customers: in fact, we had three or four inner city children who were each admitted at least ten times that year.

A quick digression: one such child, Pamela L., had a notorious mother, who when the child would start to wheeze severely, would bring her to the Emergency Room. When the intern would begin to examine the very ill Pamela, her mother would then turn around and run from the hospital. The staff would never get the history of the illness and the mother would never return until receiving a call that the child was ready for discharge days later. Later in my fellowship, partly out of frustration, I arranged for young Pamela to be accepted for a long-term admission to the asthma Mecca: National Jewish Hospital, located in Denver, CO. It was widely acknowledged that this was the country's leading institution for the care and treatment of severe asthma. The country's sickest asthmatic children were sent there from all across the country to get their chronic asthma under control. While Pamela's asthma severity (12 hospitalizations in the last 18 months, including several requiring ICU admission with mechanical ventilation) was easily enough to merit this referral, on another level, part of the motivation for referral was to get the child and obnoxious mother away from the very frustrated CHOP house staff. Ironically, in an unseen twist of fate, when I later applied to National Jewish to take the latter part of my Asthma/ Allergy training, who was I lucky enough to pick up on my service? The infamous Pamela L., of course!

Back to the beginning of my journey into a pediatric asthma specialty. Asthma treatment was very different in the 1970s or earlier. Inhalers and nebulizers, the mainstay of treatment in newer times, were just coming into use and would revolutionize care. During my residency, the major drug in use was theophylline (given orally), or its derivative, aminophylline (used intravenously during hospitalization). These medications were markedly less effective than current inhalants and tended to be nasty: they had a low so-called therapeutic index, the amount required to produce a beneficial effect versus the amount that caused side effects. And the side effects could be severe, starting with vomiting and headaches but potentially leading to seizures—even death. Much research was done on how to best administer these medications, whether by mouth or IV, and my early published medical articles all had to do with these drugs. Even when administered properly, the effects were only moderate at best—one of the reasons so many children would be hospitalized back then.

The chief of the Allergy/Asthma service was Dr. Harold Lecks, a rather dapper 70-year-old, who was not thought of that highly by the general staff (a little too dapper and a little too full of himself) but turned out to actually be quite bright. He read voraciously and was always bringing up new and obscure information during rounds, although frequently totally out of context. Also, while bright, Harold had a propensity for malapropisms.

One day, early in my fellowship, I apparently said something that had pleased him. Dr. Lecks turned to me and said, "You're pretty bright, Lotner. How old are you?"

I looked at him a little suspiciously. "Twenty-nine, Sir."

He stroked his chin and pondered. "Twenty-nine, huh? My daughter is thirty-one. I guess that would make me almost old enough to be your father."

Almost, Dr. Lecks.

Chapter 49

A Tipsy Mother-to-Be

After a lovely honeymoon, we were back in the groove, planning a possible second prestigious fellowship in Denver at National Jewish Hospital, and to enjoy the mountains and great outdoors for a couple of years. However, that outdoorsy enjoyment part was not to be; after just six weeks of marriage, Sandy and I discovered we were five weeks into a pregnancy.

"Discovered" is an interesting term here. Sandy was not only tired and distinctly not her perky self but was having daily bouts of nausea. My doctor-self knew the likely diagnosis; our geez-we-just-got-married selves were in wishful denial. A pregnancy test was in order but in 1976, this was not as simple as in today's world. Not only were there no home pregnancy tests, but it was only in the last few months that CHOP had purchased very expensive kits to be able to obtain rapid answers in the ER. Previously, we were forced to send out blood specimens for suspected pregnancy to the adult hospital nearby and results could take 48 hours to obtain.

I brought in Sandy's urine sample with me to the ER and cornered Bill Yang, one of the residents there, to aid me in performing a pregnancy test. I was now an Allergy fellow and the kits really were so new that they had not been available when I had been a senior pediatric resident just a few months earlier. Bill surreptitiously found a kit, cautioning me to be quiet lest we come under the eye of Nurse Cheryl Kramer, the loud, secretly lovable, and totally terrifying nurse in charge of the ER. Unbeknownst to me, the kits cost over $100 in 1976 terms (I believe in today's terms, this is almost akin to the purchase price of Alaska) and the ER only had a few. Nurse Kramer was VERY possessive of them.

Bill ran the test under my watchful eye (I had never seen the test performed). In this early iteration, there were four separate steps taking several minutes each, and if there was NO pregnancy, the test would turn blue. This meant, if the woman were pregnant, NOTHING would happen. And sure enough, after several minutes, nothing happened—a very unsatisfying result for such an important event. I looked at Dr. Yang, he looked at me, and I asked plaintively, "Does this mean my wife is pregnant?" Bill said he thought so, but then admitted he had only used the kit once before and he wasn't 100 percent certain either.

Although the test confirmed what medically I knew to be true, I needed better confirmation. I asked Dr. Yang to get another kit, but he was not willing to risk the wrath of Nurse Kramer. It was a shared fear, but I was a man on a mission. He pointed me to a cabinet surrounded by guard dogs (or seemingly so, to me) and told me I was on my own.

I grabbed the precious kit, sequestered myself in a small alcove, ran the test, awaited the last step results—and heard Cheryl Kramer's booming voice, "DOCTOR LOTNER!! What are you doing back in my ER??! And where are my PREGNANCY TESTS????" I glanced down at the strip while I ran out. Nothing had happened.

Sandy came home that evening, vomited a few times—didn't believe my hard-earned results confirming her pregnancy and ran to a nearby women's clinic—vomited again, and only after they had performed an identical test did she believe what was then her third pregnancy exam of the day.

Getting over our initial surprise (or was it shock?), we began to enjoy the idea of impending parenthood and settled into a few semi-blissful months, scheduled to occur the same exact week we would be moving to Denver. Things went along peacefully enough until about week 24, when Sandy went to a routine visit with her highly recommended obstetrician, the Chief of Obstetrics at Pennsylvania Hospital, the nation's very first hospital. She called me afterwards, obviously distressed. Although she felt fine, the exam found her somewhat effaced and dilated (her cervix was starting to thin out and stretch open, a sign of impending delivery, which at that stage would be catastrophic). The recommendation: go home now, don't go back to work, go to bed, and START DRINKING ALCOHOL AROUND THE CLOCK! To me, there were two obvious problems: first, I didn't believe that Sandy was actually going into labor and second, I'd be damned if my wife was going to drink alcohol! (Modern readers will be aghast at this advice as I was, with concern about fetal alcohol syndrome.)

A short word of explanation. In today's age, even those who are non-medical are well-acquainted with the dangers of fetal alcohol syndrome. Indeed, many expectant women will not touch any alcohol. But the concept of fetal alcohol syndrome was relatively new back then (although as a pediatrician, I was of course familiar with it). To the contrary, obstetricians in those days had started using intravenous alcohol in an attempt to stop incipient labor in a woman where the onset of labor was extremely premature (i.e., below 26–28 weeks) where back then, results were likely to be disastrous. Alcohol inhibits the release of oxytocin, a hormone involved in the onset of labor. It had been discovered that if a woman had very early onset of labor, high doses of alcohol (best achieved intravenously) could actually turn off the labor. I once calculated that the women were being given by IV the equivalent of four to five shot glasses of whisky the first hour, and two to three an hour afterwards. For obvious reasons, this was only continued for a few hours. When I was at CHOP, a pediatric hospital with no labor ward, the Pediatric residents were called on to monitor women at Philadelphia General Hospital, the huge municipal hospital next door, when a woman was being administered IV alcohol. Walking onto the labor ward, the resident would be met by a bevy of nine-month ripe women in active labor, crying and screaming at the top of their lungs, and at the far end of the ward, would be a young woman, not so very pregnant (only in their fifth or sixth month), laughing and chortling, drunk as a skunk, yelling things like, "Hi, Honey, how're you?"

As a resident, I could understand (sort of) the rationale for using alcohol as a one-time IV trial to turn off premature labor, but what was being proposed with Sandy was far more nefarious to me: her obstetrician asked her to go home and drink alcohol around the clock on an indefinite basis until he told her otherwise! How much? He asked her what she liked to drink and my wife, only a very occasional consumer of alcohol, replied that she really wasn't much of a drinker. He pressed on; if you had a drink at a party, what would it be? She responded that she'd probably have a screwdriver (vodka and OJ). He then ordered her to immediately go home from work, drink four screwdrivers in hour one, two more in hours two and three, then one an hour throughout the first day. (She made it through her second screwdriver before she started retching.)

I was aghast. The difference between a one-off procedure with alcohol administered over several hours vs. prolonged administration in high quantities over months was staggering. While Dr. X as an obstetrician might not have been concerned about the relatively newly described fetal alcohol syndrome, as a pediatrician (and father-to-be), I sure was.

I had never met Dr. X, but he was the kind of physician I instantly hated when I finally reached him via phone. He was the old-time type of doctor that I never wanted to be (and hopefully never was during my 45 years in medicine): egotistic, self-righteous, all-knowing. He liked to dispense advice as an oracle and resented any questioning of his pronouncements. Our relationship consisted of several phone calls over the next few weeks. Every time I would ask a question or raise an issue, he would pull rank on me. I would ask about concerns for fetal alcohol syndrome with prolonged alcohol intake vs. a one time "fix," and he would reply, "Now let me get this straight. I'm the Chairman of OB/Gyn at Pennsylvania Hospital, the oldest hospital in the United States, founded by Benjamin Franklin and one of the most respected hospitals in the country, and you're a PEDIATRIC ALLERGY … Resident?.. And you're thinking you know more about this that I do?" As the calls progressed, Sandy was not progressing at all with her incipient "labor." Thankfully, she was not consuming nearly as much alcohol as he desired (there are some distinct advantages to being a cheap drunk who can't hold much liquor). I continued to question him about her returning to work, by this point equally concerned about the loss of her income—far higher than mine at that time—than I was about what seemed to me the increasingly unlikely off-chance of the onset of very early labor. Our conversations deteriorated, ultimately culminating in what to me was our last infamous discussion (or, more accurately, our last yelling match). This heated session ended with Dr. X screaming: "Let me remind you, Mr. Pediatric Allergy.. Fellow… that I am the head of OB at the nation's oldest hospital and I have over 30 years in practice and while I cannot tell you exactly when your wife will deliver, whether it will be 25 or 26 or 28 weeks or even 32 weeks, but the one thing that I will GUARANTEE you is that your wife will deliver early and if she doesn't do what I say and she goes into very early labor, it will be disastrous and it will all be on you!"

Whew! Poor Sandy! Think of her predicament. A highly respected OB attending, recommended by several wives of other physicians vs. her young doctor husband, who had missed most of his OB rotation with chicken pox. Who does she listen to?

And poor me! Already in turmoil with our out-of-state move coming up in a few short months, working my tail off as a too-busy young physician leaving no time for anything, and now totally in disagreement with an "expert" who constantly reminded me that I was not in my field and dire consequences could result. But with concerns for our baby, I knew I had to stick to my guns.

Luckily, Sandy stabilized and gradually trusted me (and Dr. X let up a little) and returned to work. Every day, around 11 A.M., in the large office building where she worked in downtown Philly, Sandy and her friendly co-worker would go to the bar downstairs as she became the Pregnant Lady Who Drank One Glass of Wine a Day.

As to the doc who "staked his reputation" that she would deliver prematurely, she eventually delivered in Denver one week after her due date.

I'll drink to that.

Chapter 50

Jeff-isms

The Junior Attending in the Allergy/Asthma Department at CHOP during my fellowship was Jeff Greene. He was to become my closest friend during that year and later, somewhat of a life mentor. Jeff's story was a little unusual in that we had been interns together but now he was two years ahead of me. Previously, after his medical training, he had gone into the Army as a general physician, serving in Vietnam for two years. He pursued pediatrics when he returned. Because of his previous experience, he was asked to serve a pediatric internship—but afterwards, he was able to skip residency and go directly into a fellowship program at another pediatric training program in Philadelphia. So, although we had started out together during our mutual internship year, he was now two years my senior in training and almost 30 years younger than any other attending in the department. It was perhaps not surprising that we became close friends as well as colleagues.

Jeff was not only very knowledgeable about allergy and immunology and an excellent teacher, helping me considerably in areas important for my later career, but he turned out to be a mentor for me on raising a family. Our friendship blossomed while Sandy and I were engaged and married shortly afterwards. By that point, Jeff was married for several years to a wonderful woman, Gaye, and had three young boys. I got to spend considerable time with his family. I was doing so much reading that I enrolled in an Evelyn Woods Speed Reading course, thinking this would help me keep up with my medical journals. The facility was 30 minutes from the hospital but near Jeff's home on the Main Line. For a period of several months, every Tuesday night, I would drive over to the Greene's and have dinner, with three young dervishes climbing over me, before heading out for my course. (Sadly, the course failed to live up to my expectations—it was fine for light reading, but not for the technical articles I needed to digest more thoughtfully. In retrospect, the home-cooked meals and the child-rearing advice freely dispensed by the Greenes proved infinitely more helpful for me than Evelyn Wood.)

While we would eat, Jeff would dispense what I would later call Jeff-isms: pithy little words of advice that would help me raising children. This was of critical importance. As previously noted, we had returned from the honeymoon surprised to learn that Sandy was pregnant. In several months, we would be heading to Denver for me to complete my second fellowship at National Jewish Hospital and Respiratory Center, and while we were looking forward to the institution and spending time in the glorious Rockies, we knew nothing about raising a family and would be a thousand miles from any relatives or friends. I soaked up Jeff's advice as if he was offering pronouncements from an oracle and Sandy, incredibly intelligent but career-focused and with little maternal experience, always deferred to me since I was the doctor.

One of our earliest Jeff-isms that I put into play was advice on how long a baby should sleep. He offered a simple formula: four hours until four weeks, then an hour longer each week until week eight (i.e., five hours at five weeks; six hours at six weeks, etc.). I had never heard this before and am not sure where he came up with this cockamamie advice, but when my daughter Jessica was born, I decided to put it into play. We had moved to Denver just before July 1, and Jessica was born ten days later. I was on call in the hospital every third night. With a baby crying much of the night, parental fatigue is to be expected; combining that with lack of sleep from being on call made for one very tired daddy (not to mention mommy, as well). According to Sandy, Jessica was the perfect baby—at least during the day. She would breastfeed and then sleep for four hours, breastfeed and sleep for four more, a repetitive cycle that would last all day. Sadly, that cycle ended each evening near the stroke of midnight. Then all hell would break loose, and we would have crying and screaming for hours on end unless she were held and rocked. This inability to leave her alone persisted until about the time of morning when I would be leaving again for the hospital. Oh, we were tired! Like any young parent, I would have liked to hold and play and marvel at our newborn during my limited evening hours at home, but this was not to be. For about two weeks, this terrible reverse cycle continued.

Finally, I remembered Jeff's maxim about sleep. I decided we needed to alter her sleep time to the night, which would mean substituting an awake period some other time (preferably in the early evening when I was home). So I set upon my plan to keep her awake from 6 P.M. to 10 P.M. and have her sleep at night. Neither part proved easy. First, we had to keep her awake—and I soon discovered that infants are pretty determined sleepers. After her evening meal, we would hold her, talk to her and cuddle her, but after ten minutes, she would go back to sleep. I tried rocking and moving her (good for a few minutes) and then scratching the bottom of her feet (good for eliciting a Babinski reflex but only keeping her awake another ten minutes or so), and then she was off to a deep slumber. Finally, I hit on it—shampoos! A series of shampoos with slightly cool water and it worked! Holding the top of her head under cold running water for a couple of minutes produced a very unhappy little babe, but one who stayed awake for quite a while. After a few such shampoos, we were awake for hours and Jessica probably had the cleanest hair of any baby in history. Following shampoos, sleeping was relatively easy afterwards. After 10 P.M., when she was fed and her diaper changed, we initiated the ten-minute rule—if she was still crying after ten minutes, we'd get her but not before then. We turned on our rather noisy window air conditioner and set an alarm for four hours. Worked like a charm.

When we embarked on this plan, Sandy originally looked at me and asked if I were sure we should be doing this. "Of course, trust me," I told her. "I'm a pediatrician." It sure worked for the Greenes. It definitely worked for us.

Sounds cruel? (My kids think so and so did most of my friends.) Effective? Incredibly. It took three nights but by the third, we had totally transformed evenings into wake times and nights into... well, nights. And sleeping. After that, Jessica spontaneously followed Jeff's rule with no interventions necessary on our part: she slept five hours at five weeks, six hours at six weeks, and so on until at two months, she slept a full eight hours. Several months later, we were out with two couples, both with young children. One complained that their six-month-old cried all night and never slept more than three hours; the other topped it with a story of an almost two-year-old who still needed to be held much of the night. Even Sandy smiled with me at this one. (I'd still gladly trade being thought cruel for three nights compared to months of good sleep and the chance to enjoy my baby when I was home.)

Jeff-ism Number Two was about babysitters: as soon as we got to Denver, our top priority would be to find a babysitter, and not just any babysitter. He told us in no uncertain terms that we needed to find a 13-year-old Catholic girl. I was dumbfounded. "Why Catholic?" I asked Jeff. "Why not Jewish, like you and I?" He looked at me as if I was unbelievably naive. She obviously needed to be Catholic because then she was likely to have come from a large family and would have acquired a whole (albeit brief) lifetime's worth of childcare experience. And 13, why so young? According to Jeff, girls started dating much younger than they had in our generation and any girl worth her salt would probably have started dating by 14. Once they had, they would be lost to you as an effective babysitter—they had more important things on their minds. I think I smiled dumbly and was skeptical, to say the least.

How did that work out? I'd love to say when we got to Denver, with Sandy expected to deliver imminently, that I put out signs in our apartment complex advertising for 13-year-old Catholic lasses, but I didn't. Instead, to my amazement, they came looking for us. Less than two weeks after Jessica's birth, as Sandy and I were walking with Jessica strapped to my chest, two young girls from the next apartment building came running to coo over the infant. They were both very sweet and friendly. The older one introduced herself as Maureen and asked if we might need a babysitter. How old was the very young-looking Maureen? She answered she was 12, but seeing the concerned look on my face, added that she was about to turn 13. Catholic? With a name like Maureen, what do you think? Brothers and sisters? Four others and she was the oldest. And to top it off, the family lived 50 yards from us and her mother was always home if there was a problem.

Maureen was a great babysitter—for about two months. The problem? Jeff had underestimated the age at which girls started dating and soon after turning 13, the very pretty Maureen acquired a beau and lost her interest in sitting. The solution? Her sister from our first meeting, Kathleen, had just turned 12, and was gung-ho and only too happy to take over the mantle. She proved to be terrific for the rest of the year.

Catholic and thirteen? Who would have known? Thank you, Jeff Greene.

Several years later, I was long settled in Atlanta with my family of four and Jeff and his family continued in Philadelphia. He and I talked frequently. One Sunday evening, I called Jeff. A few minutes into the conversation, I could hear a commotion at the other end. Jeff interrupted our chat, unsuccessfully covered the phone's mouthpiece, and yelled, "Boys, go back outside and run around some more." We resumed our conversation.

Two minutes later, the ruckus from his end was much louder, with banging and loud voices. Jeff excused himself again, and although his hand covered the phone, I could easily make out his directive: "Boys, I just told you! Get back out there and keep running around the block! Come on!"

When we resumed, I was naturally curious. He replied, "We've got three sons, ages ten, eight and six. They're all really, REALLY active. If they don't burn off that energy before they come in in for the evening, we have a terrible wild night. So we have them run around the block a few times."

"I take it they're not into that today?" I asked.

"No, it's raining cats and dogs outside and they just don't want to run!"

I loved Jeff. (Sadly, many years after his earlier tour in Vietnam, it was learned that he had acquired Hepatitis C from a transfusion when injured, and he was to die way too early.)

Chapter 51

The Somewhat Unusual Birth of Our Daughter

We had just moved to Denver and Sandy was imminently due to deliver. I had started my fellowship at National Jewish Hospital, unofficially the nation's asthma center in a day where asthma treatment was not as advanced and children were constantly hospitalized with asthma attacks. NJH was considered Mecca for asthma specialists, and I was delighted to be accepted into their fellowship program.

The confounding factor was this somewhat unexpected pregnancy. I had done my initial year of Pediatric Allergy/Asthma fellowship at CHOP and felt I had excellent training. But Mecca was Mecca—one did not turn down the chance to go to such a prestigious program when opportunity presented itself. And so, our plans were set.

We would get married (check!); I would apply to NJH (check!); I would be accepted (check!); Sandy would find a great job (check!) and we would have a couple of great years in Denver with mountains, hiking, and open skies—things we both loved—before starting our family. Okay, not so fast on that check. They say man plans and God laughs, and he probably had a good chuckle on our account: we hadn't quite counted on that pregnancy so early in our marriage. (I like to say that we got religious on the honeymoon and used a "holey" diaphragm, but Sandy hates that joke.) In any case, while Denver and the fellowship were lined up, we suddenly found that with my new position to start July 1—and Sandy's due date of July 4—life was a tad more complicated than planned.

The pregnancy itself had been complicated and stressful, but things had been a little quieter in the latter months as it was clear she was not going into premature labor. Of course, quieter is a relative term. Not only was I busy with my fellowship at CHOP and planning for our new life to follow, but I had to go to Denver alone, meet with my program directors, orient myself to a strange city, choose an apartment for our move two months hence, and find an obstetrician to deliver Sandy almost immediately after our arrival. In total, I had all of three days to accomplish everything. Somehow, everything got done. Of all the tasks, interviewing OB-GYNs was certainly the most interesting. Reflecting back after 45 years, I can still acutely recall my discomfort of sitting alone as a single male in a gynecologic waiting surrounded by a bevy of young expectant mothers, all looking at me askance. I was definitely an outsider. I spent several hours sitting and smiling stupidly, thinking of things I could say (like "Our baby is due in two months and I'm not even showing"). Somehow the practice that I picked for Sandy (and that would take us, as some practices refused to deliver a woman they had not followed) turned out to be excellent.

The physical move to Denver was quite stressful. I had to transport our car from Philly to Denver, normally a trip that would take at least two days. Sandy was in her 39th week, and while I did not believe her Philadelphian obstetrician correct when he guaranteed an early delivery, his certainty of that fact weighed heavily on my mind. In the days before cell phones, personal computers, GPS, or ready internet access—and with driving to be guided only by a hastily purchased Rand-McNally *Road Atlas*—I was to embark on this trip solo. I was certainly not bringing my wife with me, perhaps to deliver in a Nebraskan wheat field, attended by her idiot physician husband. No, Sandy would fly out immediately after my arrival, and the trip would be punctuated by my stopping in Kansas or Iowa every few hours to place a call home, making sure she hadn't delivered in the interim.

Even getting her on a plane was no easy task. The airline demanded a physician's letter guaranteeing that she would not deliver within 48 hours of flight. Since we (okay, I) had been continually fighting with her OB, he naturally refused to write such a note—and indeed, what sane doctor could forthrightly "guarantee" that a woman in her last week of pregnancy would not deliver at any given point? (Well, I would, as it turns out.) Eventually my exceptionally pregnant wife, longer horizontally than vertically at this time, managed to board a plane with a letter from a pediatric allergist on a Children's Hospital prescription pad, stating in no uncertain terms a "guarantee" of non-imminent delivery. Somehow it worked, with the airline taking it at face value.

I left Philadelphia in my stuffed little Chevy Vega death-trap and miraculously picked up a hitchhiker, who—even more miraculously—was headed for Denver and who was as insanely eager to get there as I. We drove for 30 hours straight, stopping only for phone calls, coffee and restrooms. I was a wreck on arrival and Sandy flew in the next day, after an easy two-hour flight, looking as cool as a very pregnant cucumber. Somehow, she liked Denver and the apartment I had picked sight unseen. The next day, she had the first and only meeting she would have with her new obstetrician prior to delivery. Amazingly, she loved her new doctor, picked by her solo male husband. It was all good.

Since Sandy was predicted to deliver almost upon her arrival and I was starting a program that required my staying overnight in the hospital every fourth night, I cannily managed to trade and avoid call the first ten days. My co-residents were wonderful about working out these on-call shifts, but Sandy refused to deliver early as guaranteed by her earlier physician. (He may indeed have been the Chairman of the nation's oldest hospital, founded by Ben Franklin as he repetitively pointed out—but to me, I will always think of this doctor as an ass flying a kite.) By the time July 11 rolled around, because of all my earlier swaps, I found myself stuck taking call and staying overnight in the hospital every 48 hours.

Sandy's call came at 4:30 in the morning as I slept in the doctor's room at NJH. Her contractions had started, were coming every eight minutes or so, and she was ready to go to the hospital. I knew the contractions were too far apart and reassured her that we had time. I didn't want to call in my new friend and co-fellow, Bill Scott, to come in and cover for me so early. I'd wait until Bill was scheduled to arrive at 7:30, leaving immediately upon his arrival and we'd head for the hospital. But first, all agog with anticipation, I would get myself ready to make an instant getaway. I got up and thought I was pretty cool and calm, all things considered—after all, I was a hot-shot young physician who dealt with sick and dying patients, and this was just a delivery, nothing to be excited about. So, I calmly headed into the shower. After a few seconds, I noticed there was something unusual about this particular shower: I could see my feet clearly! That might not seem odd but in those days before LASIK, I wore glasses constantly and could barely see without them. Seeing my feet clearly while showering was a novelty. Sure enough, I realized I was wearing my glasses in the shower. With those glasses, not only could I see my feet but I could see the socks I had forgotten to remove before showering! How stupid! Long gone was the perception of calm and collected, replaced by a thankfulness that at least I wasn't fully clad in my pants and shoes while I showered.

After Dr. Scott's arrival early that morning, I zoomed home in record time and realized that we were still way too early. However, Sandy insisted on going to the hospital and I agreed, but by this time I really had calmed down. On the way, we went grocery shopping and then sat inside the car as we entered a drive-through car wash. With a clean car, we proceeded to the hospital. I suspect we may be the only couple in recorded history to get a car wash on the way to having their first-born child.

On arrival, we waited for the action to begin as Sandy experienced contractions every six minutes or so. We were prepared: we had taken a whole series of Lamaze classes and I was set to be a partner and a coach. (Picture the whole nine yards: I was wearing my baseball hat and had my coach's whistle around my neck in order to cheer on my team.) A couple of painful contractions, and Sandy—who had practiced for this for months, to do it all naturally, together, a team!—opted immediately for an epidural. Suddenly, I was a coach without a team. Here I was, all pumped up—I had trained for this role! There was no one to coach! (I began to appreciate that in this particular sport, the coach's role was vastly inferior to that of his only player.) As labor s-l-o-w-l-y progressed, and my player no longer knew when she was contracting, I took to randomly blowing my whistle and attempting to coach other women on the ward, much to their annoyance.

As 8 P.M approached and we had been there for 12 hours, Sandy's OB decided to do a C-section for "fetal distress," occasioned by an elevated fetal heart rate. Looking around and realizing I was the only pediatrician in the room, I called for a time out and a conference (I may not have had an active team but I was still deep into the sports analogies), explaining that unless there was something else going on, as the pediatrician, I was concerned about a slow fetal heart rate (bradycardia), not a mildly elevated one (tachycardia). I may have been a little selfish; I suspect that my reluctance to move ahead with a C-section was to avoid having my pretty wife with a long abdominal scar if not needed. The OB appropriately but reluctantly agreed to give it a couple more hours. Thankfully, my "team" came back to life and a healthy and beautiful baby Jessica was born after 17 hours of labor.

The rest of Sandy's and Jessica's hospital stay was unexciting but interesting. Knowing almost no one in Denver, aside from myself and one visit from our new friends, the Scotts, Sandy's only visitor was a Black minister. As it turned out, after delivery Sandy shared a room with a very nice young Black woman, who was nearing discharge with her baby. When her minister came by and learned that Sandy knew no one in this new town, he continued to visit her daily, even though his own parishioner had departed. Nice man—and for a short moment, we considered being the only Jewish members of a Black Baptist congregation!

Chapter 52

Saturday Night Fever

Jessica was ten weeks old and was spending the evening in the Intensive Care Unit at National Jewish Hospital—again. It was her fourth stay in the ICU in as many weeks, and she had never been better!

A word of explanation is clearly in order. National Jewish Hospital is a venerable institution that has gone through many iterations and many sub-titular name changes. It had begun in the early 1900s as a tuberculosis sanitarium/hospital when there were no good treatments for tuberculosis, but it was known that mountain air (i.e., low oxygen) was beneficial in the treatment of the disease. As medications eventually began to treat TB as a serious problem and the disease became less pervasive and more easily curable, the hospital later evolved into one of the world's leading asthma hospitals. In later years, it would become a center for not only asthma, but all immunologic and respiratory diseases.

I did my fellowship in the waning asthma years, when the hospital was frequently given the unofficial title of the National Asthma Center. Before current inhaled generations of asthma medications were developed, asthma was a nasty disease with few effective acute treatments, leading to many severe patients requiring repetitive hospitalizations. Not infrequently, a "bad asthmatic" might have several hospital stays in the course of a single year.

During my first allergy fellowship year in CHOP, I had two patients who were respectively hospitalized ten and 12 times in a calendar year, each with several ICU admissions for mechanical ventilation or isoproterenol infusions. In these days, National Jewish (NJH) proved to be a national resource. Terribly ill patients, the worst of the worst, could be sent there for longer-term admissions in an attempt to get their asthma under control on a more meaningful basis. A decade prior to my fellowship, it was not unusual for some of these patients to have stays in Denver that would last 12–18 months; by my era, treatments had begun to improve and insurance would dictate shorter stays, but several-month residencies were not uncommon. We used a holistic approach to treatment, a word not often heard at that time. Patients would be assigned to a team with a physician, psychologist, nurse, social worker, and a childcare worker, among others. The child and the family would be examined from all aspects to make sure medical care was optimized, unusual diagnoses not overlooked, and all family and social aspects evaluated.

While termed a hospital, most of the patients were fine on a day-to-day basis. During longer stays, patients would have tests (both medical and psychological), meet with multiple individuals, and have classroom time to keep up with their appropriate schoolwork. The arrangement sometimes felt more like a boarding school than an acute care hospital.

NJH did have an ICU, but it was not the typical ICU setting of any major hospital. Since the wards where the children spent their time felt more like dormitories than hospital rooms, any child who became acutely ill (with a typical asthma attack that might have required routine hospitalization in any other hospital) would be transferred to our only traditional hospital ward: the ICU. In contrast, a patient severely ill enough to require a true ICU admission—in what is termed respiratory failure and requiring mechanical ventilation—would be transferred to the pediatric ICU at the University of Colorado Hospital several blocks away. (This was rarely needed.)

Accordingly at NJH, our ICU was often a quiet place. We did an excellent job of keeping most of the patients under good control, and while some wheezed frequently, they were rarely at the point that hospital admission (or, in this case, ICU admission at NJH) would have been necessitated.

The hospital was naturally excited to have the birth of a new baby to an integral staff member (I was one of four new fellows on the pediatric side that year), and Sandy and I had brought baby Jessica over once before. When she was six weeks old, on our way to dinner at a restaurant and without a sitter, we decided to make a quick stop at the hospital to let the nurses coo over our delightfully cute infant. The restaurant was only four blocks away.

When we reached the ICU, entering with a little trepidation (I knew it wasn't a "real" ICU, but still, the name was so suggestive to anyone in medicine), we were greeted by four nurses who went absolutely crazy over the baby. They passed her from one to the other, laughing and cackling, their faces lighting up. As I looked around the unit, I realized that they did not have a single patient in the room. Glenda, the very personable charge nurse, turned to us and excitedly exclaimed, "Why don't you leave her here while you go out to dinner?"

Why not indeed? Well, I could think of lots of reasons, starting with the obvious: she wasn't sick, she wasn't a patient, she was only six weeks old, what if something happened, and wasn't this illegal somehow? The ever-enthusiastic nurses had a different set of answers: they were all trained pediatric nurses, they loved babies, they had no patients, we would enjoy a meal more without a baby crying, I had a beeper that allowed them to reach me instantly and we were close enough that we could back in a few seconds. We didn't need much convincing—Sandy and I were sold. Jessica and the nurses spent a great three hours together in the ICU and we enjoyed our first fine meal since moving to Denver.

The situation proved so mutually enjoyable that the nurses begged us to bring her back the next weekend and we did. And the next. And the next.

It was Monday morning in the hospital, and the Chief Physician, Dr. Richard Johnston, an excellent immunologist, was leading rounds. All the memorable new patients of the previous several days were presented, their cases discussed, and their treatment planned. Finally, the conference was about to disband when Dr. Johnston stopped everyone from leaving. He stated that he had recently become aware of an unusual and very perplexing patient in the hospital, with an interesting complaint and felt that we needed to discuss the child. To lead the discussion would be none other than...Dr. Lotner.

He called me up in front of 20 or so colleagues as I nervously wondered what was going on, and whether I would have any meaningful ideas about this unusual case. With no preparation or forethought, the situation felt ripe for me to make a total fool of myself.

Dr. Johnston proceeded. "Dr. Lotner, I've recently learned that we have an infant with a very unusual case of apparent periodic fever [*Note to the reader: there are pediatric disease with fevers that recur at relatively set intervals, but not like this*] that occurs only on Saturday nights. Apparently this infant is entirely well, but virtually within minutes, is so ill that ICU admission is required. Then almost as intriguingly, within three or four hours, the entire episode resolves so quickly that the child is discharged home to the care of her parents with no testing or follow-up involved. I personally have never heard of a case with such a precise periodicity and lack of other symptoms. Dr. Lotner, can you give us your differential diagnosis and proposed evaluation of this patient?"

Stammering and red-faced, I replied, "Dr. Johnston, you're right. I have to admit that's a rather astounding presentation and I must admit I'm almost at a loss for diagnostic possibilities. The one thing I can say about this patient with a fair degree of certainty is that between now and next Saturday, I will get to the bottom of this and I feel confident that we will not be seeing any further recurrences."

"That's a good thing, Dr. Lotner. I'd hate to think of the consequences if they were to continue."

Lo and behold, the baby with Saturday night fevers was never seen again.

Chapter 53

Welcome to Atlanta

Two years later, and after an extensive search (with no internet or cell phones, meaning that my well-conceived plan was primitive by today's standards), we were headed for Atlanta. It figured; we loved the mountains in Denver (two good job offers there), came from the Northeast (good offer there as well), adored the Seattle area (another position offered to me), and even had received an offer from beautiful Monterey, California. The only part of the country that Sandy and I were opposed to *a priori* was the South: too dry, too hot, and too redneck.

The decision was not quite as crazy as it seems. Having trained at two prestigious academic programs, I was used to practicing at a high level of medicine but it proved hard to find a group practicing at the standards I wished to keep. Several of the practices with which I had interviewed around the country were thriving .and would have been more lucrative than Atlanta, but I was concerned about their medical standards. Meanwhile, in Denver itself, I had excellent offers from physicians I knew well. One was from Jack Selner, a previous NJH alum with an excellent and growing practice. I had moonlighted for him, covering his practice every third night for a year, and it was anticipated I would join him. But I got cold feet about Denver (sometimes literally) because it was too good and too many people wanted to practice there. At the time, two national training programs in asthma existed (both equally regarded as excellent university allergy/immunology programs). The first was National Jewish, where I was doing my fellowship. The second, perhaps rated a slight rung below, was the Children's Asthma Research Institute, which was located in...you guessed it, Denver! So you had two large centers in one beautiful city with lots of trainees all eying the chance to stay, but one whose altitude made for no dust mites (the greatest cause of year-round allergy), fewer molds, and even fewer pollens. The Colorado motto was *"Tis a privilege to live in Colorado,"* which it was—but I didn't want to risk my financial future when similar cities had far less allergists per capita and far greater quantities of allergens. Also, after two years of drought in Denver, with the occasional drive out of the city revealing the distressing picture of dead cattle in fields, I was concerned about the city outgrowing its precarious water supply. (In retrospect, my friend Jerry Koepka took the Denver position I had declined and had a great practice, and Denver hasn't run out of water yet, despite four additional decades of growth.)

But Atlanta and the South? I was recruited by David Tinkelman, who had left NJH a couple of years before our arrival in Denver and had an outstanding reputation there. David was almost legendary in NJH for being very bright and for his aggressive pursuit of research (which he continued to do in private practice in Atlanta, at a time when almost all such research was performed only in academia). He had joined Atlanta Allergy & Asthma Clinic, P.C., a several-year-old practice that was making a name for itself (and would later turn into the largest and certainly one of the most innovative allergy practices in the US). David had gotten my name from Dr. Richard Johnston, the acting head of my NJH fellowship program, as a good young physician who was looking for a practice. David's recruitment pitch started at a disadvantage, however, because of my whole "thing" about the South. Luckily, he was an excellent salesman and a smooth talker, countering almost all my arguments with the fact that he himself was a nice Jewish boy from Philly, who had shared all the same concerns three years earlier. He convinced me to at least come take a look; at the very least, they'd pay for the trip.

Our visit was scheduled for early December. While our first Denver winter had been mild enough to play tennis in the city most weekends (or, of course, ski in the mountains), the second year was brutal. We had purchased a house several months earlier from another resident physician who was completing his training. The house was great, a few blocks from the University of Colorado Medical Center, and even came replete with a hefty collection of grape vines (from which we would later fashion our own wine). The selling physician mumbled something about the heating system being old and not always working well in the periphery of the house. This hadn't exactly struck fear in my heart when we bought the house in the heat of summer, but when late November and early December brought temperatures below zero and we had almost no heat, I really did have cold feet. Though he had warned us that the system was not great, he could have done so with more urgency: we didn't realize it was totally out of order until the antiquated boiler ran out of the water I hadn't known to replenish, blowing up completely.

Without heat, Sandy, baby Jessica and I spent several weeks huddled together under blankets during every waking moment, fully clothed in skiwear. From this wintry hell, when my plane flew into Georgia, it was truly a sight to behold. In those days, Atlanta was sometimes called the City of Trees. Indeed, flying into Hartsfield showed a small clump of gleaming skyscrapers surrounded by a virtual sea of trees, extending for many miles in all directions. Where Denver had been -4 degrees and barren, and our family had spent several days listening to our own chattering teeth, Atlanta clocked in at a balmy 64 degrees two weeks before Christmas! After meeting some great doctors and wives in my group and seeing large, beautiful and very affordable houses—no ski jacket required—it didn't take much convincing to decide Atlanta would be our new home.

We're still trying out Atlanta 40-plus years later, and it's been a great choice.

Chapter 54

Just Bend Over

I walked into the exam room in our Windy Hill office to encounter the patient: a curt, irascible old man.

It was 1980 and I had been in private practice almost a year. Our group, the Atlanta Allergy & Asthma Clinic, P.C. (AAAC) was quite innovative in several ways. The practice had been started nine years earlier by Dr. Gerald Vanderpool, an entrepreneur in his own rights, and one of the first physicians in the Atlanta area to open multiple offices for a single practice. While this concept was to become widespread in future years and for numerous specialties, I'm told Gerry was really the first to start this in Atlanta—which makes him a bit of a big deal.

Atlanta was later to become known as the City of Mega Practices. In the early days of managed care, as physicians tried different strategies to cope with the huge and rich corporations that were squashing the traditional small doctor, Atlanta had the largest collection of multi-physician single-specialty practices not only in allergy, but also for ENT, cardiology, urology, orthopedics, gastroenterology, and several others. The city became known as an innovator in this respect—and it had all started with AAAC.

At the time I joined the practice, I was the fifth physician in a group that had three offices, soon increasing to four. (In later years, we would expand to an almost unthinkable 19 physicians, several nurse practitioners, and 18 offices. For several years, we were the largest single entity allergy practice in the United States.)

Our group was also very ecumenical. Dr. Vanderpool was the son of a Baptist minister. Scott Carroll, who joined him several years later, was an observant Roman Catholic (who would later change denominations after a divorce). Next came David Tinkelman, who I always described as a moderately observant Jew (but I think this may only have been in contrast to my very much less-observant self). Then, Dennis Spangler, who was a WASP cum Roman Catholic. I joined the practice after Dennis, a year later, and initially described myself as a heathen Jew or a secular Jew (although I am somewhat more observant as years have passed). All in all, a fairly diverse bunch. We all were to get along well for many years—in fact, Scotty and Dennis would subsequently become my closest friends in the group.

Our mix of beliefs and backgrounds was representative of the city itself. Presently, Atlanta is a sprawling cosmopolitan city, with a diverse mix of people and visitors coming from all over the world. The economy is expanding rapidly; it is a center of international trade; Georgia Tech is recognized among leaders in many areas of technology. Presently, it's unusual in the metropolitan area to hear a Southern accent and almost unheard of on local news. While Atlanta has the largest Black population of any major city in the US and has had Black mayors for the past 30 years, many racial tensions of earlier years have been quieted for a long time. This was not always the case when I went to see the patient in 1980.

As in many urban areas, cities are more cosmopolitan at their centers and less tolerant in peripheral areas. The Windy Hill area in Cobb County, nowadays considered relatively close to city life, was a mixed bag when I arrived. While there were many up-and-coming suburbs with transplanted Northerners and high incomes, rural areas were not far away. It was not unusual to meet people with Southern drawls, particularly among older patients (often with outdated and bigoted attitudes to match).

The old man, a patient normally of Dr. Vanderpool (he with the Baptist upbringing), reminded me of a slightly updated version of ex-Governor Lester Maddox. For those too young to remember, Maddox was infamous: a colorful, controversial, nasty character who was well-known on the national scene. He was initially a restauranteur who opened a Southern-style emporium near the Georgia Tech campus, refused to admit Black patrons (at one point achieving national notoriety when he confronted Black customers, wielding an axe handle to prevent their entrance), and later parlayed his fame into becoming Georgia's governor from 1967–1971. He was exactly the type of person I visualized when I had initially told David Tinkelman that I had no interest in practicing in Atlanta.

Pat, the receptionist, apologized to me right away. The patient had been scheduled to see Dr. Tinkelman, but Dr. T. pulled rank and told her to give him to the rookie (lucky me!). She warned me the old man could be "crusty." I entered the exam room and the old man eyed me warily. Not only was he a Maddox look-alike both in build and in yokel clothing, but his deep drawl and his vocal inflections were almost a clone of the former segregationist governor. He was there because he suspected a sinus infection and had wanted to see Dr. Vanderpool, who—unfortunately for the patient (and for me)—was at a distant office that day. Reluctantly, the geezer had agreed to be seen by an associate, which on this particular afternoon would be either Dr. Tinkelman or myself. Now, Tinkelman is an obviously Jewish name; Lotner is totally nondescript.

As soon as I walked in, I could feel him sizing me up (although his stern gaze would never meet my eyes). Gruffly, he asked, "Who are you?"

As flatly as I could, I responded, "I'm Dr. Lotner."

Out of the corner of his mouth, he almost spat out the words. "Thank God! I thought I was going to get the Jew!"

I was stunned, but only for a moment. "Well, sir, I guess this is just your lucky day. We should get that sinus infection cleared up in no time. Now if you'll just bend over and drop your pants, I think we'll start off with the rectal exam!"

"Is that really necessary, Doc?"

"Not always, Sir. But in your case, I have the strong feeling that it's going to be the key to the whole evaluation."

I've told that story so many times over the past four decades that I wonder what I really answered. As some of my patients would say, my career has been "blessed," and over the course of my professional life, when patients cared at all, I'm thankful that there were many more who were happy to get a Jewish doctor ("Jewish doctors are the smartest, Doc") compared to the old-time segregationist anti-Semites, like my Lester Maddox clone.

Patient X learned a valuable lesson that day. There's no room for anti-Semitism in our world—and as it turns out, the same is true for the exam room.

Chapter 55

Which Eye Has It?

Mitzi lived down the block and had asthma. Before she became my patient, she was our babysitter.

We had been living in Atlanta for a year, had two children under four years of age, and desperately needed babysitters. We met Mitzi through her mother, Leeanne—a bright and vivacious woman who lived just a few houses away. Mitzi was 14, pretty, intelligent, and more than a little dramatic (as many teenagers tend to be). But the need for babysitters was ongoing and we worked her into our rotation of regular sitters. In a neighborhood with many young families, the competition for good sitting was intense.

We also learned about the family through neighborhood events. Leeanne, something of a local media personality, lived with her second husband, Mitch, who brought Mitzi's half-sister Susan into the mix. However, several houses beyond lived Leeanne's original spouse, Drew, along with his wife and two teen daughters, bringing a second half-sister for Mitzi. Everyone seemed to move back and forth with great fluidity, and I, with little sense of gossip or social structures, had no idea how anyone was actually connected in this seemingly free-flowing group.

This normally would have been of no concern until Mitzi came to see me as a patient. She had episodic asthma, generally going from being totally well to suddenly having acute episodes arising out of the blue. These episodes were fairly severe, frequently not responding to usually effective treatments, and often leading to emergency room visits or occasional hospital stays. After working with Mitzi for a while, it became apparent that most of her episodes were brought on by emotional outbursts. She was a very highly-strung young teen, excessively theatrical, and it was during emotional outbursts over some perceived issue that she would experience her sudden acute attacks.

A quick word about asthma is needed here. When I first entered the practice 40-plus years ago, asthma was considered a psychosomatic illness by some groups in the world of medicine or psychology. It isn't. But there had been much written earlier about the personalities of patients with asthma, the emotional issues, and secondary psychological types that in some circles, asthma sometimes carried a stigma of not being a "real disease." This stereotype couldn't have been further from the truth.

Asthma is an inflammatory condition of hyperactive lungs, sometimes described in shorthand as "twitchy lungs" where, due to immune changes, the lungs can easily clamp down and go into spasm. The illness is clinically characterized by wheezing, chest tightness, cough and mucus production. While asthma is a heterogeneous disease (meaning that it varies greatly from patient to patient and there is no one pattern that fits all), multiple types of stimuli can trigger episodes for many patients. Perhaps chief among them are allergic exposures and certain viral infections; other examples will include cold temperatures, exercise, and irritants such as smoke or pollution.

For some, psychological stress can serve as such a trigger—but conversely, more often the disease caused the psychological changes. In a child who was chronically ill and had severe attacks of breathlessness that might come on with great frequency, it would not be unusual to have depression or other psychological issues develop. In fact, as asthma care improved with the development of nebulizers or inhalers that could reliably give quick relief to previously untreatable attacks—and asthmatic children could start to live more normal lives, participating in sports and activities previously denied to them—the old myths about asthma as a psychosomatic ailment rapidly faded from view. In my early years in practice, I was pleased that many parents who saw a stigma to their child's illness ("If it's psychosomatic, it's not a real disease") had their concerns abated as we gained control their child's disease.

Mitzi was the exception. Having treated her for a few months, it was clear that her problems, a combination of asthma and hyperventilation, were almost entirely brought on by her frequent psychological misadventures. In children, allergic asthma often predominates, but Mitzi had no signs of allergy. (Not all childhood asthmatics are allergic, but the majority are; this is not as true in adults with asthma, particularly older ones, more of a mixed bag.) She also did not respond to the usual treatments. She would get upset about a family or teenage issue, start to get herself worked up, hyperventilate, and trigger asthma (hyperventilation panic attacks could mimic asthma at times; she truly had both). As she would get more panicky, she would not follow directions to slow down her breathing, and would not respond to breathing treatments, yelling and flailing. She had very few episodes triggered by the more typical exacerbating factors for most people: dust, smoke, viruses, odors, etc.

After working with the family for a while, I gently suggested to Leeanne that they see a psychologist, as I suspected much of Mitzi's problems were indeed emotional and behavioral. She readily agreed and asked for a recommendation. Having recently met an earnest young psychologist at a hospital lecture, I referred them to Dr. Rick Holmes, who had indicated his interest in working with asthmatic patients. Rick cut a rather dashing figure: he was tall, handsome, and wore a black eye patch. His office was only a few miles away and I readily offered his name.

A period of about six months elapsed before I encountered Leeanne and husband Mitch at a neighborhood gathering. I was curious; I'd not heard anything back from Dr. Holmes nor from the family. Over a glass of wine, I gently pried Leeanne as to whether they had followed through and if so, what their experience had been with Dr. Holmes.

Leeanne was her usual quick-witted, perky self. "It was a strange thing, Doc. The first session, Mitzi and I went and Dr. Holmes asked us lots of questions. At the end of the hour, he said, 'You know, I think there's more going on there than I'm aware of. Could you possibly bring in her biological father next week?'

"So the next week, Mitzi and I went back, this time with my ex, Drew, and his wife Ellen. At the end, Holmes said, 'You know, this is pretty complicated. Can I induce you to bring in your husband and your other daughter for the next visit?'

"So, a week later, Mitzi and I, along with Drew and Ellen, and my husband Mitch and my other daughter, Susan, all showed up and spent an hour with him. It was pretty chaotic. Finally, he said, 'I think I've almost got the picture and we're making progress but next week, I'd like to meet her other two half-sisters, so I can really see how all the pieces fit together.'

"Our last visit was an unmitigated disaster. We now had so many of us that we needed three cars to get us there. Just before we entered the room, Drew, Mitzi's dad, turned to us and said that last week, he was pretty sure the eye patch had moved from one eye to the other. I think we all spent that last session staring at the patch and not paying any attention. That was it. We decided after we got out that we wouldn't go back—or if we did, we would need to buy a Volkswagen bus."

In another year, Mitzi had largely survived her adolescent hormones. Her asthma issues had also greatly improved. The next time I ran into Dr. Holmes at a hospital meeting, I had the nagging feeling that his eye patch was on the wrong side.

Chapter 56

Why is that Man so Fat?

It started with a routine page from my answering service.

The call came when we had been living in Atlanta for about a year. On a beautiful, summery Sunday evening, I was babysitting Jessica (who was three at the time) while Sandy was out folk dancing. The patient left a message with the answering service that he had an ear infection and needed an antibiotic called in.

When I returned his call, the patient explained that his ear was somewhat uncomfortable and that my senior partner, Dr. Vanderpool, would always call in an antibiotic when he got this way. I explained that I did not know him myself and was uncomfortable treating infections over the phone, particularly in adults who did not often get ear infections that actually required an antibiotic. The situation did not sound critical, but we would be happy to squeeze him in the next morning if he wasn't feeling better after taking some decongestants I suggested. The patient was unhappy with my suggestions and persistent—though he didn't feel he was ill enough to require an ER visit, he made it clear that he most definitely didn't want to wait until morning.

This took place almost 40 years ago. There were no urgent care facilities yet, and it was starting to be recognized that antibiotic resistance from overuse and improper use was becoming a major problem. Having recently graduated from top training programs,

I was more reluctant to use them indiscriminately, particularly at that stage of my career. We also realized that we had some problems in those days before computers: certain patients seemed to exist only in after-hour phone calls for medications or advice, almost never to actually be seen in the practice.

Since our practice had several office locations, I was happy to learn that the patient was normally seen at an office barely a mile from my house. So, rather than being confrontational, I offered a compromise: if he didn't feel he could wait, I would meet him at the Sandy Springs office in half an hour, at 8:30 that evening. To my surprise, he was delighted with my suggestion. Thus as the sun began to set, dressed in old shorts and throwing my three-year-old toddler, Jessica, into the car, I zipped to the office in anticipation of the patient's arrival. This should be fun.

When I arrived and unsuccessfully inserted my key into the lock, I realized to my horror that I had received a note two days earlier informing me that the locks had been changed after an attempted break-in (there were five doors to this sprawling office) and I would be provided a new key at our practice meeting in a few days. Our office setting was an elevated complex sitting on a flattened area off the main suburban drag, visible below. The patient, Cary (a jovial and very overweight fellow), arrived similarly clad in shorts, as I frantically and unsuccessfully jiggled the key into the impenetrable lock.

Thankfully, I had a portable otoscope in my car. I explained that we were locked out but, if he didn't find it too weird, I would examine his ears in the parking lot, under streetlamps and moonlight. Cary said that was fine with him and he was happy with anything I would do; in fact, he was amazed that I hadn't just made up the part about meeting him and figured he would arrive and find himself all alone. Little Jessica wrapped her arm around my leg as I started to insert my otoscope in the ear of the 5-foot-8, 270-pound patient. As I started to peer in, she said loudly, "Daddy, why is this man so fat?'"

Having heard her very clearly, but biding for time and hoping maybe I'd heard incorrectly, I said, "What did you say, Jess?" This time she positively yelled: "Daddy, why is this man so FAT?" Cary graciously added, "It's okay, Doc, she's only stating the truth." Totally embarrassed, I offered to write a prescription for Cary—I no longer remember the details, I'm fairly sure he didn't have a bad ear infection but I'm equally sure that under the circumstances and given my embarrassment, I would have given him anything he wanted.

Not content to leave well enough alone, I asked the patient if there was anything else bothering him. "Why yes, Doc, now that you mention it, my chest is a little congested. Would you mind listening to it while you're at it?" Well, that was easy and something I would normally be doing anyway had we been IN the office, rather than out here, examining under a full moon. I went back to get my stethoscope from where I kept it in the car.... and it wasn't there! Then I recalled I had taken it out to listen to a neighbor earlier and left it by the door to put back later. Cary indicated it was no big deal and he was sure the antibiotic would take care of it, but I wasn't happy. I briefly considered having him strip under the streetlamp and listening to his chest with my ear but decided that was too weird—even given the already strange tenor of this evening.

So I ran around the building, trying the key in each of the five locks, and to my great relief, finally found that one lock had not been changed and which my old key fit. I opened the door, only to have my joy immediately turn to dismay when the glaringly loud alarm went off instantly. Apparently, the alarm delay only worked if a particular door was opened—opening any other door resulted in an immediate triggering of the system. I quickly ran through the building, shut off the alarm, allowed Cary and Jessica in through the main door, quickly listened to him with a stethoscope, and sent him on his merry way. I wrote up a quick note for the staff, reset the alarm, smiled as I grabbed little Jessica's hand, and opened the door to find two policemen standing five feet away and with guns drawn and pointed at us!

Luckily, I was able to trade Jessica for a Get Out of Jail Free Card.

Why is that man so fat, indeed!

Chapter 57

That's a Lot of Surgeries!

Several months after starting my practice, I had noted, not surprisingly, that most of my younger patients had very little listed on their history sheets. While the older patients had a variety of ailments (cardiac, diabetes, cancer, etc.), most younger people, aside from their allergies and asthma, had little other medical history. Maybe an occasional surgery here and there or another ailment, but their medical histories were generally short and sweet.

That afternoon, my new patient (let's call him "Rob") was different. Rob was 32 years old. His allergy problems were quite straightforward, having developed severe rhinitis and sinus issues since moving to Atlanta (much like myself), but his list of surgeries went on and on. I looked at the young computer exec in front of me—a stocky six-footer in a suit that looked too small—and wondered what he was doing with page after page of operations.

Rob explained that in the Midwest, he had played the offensive line at his smaller but well-respected college and had considered himself lucky to be drafted in one of the later rounds by the Dallas Cowboys. He never made the team but played two years on their taxi squad. This would have been back a decade earlier, in the early 70s—and while most sports fans would have considered even this limited exposure to professional football as quite glamorous, I knew he wouldn't have made much money at it back then.

His past surgeries were substantial. Both knees had been blown out, and while he had undergone several additional orthopedic procedures, his most serious problem had been a severe ankle injury requiring multiple surgeries. This left him with two steel rods in place, a permanent limp, and the inability to ever again do some of the things he enjoyed, like skiing.

While this was bad enough, the surgeries did not account for most of his listed hospitalizations. His biggest problem had been with kidney stones. It's obviously important to be well-hydrated when involved in heavy exertion—but Rob stated that the only thing he liked to drink (nay, *loved* to drink!) had been milk. Boy, did he love milk. During college, following a strenuous practice session in hot weather, he would inhale two gallons of milk. After a while, he started having kidney stones from all the calcium, which repeatedly would leave him writhing in pain and occasionally hospitalized. He had experienced these calcium oxalate stones on 17 separate occasions before the repeated verbal lashings of doctors, coaches, parents, and teammates sunk in and he realized he could not keep up his incredible milk intake. So, reluctantly, he had given up his milk and switched to water. The only problem? He despised water and never drank enough of it. (No wonder someone would later make a fortune on Gatorade!) His last 14 trips to the ER (and subsequent hospitalizations) had been for uric acid kidney stones, the kind that would be seen with severe dehydration.

So, here I had this bright 32-year-old computer exec—in what should have been the prime of life—with permanent rods, limps and pains, overweight, unable to exercise as he would like, and with more hospital trips than most would make in a lifetime.

He had chased the American dream—playing professional sports, and in particular, NFL football—and had come much closer than most of us ever would.

I couldn't help but ask. "Rob, looking back…was it worth it?"

He looked at me coldly. "What do you think, Doc?"

Maybe that's why I never considered a career in professional sports. I also hated getting hurt.

Chapter 58

Toilet Training, Part I, II, III

PART I

Danny, my son, was almost three and we were at a Braves game in the old Fulton County Stadium. He had just learned to pee in the potty and now needed the restroom.

During a lull in the action (pretty much the whole game for the Braves circa 1983), I took him into the men's room. Fulton County Stadium was never renowned as an architectural marvel and the restrooms were certainly not things of beauty. While there were a few stalls with toilets, instead of the individual urinals of today's arenas, there stood a long continuous trough that, on a crowded day, might accommodate 15 patrons at one time. This was not a crowded day; we were the only ones in the facility. The only problem was that Danny was so short, he didn't quite reach the trough. Dutifully, I led him into a toilet stall and we both proceeded to relieve ourselves, Danny finishing first by a few seconds and wandering out of the stall.

When I walked out, I was horrified to see where Danny stood. At the trough stood an immense Black man who looked like he could have started at offensive tackle for the Falcons, probably 6-foot-4 and 260 pounds, peeing away into the trough. And Danny?

Why, he had his little arm draped around this guy's huge calf to support himself and was leaning forward and looking upwards as the stream cascaded downwards. And the guy had his hands on his hips, leaning slightly backwards, peering down at Danny and looking oh-so-very proud.

I thought I was going to die.

Part II

Several months later, we were back again at the Stadium, this time with friends. Dick Baldwin was a pediatrician, a good guy and a good doc who referred me a lot of asthmatic patients. His son, Patrick, about three-and-a-half years old, was just a couple of months older than Danny. Dick had called me about taking our sons to a Braves game together and I thought it was a great idea. It would be a chance to enjoy myself, show off my son, and entertain a referring physician.

That Wednesday afternoon was sunny and hot, and befitting the Braves, perennial last placers in those years, the stands were almost empty. Dick and I picked out a section of the stands—yes, we had an entire section to ourselves—grabbed a couple of beers, and stretched out.

This was to be a big day for Danny and me. A full year slower than his sister had been, and slower than almost all the other children in his nursery class, my son was (finally!) totally toilet trained as of a week earlier. We were making our first outing after that momentous milestone and for the first time, Danny was wearing "big boy pants" and no diaper. I did not have backup. After five years of carrying diaper bags for one child or the other, it was liberating to have free hands. Yes, I was enjoying that beer.

The game started and Danny wandered around, making paper airplanes out of trash. I wasn't sure if he actually knew what direction the game was. Dick's son Patrick, on the other hand, stared intently at the field and said, "Hey, Dad, is that Claudell Washington in centerfield?"

Another half inning went by. Patrick rattled off the names of Elio Chacon, Bob Horner and the rest of the Braves infield; Danny ran around trying to catch imaginary butterflies.

After another few batters, as I luxuriated in the cool beer slaking my thirst, leaning back in the warm sun, Dick tapped me on the shoulder. "Gary, I know you said Danny is toilet trained, but he's doing a heck of an imitation of someone assuming the position behind us."

And so he was. It was the second inning and two rows behind us, he had squatted and just had one of the largest, ugliest movements ever. There I was with no diapers, no backup, and one very soiled pair of "big boy pants."

A man does what a man has to do. Lying him down between rows, I discarded the underwear, cleaned him with the instruments available to me—in this case a can of beer and a bunch of napkins—and prayed we would make it through the rest of the game. We lasted another inning.

I thought I was going to die.

When we arrived home, pulling into the driveway, Sandy came out to greet us. She smiled brightly at our son and asked him how he liked it.

Running toward her and still carrying his little baseball glove, he threw his arms around her neck and squealed, "Oh, Mommy, I love FOOTBALL!"

Part III

Sandy told me we needed a new carpet; I disagreed. So now, not surprisingly, we were out carpet shopping. It was a family expedition. This was several months after the incident above and Danny, turned four, was long since toilet trained.

The carpet section in the department store was crowded and we waited for a salesperson to get free. Never a good shopper to begin with, I grumbled while we waited. Sandy read and Jessica and Danny, seven and four respectively, climbed mountains of rugs and did swan dives. A good 20 minutes had elapsed before a salesperson finally was free to assist us. He introduced himself pleasantly and apologized for the wait. I was ticked off and having none of it, so I pointedly introduced myself as DOCTOR Lotner. I rarely pulled the "Doctor" card, but I wanted him to feel my righteous indignation. I was an important person he had kept waiting.

As we started to talk, Jessica, usually well-behaved, came running over and tugged on my pants leg. "Daddy!" she cried insistently.

"Not now, Jessica. You guys play for a few minutes and then I'll be with you."

She started to run off but made a rapid U-turn. Again, she grabbed at me. "But, Daddy!" she screeched.

I was a little irritated. Jessica was usually better than this. I couldn't believe she was doing this after the long wait for the salesman.

"Jessica, I'm a little unhappy. Can't you see that Mommy and I are talking to this nice gentleman? Can you please wait just a few minutes?"

She started to run off, then turned back and this time yelled, "But, Daddy, Danny is peeing on all the carpets!"

And there he stood, high on a pile of lovely area rugs, peeing away.

I knew I was going to die.

This time, we all ran.

Chapter 59

Hearing Voices

When I entered the exam room, I met Marian, a pleasant older woman in her late 60s, complaining of headaches and stuffiness. She was normally a patient of one of my associates, but I was covering the office that day. Although she did not feel herself to be terribly ill, she was a little uncomfortable and wished to be seen.

After a short history, I started my physical exam on this very nice, well-dressed, rather petite woman. When I needed to examine her throat, I did the normal doctor routine, asking her to open wide and say "Aah." What came out was not the usual gurgling or choking sound that people make, but a piercing, perfectly pitched resonance: loud, crystal clear, seemingly emanating with gale-like force. I was almost propelled backwards, felt my contacts vibrating, and suspected all the windows in the office (and several surrounding buildings) were likely chattering.

When I recovered from my visible shock, I stared and Marian smiled. I asked her just what she had done career-wise in an earlier iteration of her life. She smiled and answered that at one point she had been a featured soprano with the Metropolitan Opera in New York. I laughed and told her that would have certainly been my guess, and while she had hit a perfect A, in the future, she might keep in mind that when asked to say *Aah* by a doctor, the goal was merely to see the back of her throat—not to see if she could still shatter glass.

Good to know she still had it, though.

Another patient who I cared for over a number of years was Jane, an incredibly sweet woman who I first saw in her early 60s. From the moment she walked in the door and started talking, I knew I had heard her voice before. While I knew we had never met previously, I couldn't shake the feeling I knew the melodious voice.

"It's from your phone, Doc."

"My phone?"

"Yes, I'm the person who does all the phone announcements. I've been doing it for twenty years."

Sadly, younger readers will not remember this, but before God gave us Siri and Alexa and computerized voices—indeed before cell phones ever descended from the great Motorola or Apple factories in the sky—actual human voices were recorded for phone announcements. And so, when you received a message, such as "The number you have dialed is no longer in service," or "The number you have called has been changed to a non-published number," Jane was the person whose voice had been recorded. Considering that at the time phone numbers remained local to discrete neighborhoods and every time someone moved more than a short distance, new numbers were requisite, Jane's recorded messages were heard by millions almost daily. She was also the voice behind many TV and radio advertisements, including one for cat food that I had heard often enough to memorize (despite never owning a cat). I felt I had known her, or at least her voice, all my life.

We became good friends over the dozen years or so that I cared for her. Her problems were not serious but interfered with her work. Moderate allergies left her with enough throat drainage to cause hoarseness and choking. Antihistamines were too drying for her throat; the allergy injections she took helped on a longer-term basis, without the usual side-effects of medications. When she would come in for the occasional check-up visit, I would walk in and say, "The Voice!" She would sweetly answer in that crystalline tone I knew so well, "You're the one who keeps it that way, Doc."

When she passed away a number of years later, I could imagine trying to reach her and receiving a message in familiar tones: "The person you are trying to reach is no longer available and has been moved to a non-published location." While it's been 30 years since I've last seen her, I can still close my eyes and hear that voice in my head.

Somewhere in my brain, I knew that even in heaven, Jane still had it!

Chapter 60

You're Supposed to
Spray It in Your Nose?

Joan was the kind of patient I could really identify with.

While I had a lot of pride, particularly in the early years of my career and before medicine changed for the worse (less personal, less time, more constrained by rules of insurance companies and government), I really felt I knew my patients without even looking at their charts. Importantly, this meant as people, not just as names or disease states.

Still, some were easier to identify with, and Joan was one of these. She was a bright, single Jewish woman with a good sense of humor, about my own age and a professor at Georgia Tech—a terrific and highly respected institution. She was also a bit of a klutz. We seemingly had a lot in common. In my earlier years in practice, I saw Joan frequently. Not only did she have fairly severe allergies, but she was a little neurotic (as I said, we had a lot in common).

One particularly heavy spring pollen season, Joan was having a bad time of it and I prescribed a nasal steroid medication. Nasal steroids, like today's Flonase or Nasacort, mainstays of current treatment, were fairly new back then and a bit of a hard sell to patients. Although multiple studies had shown they were more effective than the ubiquitous antihistamines, America remained a nation that preferred pills, not sprays. Furthermore, these newer medications were the opposite of nasal sprays previously on the market, like Afrin, a decongestant. Afrin worked instantly but could not safely be used long term. Conversely, the nasal steroids of the day, Beconase and Vancenase, were extremely safe long term but had to be used for several days before they typically proved effective. Americans wanted instant relief from their medications!

With Joan's flare-up, I gave her samples of a brand-new nasal steroid, Nasalide. Her antihistamines all made her drowsy (this was in the dark days of the mid-1980s and "newer" non-sedating antihistamines like Claritin or Allegra were not yet around), and she had previously "failed" a trial of Beconase. ("Failed" as in stopped using it after one day because she saw no relief, although as she coyly said to me as she smiled, "I know you said I had to use it for a few days before it might help—but Dr. Lotner, I couldn't wait that long!")

Now, the newer Nasalide had one advantage over the other cortisone nasal sprays—it burned like heck as it went in. It didn't work any better or any faster (it was a "me too" drug if ever there was one) but the preservative it contained tended to sting for a lot of people. This would hardly be a characteristic that one would intuitively think of as an advantage (which would you prefer, a nose spray that feels good when it goes in or a similar product that feels pretty uncomfortable when used?) but to my surprise, in the early days of use, a significant percentage of patients liked the more-uncomfortable Nasalide. Somehow, the burning sensation seemed to indicate that the drug was doing something quickly, while they couldn't "tell anything was working" when they sprayed the more comfortable ones.

I gave Joan the sample and knowing that she was very bright but just a tad klutzy, I even demonstrated the technique for using the inhaler—a slightly altered method than for similar products. She smiled sweetly as I mimed how to use it, commenting I was cute when I acted this out.

Several weeks passed after this fairly unremarkable visit before

I received a thick packet from the FDA asking me to fill out adverse drug reaction forms on Joan and her Nasalide. The form was outrageously long and had to be filled out in six copies. This being long before medical office computers and terms like the "internet" or "online," I was clearly looking at a long project! What's more, I had no idea what possible side effect could have arisen from this type of drug—and assuming there was a side effect, how did the FDA know about it? I had never received a form like this to fill out and indeed, it was the only such FDA document I ever encountered in my 40-year career.

When I called Joan to find out what happened, I was first met by an embarrassed silence. She told me that it was really nothing, and could we just ignore the whole episode? I explained to her that the package had arrived with more postage than the mortgage on my house, and enough warnings to physicians not to ignore (I no longer remember all the details, but I'm pretty sure they mentioned slaying of the first-born), that I must complete these documents. She remained very reluctant. I pried a little more slowly.

Why was the FDA even involved? If there was a problem with the drug, how did they come to be aware of it? It took a bit to get it out of her, but it turned out that "It was nothing" involved going to the emergency room at Emory University Hospital. Really? What reaction? She still wouldn't tell me.

Could it be she was the first person I had ever heard of having an anaphylactic (severe allergic) reaction to a nasal steroid? No.

Minor nosebleeds could occur with these meds, usually not too bad and usually after prolonged use. Had she experienced a gusher? No.

These meds were nice because although they were cortisone products, they worked almost entirely locally and with none of the potential side effects of cortisone. Could the miniscule amount have somehow…? No.

Somewhat frustrated, I blurted out: "C'mon, Joanie. You gotta give me something here. I've got an hour of forms to fill out and have no idea what the problem is. You're a damned professor at one of the nation's most respected technical universities. You're really bright. I know you're embarrassed but help me out over here."

"Well, Dr. Lotner, remember when you told me it might burn and you showed me how to use it? I thought you were really being sweet when you showed me that. I thought it was funny and really didn't pay much attention.

"When I got home and tried to use it, I put it in my nose—the wrong way, it turned out—and when I tried to spray it, it didn't work like the other brand, so I twisted it and it came out of my nose and I shot it directly into my eye. My eye burned SO badly and then it started to swell up and then I rubbed it and it burned more and I rubbed more and it swelled shut and I got my neighbor to drive me to the ER where they flushed it out and told me I would be fine. I thought the doctor was laughing at me as I left and I really had no idea they would be sending you papers to fill out."

My mind staggered at the idea of how badly she had to have attempted this to have a tube meant to be inserted an inch into a nostril somehow miss the nose completely.

I probably would have laughed too, but the thought of all those forms awaiting me was too sobering. I felt vaguely better that my friendly professor may have been at a highly respected technical institute but was a professor of English Literature.

For the rest of my career, I made sure that either a nurse or myself personally demonstrated the use of every device to every patient—sans cuteness.

Chapter 61

Never Tell a Lie.
(Well, Almost Never.)

Chris was the type of patient who was not hard to like. She was young, pretty, outgoing, and invariably upbeat. I was in practice about five years and in my mid-30s. She was a couple of years younger; her husband was a youth minister and they seemed to like many of the same things as Sandy and me, particularly outdoors and hiking. A long-term asthmatic, her chronic asthma was now under excellent control. Since I loved to talk with my patients, parts of her visits would have her animatedly describing to me adventures she and her husband were planning.

About a year after becoming my patient, Chris eagerly started describing their big adventure to come: a two-week hiking and camping trip out in Colorado, just the two of them, including several days in a designated wilderness area. It was hard not to catch her contagious enthusiasm, and sometimes, when she would come in for allergy injections (with a mandatory 30-minute wait afterwards), she would ask the nurses if she might talk to me for a minute and she would excitedly add more details. I found myself looking forward to hearing of their trip.

A month or so elapsed and one evening, through the waiting room glass, I spotted Chris signing in for her injections. She was on crutches, wearing a boot, and had a cast that extended from her foot to the top of her thigh. It was one of the larger casts I had seen since my training days several years earlier.

I motioned for her to come over, and with some difficulty, she hobbled my way. Despite her obvious discomfort, she was her usual perky, upbeat self. Naturally, I inquired about what happened and she told me the details. In fact, she told me *every* single detail. When she finished her tale, I looked at her and said:

"Chris, that is an absolutely horrible story. I know you're not supposed to lie and I think your candor is admirable. However, there are times where lying is not such a bad thing, or omitting a few details is perfectly acceptable. Under the circumstances, I think just telling people that you went on an adventure camping in the wilderness and suffered a bad fall and broke your leg in two places is as much as anyone needs to know."

All of this was true and somehow seemed much more appropriate than the mental picture I had as this attractive young woman described her mishap. On a steep rocky hillside, she and her husband had set just set up their camp for the day. She had to relieve herself and found a steep but open spot near her campsite. Squatting down, with her jeans and panties around her ankles, she reached backwards to where she had put some tissue. Unfortunately, in that action, she lost her balance and had tumbled backwards a couple of times, butt over heels, eventually falling over a log—and remained lying there with her posterior up for nearly an hour until her husband could come to her rescue.

Somehow, the visual image did not do justice to the situation.

In medicine, I always tried to establish a continual flow of honesty within the patient-doctor relationship—but there are times that obscuring the details a little can be very helpful.

Chapter 62

A Who-What Mole?

Our kids were older now—Jessica eleven, Danny eight—and we had decided our family was complete. Or had we? Every once in a while, Sandy would find the urge to have a third. Occasionally, I would entertain similar sentiments, but the timing for the two of us generally did not coincide. Until one moment, somewhat amazingly, we both had the same urge at the same time.

Here we were, a few months later, and Sandy was pregnant. Unfortunately, she was having a very hard time of it. Neither of her previous pregnancies had been this uncomfortable. While it had been a number of years and our memories were collectively fuzzy and we both recalled a good deal of nausea with her first pregnancy, this was clearly different. Her nausea was constant and massive and by ten or 11 weeks, she seemed to be showing, considerably sooner than the usual 16-week time frame. Before departing on a scheduled two-week summer vacation with the kids to Maine, Boston and Albany, we scheduled an appointment with Sandy's OB-GYN, Dr. Maury Fradkin—a very kind man and a good friend. Maury agreed that things seemed a little excessive, drew some lab tests, and wished us well on our imminent vacation. The results would be waiting upon our return.

I will not write much about our vacation here—a saga that will live on in Lotner family memory and a fortnight's journey that could be the subject of its own novel. Pertinent to the current discussion, amidst an adventure that was at times hysterical and at times pathetic, while the other three family members had a generally great and hilarious vacation, poor Sandy spent much of her time deeply uncomfortable, vomiting repetitively. We would check into a quaint inn in Kennebunkport, I would comment on the cuteness of the room, and Sandy would vomit. We would arrive at a great restaurant, seduced by the aroma of Maine lobster and butter, and she would retch. We would find a beautiful mountain trail to hike, the wind sweeping at our faces—and, well, you get the picture.

By the time the trip concluded, Sandy was exhausted and her abdomen had swelled even more markedly. She was huge for someone just starting her second trimester. Twins? Triplets? Somehow, I didn't think so. We were soon to find out. Her appointment with Dr. Fradkin was to be the day after our return.

We sat down in his consult room and Maury solemnly informed us that Sandy apparently had a molar pregnancy, a so-called hydatidiform mole. Sandy understandably looked confused: a whatchamacallit mole? I frantically scanned my memory to see what I could remember about this condition, last encountered in textbooks in medical school 15 years prior. What I recalled was that it was a rare condition, somewhat common among certain groups of Asians (possibly one in 1–2,000 pregnancies) but markedly less so in Caucasians (one in 50,000). The only reason I remembered it at all was because, with a name as bizarre as "hydatidiform mole," I knew it would inevitably appear on my medical school exams. (It did.) In a molar pregnancy, there was actually no pregnancy at all—or no fetus, at least. Instead, the placenta grew by itself and enlarged at a massively increased pace, thus accounting for the distended appearance at such an early stage. This growth was invariably accompanied by an excessive amount of nausea and vomiting, as Sandy had so dramatically exhibited the past weeks.

The condition was a serious one. While for reasons that I could never quite understand, it was not considered a cancer, it could spread and actually metastasize to areas like the lungs. Treatment was with a D and C (curettage) procedure, followed by close monitoring—but if the condition had spread, chemotherapy might be required.

All of this was confirmed by Dr. Fradkin, who went on extensively about the condition, the monitoring, and the treatment. He would treat Sandy the next day with the D and C, the surgical scraping out of the uterus, usually a minor procedure. Subsequently, we would be following blood levels of the hormone HCG (human chorionic gonadotropin), normally elevated in pregnancy but massively so with a hydatidiform mole. The testing schedule would be rigorous, with samples collected weekly for 12 weeks, moving to every other week for several months, and less frequently thereafter. While Maury would be seeing us, Sandy would also be followed by a gynecologic oncologist, who would take over her care if the course was not smooth.

I was extremely impressed with Maury's detailed and extensive presentation for a condition that I had considered quite rare. Curious, I asked him how many cases of molar pregnancy he had seen during his years in obstetrics.

He looked at me studiously, and answered, "I've been in practice for 17 years now. Counting Sandy, one."

I was shocked. "But, Maury, you sounded so knowledgeable about this; you sounded like you knew everything about this condition."

"Hey, knowing you were coming in this morning, what do you think I was reading about at two in the morning last night?"

It was to be an adventure together and happily, one that went well. The next day's curettage procedure went smoothly and Sandy was feeling better shortly afterwards. The clinical improvement was dramatic. Then began her arduous schedule of blood samples and monitoring.

A few weeks later, I accompanied Sandy back to Dr. Fradkin's office for a follow-up visit. He was enthusiastic, almost jumping out of his seat. A quiet, thoughtful physician, I had never seen him so animated. He called me over and asked me to look at the lab tests together with him. He showed me the first one: 54,411 as the initial level for hCG; a week later, readings at 46,372 followed by 40,317; and finally, yesterday's reading of 33,982.

"Look at how they've come down! Isn't that great?"

It was hard not to get caught up in his enthusiasm. I said, "Maury, that's terrific! Sounds great. The only thing is, hCG is out of my field and I actually haven't seen an hCG level in 15 years and don't remember what's normal. What are we shooting for here? Twenty thousand? Ten thousand?"

He looked just a tad deflated as he answered: "Zero." Or maybe I just sensed he echoed my own deflation.

Sandy did great. It took several months for the hCG levels to finally hit zero and the blood tests were able to end.

Somehow, neither of us ever again shared the simultaneous urge to expand our family.

Chapter 63

Make Sure You
Wear Clean Underwear

I awoke early one morning to make the 42-mile drive to my Stockbridge office to start seeing patients before 8 A.M. In the dark, I showered and got dressed, pulling out a clean pair of underwear from my drawer. I dutifully put them on, but before I did, noticed several small holes and a thought came to me.

At an early age, my mother had drummed into me, "Make sure you wear clean underwear." I'm not 100 percent sure when she started telling me that, but I know I was very young. Knowing her, it might even have been in utero. If I ever asked why (which I did frequently), the answer was unvarying: "You always should have on clean underwear in case you have to see the doctor." I remember wondering as a small child if doctors, who were pretty smart folks, didn't have anything more on their minds than checking the cleanliness of children's underwear. Surely they must go to medical school and study subjects more interesting than the hygiene of undergarments.

In second grade, I remember the ignominious day when, while playing punchball on a hard cement school yard, I ran and bent for a ball as fat Mark W. came barreling into me from behind, knocking me down on the pavement and snapping my forearm. My mother was called, and because we did not have a car back then, walked with me for the six blocks to the doctor's office.

Already whimpering, as we walked up the concrete steps to his doorway, I tripped again, catching myself—with my damaged, outstretched arm. I screamed for several minutes and when I finally was able to stop, my mother asked me if I was okay; as I sniffled that I was, she asked, "Are you wearing clean underwear?"

Now 40 years later, I contemplated my holey underwear before going to work and made a decision. While the pair was clean and the only one who would ever see the holes was me, I thought to myself: *I'm not a sniveling little boy, I'm a grown-up, a doctor no less, someone admired by people and I'm going to act like it!* So, I threw out my old underwear with the holes, put on a brand-new pair of undies that were spanking clean, and off I went.

I was having a busy but unremarkable day seeing my patients until about 10 A.M., at which point I was bowled over by my first kidney stone ever. The pain in my right flank came in waves that would take my breath away, sometimes driving me to my knees. I called in Gail, my head nurse, and asked her to cancel my afternoon patients as I would be going to the emergency room with my kidney stone. She first inquired if I had ever had a kidney stone before ("No") and if not, how did I know it was a stone ("Trust me, I'm a doctor, it's a kidney stone"). Showing more sense than I exhibited, Gail asked if I was in that much pain (I was back down on my knees at that point, as the next wave hit), why was I not canceling the rest of the morning patients, most of whom were already sitting in the waiting area? I, who prided myself on never missing time with my patients, responded—stupidly but truthfully—that I thought I could get through the rest of the morning and that patients would rather watch me writhe in agony than have to reschedule for weeks later.

After two very long hours, having somehow survived the morning patient onslaught, I was confronted by a choice that might have seemed easy to a wiser man, but presented me with great mental anguish. Which emergency room to head to? There was a reasonably good hospital half a mile down the road, or there was Northside Hospital, closer to home and where I was on staff—but a daunting 42-mile drive away. Now, when you're having shooting pains in your back, most people might have found this a straightforward question. But not me! While I saw the obvious merits of staying nearby, I also considered that if I required a narcotic injection, as seemed likely, I'd have rapid relief but then would be confronted with the logistics of the aftermath. I would not be allowed to drive after an opiate injection, so I would have to call Sandy, who would drive 42 miles to pick me up and another 42 miles to drive me home. Although the next morning would have me in a closer office, my car would still be at the distant hospital—so again, Sandy would be forced to drive me and then return by herself, another 42 miles in each direction. Suddenly, the pain of my kidney stone seemed less daunting than the thought of making Sandy drive all over God's green earth (and the inevitable days of complaints I would subsequently be forced to endure), and suddenly Northside Hospital seemed much more reachable. Besides, I convinced myself the severity of the pains had started to abate somewhat.

In retrospect, I have no idea how I survived that drive. My intuition that the pain waves had decreased proved sadly wrong about the time I hit the interstate, and I'm sure over the next 40 minutes, drivers nearby must have marveled at the sight of a driverless car (in 2004) as another spasm would have me buckling over, my head momentarily disappearing below steering wheel level. But made it I did, and having proudly parked in the physicians parking lot, headed to the ER to check myself in. To my dismay (who the heck shows up at an ER at noon on a Monday unless they're really sick?), I was confronted by seeming hordes of waiting patients. As I signed in between spasms, I was told by a sympathetic but unhelpful clerk that there were no available ER rooms. While they would normally try to get me in right away (considering the pain of a stone and my status on staff), I'd just have to tough it out until a bed opened up.

The waiting room was not only vast but oddly shaped, with

several nooks and crannies. I dragged myself to the furthest corner and sat beyond a bend to avoid the spectacle of being the only grown man in a suit buckling to my knees every two minutes or so when the next painful wave would arrive.

As I hunkered down in the ER, I recalled my lecture 30 years earlier in medical school: that a kidney stone was one of the three worst pains knows to Man; it was kidney stones, torsion of the testes (that one hurts just thinking about it), and intussusception (a twisting of the intestine, similar to making a sausage, with subsequent death of part of the gut). What I remembered most were the intellectual discussions that followed with my friends afterward: did "known to Man" include Woman? How did they measure the pain to exclude other viable candidates? Regarding the gender issue, we decided this was probably man with a small "m," to reason for childbirth's exclusion. And as to methodology, we figured it involved paying some very poor medical students, similar to ourselves, who were willing to trade pain for dollars. "Sure, $25 dollars and I'll let you somehow give me a ruptured appendix and rate it for you." Or, "That needle in my eyeball— that was something! But that torsion of the testes? That was a ten!"

Back to my hidden corner of the ER. There I sat. And sat. And sat. After 45 minutes or so, I decided my strategy of making myself semi-invisible might not be wise and that a new tactic was called for. So, I marched back to the admissions window to inquire whether a bed was ready, and as the clerk apologized but informed me that they were still exceptionally busy and I'd have to continue waiting, the next nauseating wave hit. This time I fell down on my knees, head to the ground, and started pounding the floor with my fist, yelling, "Oh, God! Oh, God!" The din in the ER waiting room suddenly quieted and I could sense all heads turning. Suddenly, a nurse with a wheelchair appeared and I was wheeled into the back (Yes!), but I would be placed on a gurney— smack dab in the busiest section of the ER—until a room opened up. She handed me one of those open-air hospital gowns that everyone "loves" to slip into. I was instructed to change in the bathroom, wearing just the gown—open in the back—and my underwear, before making my way back to the conspicuously placed gurney.

I lay on my gurney for 20 minutes or so, weakly waving at familiar staff between spasms. Then suddenly… the mother of all spasms! The pain and nausea briefly took my breath away and suddenly, I was down off the stretcher, on my knees on the floor, my butt up in the air, pounding with fists again. Slowly I realized as everyone looked, that my gown was open, my backside up—and I was wearing my brand-new, sparkling clean underwear with no holes—and damn it, there was my underwear, in all its glory, for all to see.

As I lay there bottom-up, the nurse ran over and said, "Dr. Lotner. Are you OK? I can't tell if you are you laughing or crying?" Not totally sure myself, I answered, "Believe it or not, I'm laughing!" And I thought, *Thank you, Mom. I will always, ALWAYS wear clean underwear!*

You never know when you are going to see the doctor!

Addendum: A little later, after seeing me and ordering some films, the ER doc asked me if I wanted to see my stone on the scan. You bet I did! Although a physician, this was out of my area and I had never actually looked at a stone on a scan. I knew I was a big strong guy and this stone was going to be like a smaller, but still very substantial, version of the Rock of Gibraltar. He pointed at the screen and said, "There it is." I looked but somehow missed the boulder. He pointed again and when I remained confused, offered a magnifier. And there it was—all 3-point-something millimeters of it, a piece of dust about the size of the exclamation point at the end of a sentence. He told me that people were often dismayed to see the size of a stone, but it was perfectly big enough, if lodged in the wrong place, to cause agonizing pain. I remained unconvinced and had further respect for my wife and all women who have succeeded in childbirth with 8-pound behemoths compared to my runty little punctuation mark that had brought me to the floor. I passed the stone uneventfully two days later and with minimal medications.

Chapter 64

Magenta

At a certain stage of my career, I enjoyed giving lectures on asthma to other physicians—generally to pediatricians and sponsored by pharmaceutical companies. This was particularly true before the FDA changed their rules and I was allowed to use my own slides about asthma, rather than exclusively relying on the drug company's slides as later mandated by the regulatory agency. I was always bothered that asthma, affecting ten to 12 percent of children, was misunderstood on certain levels.

My major concern was that asthma is a long-term inflammatory disease that in some instances can cause chronic lung damage, much like cigarette smoking. Despite this, most physicians tend to treat the disease symptomatically rather than address the potential for long-term damage. (Imagine treating heart conditions only when patients experienced chest pains rather than addressing underlying issues, such as cholesterol or obesity.) In asthma, by far the most prevalent significant childhood disease, it is particularly early on that the potential to prevent damage may exist. Yet many pediatricians are used to seeing children get better and are not as inclined to treat as chronically as their internist colleagues. It was this issue that I meant to address in my lectures.

I do not mean to get into a technical discussion of asthma nor to imply that most asthmatics will have long-term lung damage, but a few brief words are needed. Lung functions need to be followed in asthma, just as EKGs and blood pressure readings need to be monitored in cardiac or hypertensive patients. They are easily monitored from age six onwards. They reveal that in a normal population, lung functions increase, reaching their peak around age 18 and then starting a slow inexorable decline over the rest of life. This is normal, but certain conditions may accelerate this deterioration. In smokers, lung functions progress downward more rapidly and in some patients who develop emphysema, the patient will become progressively symptomatic with shortness of breath, wheezing, etc.

Similarly, asthmatic patients tend to have a drop-off in their lung functions more rapidly than healthy patients (although not as dramatically as smokers). Those who do may eventually experience chronic symptoms in later life and some non-smoking asthmatics may resemble patients with smoking-induced chronic lung disease. This does not occur in the majority of asthmatic patients, but often enough that monitoring of pulmonary functions—at least occasionally—is warranted. Occasionally, even patients considered to be mild symptomatically may undergo such a progression later on. Sadly, because many asthmatic children get better clinically in teenage years at around the age they leave the pediatrician's care, pediatricians tended to assume they all would do well later and generally neglected to measure the important lung capacities or treat them longer term. While this was fine for the predominance of asthmatics, it was a disservice to the subset of patients who may have more progressive disease when the symptoms return later in life, as it often did.

My lectures emphasized that asthma was not always as benign as doctors assumed. My favorite slide showed the pulmonary functions increasing from age five to 18, then dropping downward afterwards. In blue was a line for normal children; significantly below that in red was a line for asthmatic children; and in between, the most significant line—a vivid pink hue—showed the functions in children deemed by the pediatrician to have "outgrown" their asthma. To the vast surprise of many pediatricians, who had always assumed these "outgrown" patients had normal lung functions, these patients only averaged about 85 to 88 percent of the capacities of normal children and would go further downhill in their adult lives.

This graph was startling enough that it would often draw an audible gasp whenever shown.

One evening, I was giving the talk to a particularly large audience, with at least 40 or more pediatricians and family doctors in attendance. When I got to "the" slide, there was the usual collective intake of air, but from the back of the room emerged a semi-garbled murmur of something like, "Mmmmaa."

"Excuse me," I said. "Did someone have a comment?"

It was louder this time.

"Mgnet!"

"Magnet?" I queried. "Please speak up."

A pediatrician, a petite woman, stood in the rear and this time yelled: "Magenta! You said it was the pink line. It's not pink, it's magenta!"

Not exactly the point I was trying to make. So much for the powerful intellectual impact of my argument.

Two weeks later, I gave a similar lecture. This time when I got to the key slide, the one to shock doctors out of their complacency, I said: "Here in the magenta line, you will see that many of those kids who you convinced yourselves have outgrown this disease are only averaging 85 percent of predicted lung functions—even though you have deemed them healthy."

This time, from the back of the room, came an unmistakable cry from another female physician: "Fuchsia! It's not magenta, it's fuchsia!"

I'm only letting men in for my talks in the future. We only understand primary colors.

Chapter 65

Mary, Quite Contrary

"I've got your friend here and she's having an anaphylactic reaction to this new medication you prescribed!"

The call was from an ER doc I knew at Northside Hospital, the very good local hospital where I had been on staff for over 20 years. The patient, Mary, was a close personal friend, the wife of one of my closest buddies, and one of Sandy's many semi-connected cousins—so many times removed that I had no idea of the actual connection.

I couldn't believe it. Mary, at that time an occasional patient, had contacted me a short while ago saying she was having some spring allergies during Atlanta's traditionally heavy pollen season. Mary hadn't responded to more typical treatments and I had given her a sample of one of my favorite new mediations at the time, Astelin (azelastine) nasal spray. The sample was to last her a few days until she was scheduled to see me—indeed, she was scheduled for that very morning until she was sidetracked by this emergency situation.

Azelastine was an interesting drug. An antihistamine, it had originally been used in Japan as an anti-asthma pill, where it had some effectiveness. That in itself was curious, in that antihistamines typically did not have an effect on asthma—but this medication did. Unfortunately, excessive drowsiness accompanying the oral administration had led to the disuse of the medication in that form. Then, someone had come up with the bright idea of trying it as a nasal spray: to the surprise of many, it worked extremely well in the U.S. (other antihistamines tried nasally had not fared as well), not only helping with typical allergy symptoms but also with congestion, one of the most difficult symptoms to treat. The drug had very few side effects when administered this way. In the short time it had been available, I had prescribed it frequently and generally with very good results.

The call from the ER physician was a surprise to me and him. While Mary was in no danger in the ER, she had clearly suffered anaphylactic symptoms within a few minutes of her first sprays with this medication: itchiness, hives, throat tightness, watery eyes, and a tight cough. He had treated her easily with injections of epinephrine, oral antihistamines and steroids, and she was starting to feel better. His call was not only to alert me of the problem but one of puzzlement as well. He had looked up azelastine and found it a surprising drug to be causing an allergic reaction. I agreed. While almost every medication has been found to cause anaphylaxis in someone, including antihistamines, these reactions were extremely rare for this class of drug. Indeed, I hadn't been able to find a single case of documented azelastine anaphylaxis in a quick scan of the literature.

Yet the timing was damning and certainly pointing in that direction. Mary had arisen that morning, eaten toast and butter, poured a cup of her usual tea, and then used the nasal spray. A few minutes later, the reaction had started.

Later, once she had been released and sent home, Mary confirmed her history. Her tea was the same as usual and without condiments; there had been nothing other than her usual butter on the toast. The bread was a different brand than her usual bread: an Arnold's low-carb white bread with no seeds. While this wasn't to my taste, it certainly sounded as bland a meal as possible. That was it aside from the new medication. Certainly, the drug was the most obvious culprit.

Mary was game to test this out: two weeks later, we brought her in, I diluted a drop of the nose spray, and improvised an allergy skin test to it. We waited with a bit of trepidation, and in a few minutes...nothing! No reaction! Now, when performing an allergy skin test to an allergen (such as ragweed or cat dander), the test has been standardized. Dilutions of the appropriate materials have been tested on both known allergic and non-allergic individuals and the dilutions made to a concentration where allergic patients typically exhibit a raised welt and redness, while the non-allergic individuals do not. In improvising my new test, there was a chance I made it too dilute—but typically, in a severely allergic individual, we would have expected to see something. Instead, we were stuck with a presumed but unconfirmed cause. Despite my skepticism, we would consider her allergic to the medication, with strict avoidance in the future and she would carry an EpiPen.

The next call from the emergency room was several weeks later, this time with a more severe anaphylactic reaction—all the same symptoms but coming on more quickly and intensely, eventually with her blood pressure falling slightly. This time, even more medical treatments were required before she was able to leave quite a number of hours later. The trigger? She had no azelastine, and again had just eaten toast and butter—pretty unlikely causes.

The next week, we brought her in for some food testing (all negative) and a closer history. Again, no condiments and the only unusual thing was that, for the first time in several weeks, she had gone back to the Arnold's low-carb white bread. A little suspicious—but again, how bland can you get? She probably fell into the category of idiopathic anaphylaxis, one of those fancy Latin terms that doctors use that loosely translates to, "We don't know what the hell caused it." Sadly, there was a significant subset of patients with allergic or allergic-like reactions that, despite testing, the etiology (or cause) could never be determined. These patients were obviously frustrated and frightened, and the allergist was just as bothered. The patients carried EpiPens at all times, praying they would never have to use them. The allergist was not only fearful for the patient but also felt like he had failed to identify something that should have been within his grasp.

The call came from Mary about two weeks later. "I think I've found it! I think I'm allergic to wheat protein!"

Okay, wheat protein? What the heck is wheat PROTEIN? Aren't all breads pretty much made with wheat? Isn't wheat protein contained in wheat? Mary went on to explain that she had gathered all the labels of every bread she had remembered eating over the past few months and in the extensive lists of food products, preservatives, additives, etc., the Arnold's listed "wheat protein" and none of the others did. No other ingredients stood out as being unique to this bread. Interesting—but boy, that sounded like something breads should have in it. I tried looking it up but could find little about the substance. It wasn't gluten, but certainly sounded like something people should expect to be exposed to with a fair degree of regularity.

On the off-chance Mary was correct, we decided to improvise another test. This time we brought her into the office with a couple of pieces of bread: one from the offending loaf, the other from a competitive brand that did not list wheat protein. We made sure she did not handle the bread herself. I wet the pieces of bread, rubbed a little on each forearm, stroked the skin beneath each drop gently with a needle, and...within a few minutes, a moderate hive and a few sniffles. An allergic reaction to white bread!

The only thing needed to confirm the wheat protein diagnosis was to actually get a sample to test. Having no idea where to get this, I decided to go to the source: Arnold's Bakery in Brooklyn, New York. It took a few calls to get the pleasant individual who served as their Science Officer on the phone. (My mind boggled—really, a science officer in a bakery?) I explained about my patient and asked about her experience, if any, with reactions to wheat protein. She had never heard of any with her bakery's particular products but was vaguely aware someplace in the past of having heard about reactions to "wheat protein." I convinced her that we had no interest in suing the company but would like to get just a little bit of the wheat protein to do a confirmatory test on Mary. I carefully explained that the amount I needed was minuscule, maybe a match-head size sample sent in a plastic bag. Two weeks later, my nurse brought in a huge parcel to my office containing my "minuscule" specimen, a 20-pound jar of "wheat protein"; enough, I'd suspect, to make loaves of bread to feed the entire French army for weeks.

Mary, brave and a trooper, was as eager as I to confirm the diagnosis. When she returned to the office, out of this humungous bottle of wheat protein, I drew the smallest sliver and put it into a test-tube with saline. After mixing it well, we took a few drops of this material and again diluted it with saline, repeating the procedure a third and fourth time. This would be a non-standardized test, and the last thing I wanted to do was to start with a big-enough dose to possibly trigger a severe allergic reaction in my good friend. Having no idea where to start, I felt I had diluted this enough that any reaction would be unlikely to be significant; indeed, we might have to work our way up sequentially to stronger concentrations before any reaction might occur.

A drop on the forearm, a little stroke through it…and in a few minutes, the arm was swelling and itchy, the eyes and nose runny, itchiness all over, a little throat tightness—and full-blown treatment with epinephrine injections and several other drugs was required to break the cycle.

Diagnosis confirmed: severe anaphylaxis to wheat protein. Who knew? One of the more interesting allergic reactions of my career—and the diagnosis was made by the patient!

Mary has done well over the years, fastidiously reading labels and avoiding wheat protein.

On a related note: if anyone is in the market for a 20-pound jar of wheat protein, have I got a deal for you!

Chapter 66

Whatever it Takes, Doc!

The uncomfortable-looking woman squirming in my exam room had not been seen in our practice in over two years. A quick look through her chart revealed that she had five successive "no show" visits, failing to keep an appointment without cancelling in advance. (We really were too lenient about enforcing "no show" fees.)

She was beside herself, frantic and angry. Frantic: she had a bad sinus infection that was driving her crazy. Head pressure, colored mucus, bad headaches, missing work—she had the whole kit and caboodle. Furthermore, it had been going on for well over two months. Angry: she had been to two doctors already and neither had been able to get her better. "Doc, I don't care what it takes. Just do it. I'll pay anything! I've got to feel better."

I asked about her treatment. The first physician, her internist, had prescribed amoxicillin, a very reasonable starting antibiotic for sinusitis, but certainly not the strongest. She had taken the course but felt little improvement.

After two weeks of suffering, she went to see a good friend of mine, Dr. Ramie Tritt, an ENT. He had treated her, but again she failed to improve. I knew Ramie well. He was generally fairly aggressive in his treatments. And what had he prescribed? Amoxicillin. Really? The same med? I was amazed. She spent some time bad-mouthing both her doctors, who, despite her obvious discomfort, had failed to make her better. I could understand the original treating doctor but was quite surprised that the ENT had not taken a different approach.

I quickly examined her, noting marked congestion, purulent discharge in nasal cavities and posterior pharynx, and tenderness over sinus areas—almost certainly confirming a diagnosis of sinusitis. I prescribed nasal decongestants and nose washes, a few days of cortisone to shrink her very swollen membranes, and a significantly more potent (and more expensive) antibiotic. But before writing the actual scrip, I checked with the pharmacy formulary book from the patient's HMO to make sure the antibiotic would be covered and affordable. Thankfully it was both. I told her exactly what I wanted her to do and how to take the medications. "I will, Doc. Whatever it takes, Doc! I just have to feel better. It's been so long. I'll do whatever you say!"

She looked at me gratefully, and then threw her arms around me. I smiled—I'd be able to brag to my friend, Dr. Tritt, in our next phone call how he had failed to help a patient who I subsequently cured.

An hour passed. As I sipped coffee in my office during lunch, I heard my nurse animatedly talking with a pharmacist over the phone. From what I had overheard, it seemed to be a formulary argument concerning this patient, a not uncommon occurrence. This was about 20 years ago, in the earlier days of managed care. One of the things that was beginning to make the practice of medicine extremely unpleasant was the development of insurance formularies: lists of drugs that the patient's insurance would cover. Although other drugs might be approved by the FDA and might be more appropriate, prescribing drugs "off formulary" frequently made them too expensive for the patient. The absolute bane of doctors and nurses were endless waits on phone calls followed by daily arguments with low-level insurance company employees to get drug coverage needed by patients. I thought this might be the case here.

Angrily, I yelled for my nurse to hand me the phone. I had actually taken the step in advance of checking that the drug would be covered. How could it not be? I barked into the phone at the pharmacist that I knew the prescription was on formulary. What was the problem?

The pharmacist was exceedingly polite and apologetic. "It's not that, Dr. Lotner. The med is covered all right, but it's got a $25 co-pay. Your patient only wants one with a $10 co-pay!"

The light bulb went off in my head. This lady who never kept her appointments and railed about the incompetence of her physicians—there was something else going on over here.

I quietly asked the pharmacist, "So what's the antibiotic that's $10 on her plan? No, don't tell me. Let me guess. Amoxicillin?"

"Exactly, Doc. But I don't think that's going to get her better after two rounds of it already."

"Neither do I, my friend, neither do I. But give her the $10 Amoxicillin, and in another month, when she sees someone else, she can badmouth me along with Tritt for failing to get her better."

No, it certainly wouldn't—but the patient demanded her $10 amoxicillin and, I'm sure, went to another doc to complain about how no one could make her better. Whatever it takes, whatever it costs. Just don't make it more than ten dollars.

Doctors were often amazed and angered by studies revealing that patients were willing to pay far more out of pocket to treat their pets than to treat themselves. I was willing to wager my patient would have paid $25 if her cat was involved.

Chapter 67

Time for Dinner

My wife, Sandy, has proofread several of the anecdotes in this little treatise. She won't be editing this one, or hopefully seeing it at all, for one major reason—my self-preservation!

Sandy is a wonderful wife, mother, grandmother, friend, cousin, lawyer, advocate, activist and many more. She is a bundle of energy that seemingly goes from one project to another, often at a frantic pace. She is the glue that holds together a large network of cousins and friends, the go-to person when workers are needed on committees or when a mentor is needed for a younger person.

One role she had not embraced (or at least, not at an earlier stage in our family life) was that of being an eager cook. She didn't enjoy cooking, didn't have the time for it, and the results often reflected her lack of enthusiasm. As for me, who had once blown up an entire kitchen making hot dogs and never attempted a meal again for the next 20 years, I hated the cleaning up after our family's meals. Thus, we ate out with a fair degree of frequency in those days and the kids, at an early age, become connoisseurs of a large variety of foods of all ethnicities.

When the kids were younger, we were always very busy. Both Sandy and I worked long and hard hours at our respective professional careers, me in medicine, her in law; the kids studied hard and had a full plate of activities that we were constantly juggling. When Jessica was about 11 and Danny eight, Sundays had so many activities that it was often hard to squeeze everything in. This particular season, soccer was king. We often had one child's game in the late morning, another to follow in the afternoon, and homework time afterwards. Our typical routine on these busy weekends invariably found us running out for Thai, Mexican, or pizza for a quick Sunday dinner after soccer.

This weekend was different. The early March weekend was rainy, cold, and thoroughly miserable. All activities were cancelled and we sat around finishing schoolwork, reading newspapers, tinkering, etc., with many extra hours at hand. Late in the afternoon, as I sat there finishing a crossword and the kids were reading books, we heard busy sounds mysteriously arising from the kitchen. The activity increased for a while and finally came the dreaded pronouncement, as Sandy loudly exclaimed: "I think I'll cook dinner now!"

Without even a moment's hesitation, Danny looked up from his reading and yelled, "But Mom! We've been good!"

In fairness, as we've gotten a little older, retired with no kids at home and have lives that are marginally less hectic, Sandy has discovered her inner (Julia) child, and not surprisingly, has become a very good cook after all—and amazingly, even I have found my occasional inner chef. But equally not surprising, I still hate cleaning up afterward.

Chapter 68

Just a Little Slow

Jessica's plane to Denver briefly flashed overhead. Silhouetted against the azure sky, it should have been a beautiful sight. It wasn't. Sadly, Jessica was still seated in the car next to me as what I imagined to be "her plane" soared westward—and as we sped toward the airport in a pathetic rush to catch it.

Jessica was almost 16, a rising high school junior—very bright and meaner than a snake. Wonderful until two years earlier, and soon to be wonderful again, she was going through an adolescent phase that can only be described as ugly. (Well, it could be described in a lot of other ways, but most of them are unprintable.) The house was frequently tense; Sandy and I were barely able to speak to her, and sometimes barely able to speak to each other as a result.

Not surprisingly, we were thrilled that she was accepted into a special college preparatory program at the University of Colorado in Boulder for gifted students. At least we would have a few weeks of peace in the house to defuse the situation—plus, her program sounded great.

She needed to fly out on Sunday morning and arrive in Denver's Stapleton Airport within a specific time frame, as the program had arranged for transport vans to shuttle students two hours away to campus. It was important that she hit this "window," or transportation on her own would be tricky. Luckily, I had managed to find an incredibly cheap flight for her on a new discount airline, Mark Air, for only $225—half the price of Atlanta's ubiquitous Delta. What a deal! The plane left at 7 A.M. In those pre-9/11, pre-TSA days, I set the alarm for 5 A.M. on Sunday morning to get us there in plenty of time.

While the planning was flawless, the execution was not. I neglected to pull the pin out on our old analog alarm clock and awakened feeling happy and refreshed the next morning without an alarm having gone off—at 6:30 A.M.! While I knew there was no possible chance of making the plane (the ride to the airport alone was half an hour), horrified, throwing caution and reason to the wind, I awakened the slumbering Sandy and Jessica, made them throw on old sweatshirts, and the three of us piled into the car, barreling ineffectually toward the airport.

The trip was not pleasant. Sandy spent the entire time yelling at me for being so stupid, and while I lamely attempted to defend myself, inwardly I was also berating myself for being so totally stupid. Jessica, clearly not pleased and still half-asleep, who spent most of her time not talking to me anyway, utilized the entire ride to hone her already razor-sharp glare.

When we arrived at the airport, miraculously getting there by 7:20—remarkably close to the 7 A.M. flight time by my standards— I prepared to park and planned that the three of us would run in and throw ourselves at the mercy of Mark Air. Sandy would have none of that:

"It's a mess! You screwed up; it's your fault; you're dealing with it. I'm staying in the car and you go in with her!'

"...But what should I say?" She was the lawyer, after all.

"I don't care! Don't come back until you work it out!"

I carefully avoided the daggers coming from her eyes, with only minimal success.

I hauled Jessica in with me and rushed to the small counter for Mark Air, finding it totally empty except for one lone receptionist. While I had almost deluded myself that my rapid driving would somehow get us there and they would hold the plane for us, the woman laughed loudly at that idea. She had good news and bad news. The good news: they would gladly honor her ticket for the next flight. The bad news: Mark Air was new and young and only had one flight a day—and we had missed it. Even if I got Jessica on the next day's plane, there would be no transportation from the program to get her to Boulder, a major hassle, and she would miss the important orientation activities.

I breathlessly explained to the representative that I really needed to get her there that day and asked about alternatives. The woman said that United Air had a plane that would be boarding in an hour and their counter was immediately adjacent to us. They might consider taking the Mark Air ticket for a fee.

Moving to the next counter, I found the United rep sitting there and looking bored. Seven A.M. on Sunday was apparently not their peak time. I was the only one at the counter.

I quickly explained that I had to get my daughter to Denver, had missed the flight, etc., and the woman looked at my Mark Air ticket, checked in the computer, and told me that if I would give her the ticket along with an additional $495, Jessica would be able to fly. Great news! At least I'd get her on a plane and, more importantly, would not be skinned alive by my wife on the ride home. Bad news! That was a fortune at the time.

I glanced over at Jessica, standing off by herself 20 feet away. My very bright daughter was listening to a new-fangled iPod, passé now but new back then, and was singing and shuffling wordlessly with her back to us. Viewed from behind, she looked to be someone with a weird neurological disease. I figured I'd press on. I told the agent that I appreciated her offer, but that was pretty expensive. Further, I could tell the plane was virtually empty, it was important I get her there today for her special program, and was there *any* way she could work with me on this?

Grumbling, the woman shuffled into the back for a minute and returned. She said she had spoken to her supervisor and they would make an exception. Jessica could fly in return for the Mark Air ticket and $225.

Now we were cooking! This I could manage. But then I looked over at Jessica again, her back toward us, writhing and mouthing words to herself from the unheard music. She reminded me of schizophrenic patients I had seen years earlier as a medical student on the psych wards, carrying on conversations with voices only they could hear. The agent looked at her, too.

I decided to press my luck, almost feeling bad as I did it. (Not bad enough to stop, but bad nonetheless.) I said to the agent, "That is really a generous offer and I really appreciate your helping me out over here. And if that's the best we can do, I'm going to take that offer. But I really feel badly about this. My daughter is a little off …a little slow. Do you know what I'm saying? She functions, but …."

The agent looked at the contorting Jessica for a moment, disappeared again into the back, and this time returned with a more senior colleague. The two of them huddled together, watching Jessica writhing by herself, occasionally yelling out incomprehensible words. After a few minutes, the manager called me over. "I'm really sorry about your daughter, Sir. I tell you what, give me $35 and her old ticket and we'll get her on the plane."

Yes!

$495 to $35! A better airline. She'd make the van in Denver and get to Boulder!

I tried to hide my glee, but the manager wasn't quite finished.

"Sir, you know, this is not a direct flight to Denver. Your daughter will have to change planes in O'Hare in Chicago, a very complicated airport, and she'll have to change terminals as well. That can be pretty hard for someone challenged like your daughter. For $45 more, I'm going to have someone escort her from gate to gate."

What? My brilliant daughter, who's been flying all over the world since she was a tyke? Someone to take her to the gate? Besides, if they spoke to her, the gig might be up.

I told the woman that was amazingly nice of her but given that we had an hour before she was to board, I was going to sit Jessica down and explain to her what was going to happen. While challenged, with enough repetition, she could usually work things out. If I didn't think she was getting it, I was going to come back and pay the extra $45 and take her up on her offer.

About this time, Jessica had finished listening to her third heavy metal album and wandered over. "What's up, Dad?" The agents looked at her.

I said, "Jess, these nice ladies are going to help us and we have a flight for you but they're explaining that you have to change planes."

Jess started to answer, "That's not a prob—"

I cut her off. "I know you're upset and this wasn't what we had talked about, but try to stay calm and I'll explain it to you."

She started to answer a little more loudly, "But it's not a big ...."

I turned to the women and said I could tell she was getting a little upset, but felt we really had things under control. I was going to take her to the gate and explain things slowly.

As we walked off, I could hear the two agents talking. One said, "The poor guy really had his hands full." The last words I heard were the supervisor's response: "It's nice to see a father being so involved with his daughter."

I left the airport quickly after getting Jessica out of sight and to the gate. Knowing how tenuous our relationship was at the time, I most definitely did not tell her about my conversation with the ticketing agents. I thought she would kill me.

A day later, chatting on the phone, I couldn't contain myself. Figuring I was risking my daughter's eternal wrath, I nonetheless chanced it, telling her the entire story. I hoped she would forgive me.

To my relief, Jessica thought the tale was hysterical. The flight had been practically empty. Every 15 minutes, one flight attendant or another would come up to her and ask her how she was doing or if she was upset. They would all lean over sympathetically and say, "How are you, Honey?" like she was five years old. She couldn't imagine what was going on. And when she changed planes in O'Hare, she could have sworn that one of the flight attendants followed her to the next plane.

Thankfully, a few months later, whatever demons had possessed Jessica for the previous few years had left. We had started out with the sweetest, most wonderful daughter until her early teen years—hosted an alien creature for the next two—and ever since, we have been incredibly fortunate to have one of the world's truly sweet, thoughtful, compassionate young women as a daughter and a friend ever since.

Chapter 69

It's My Birthday – Part I

My mother-in-law Norma was the best.

Not necessarily the best person, nor the best mother-in-law, but certainly the best source of stories of any actual person I ever met. She was a true character in every sense of the word. Often, she seemed a caricature of someone playing an old Jewish woman—and this was long before she actually became an old Jewish woman. I loved her despite these quirks.

She was one of the most pessimistic people I've ever met, so much so that one never knew when she was kidding. In the classic glass half-empty or half-full scenario, Norma never actually made it that far. She would have been more stuck on "You call THAT a glass?" or "Why did I have to be the one with THAT glass?"

Of her many idiosyncrasies, miserliness was certainly near the top of the list. I'm pretty sure I read on Wikipedia that she tutored Scrooge in the tactics of stinginess (incidentally, she was a shrewd investor and died with considerable wealth). This was a woman who, a few years earlier, was the only relative who had not sent a birthday card to her son David. When Sandy asked her about this, Norma informed her that she had indeed bought and filled out the card, but never actually mailed it. "Do you know how much they want for a stamp these days?"

For reasons totally unclear to me, Norma loved me. Sandy, my wife—her daughter—was terribly sentimental about birthdays but would frequently get nothing on the big day. Au contraire, I, who never cared for such sentiment, always received something. Now, I didn't say something nice or extravagant—she was incredibly cheap, after all—but at least something.

At some point, she started sending me tee shirts around my birthday. Not especially memorable or attractive tees, but tees nonetheless. They started out with a Joe the Camel tee, certainly an embarrassment for a physician who specialized in respiratory patients and proceeded to get worse annually. No expense was spared on the wrapping. Excuse me, let me correct that. There was no expense *whatsoever* on the packaging—remember the story above of David and the stamp—and the tees would arrive in a cut-up brown paper bag held together by scotch tape and addressed in crayon. (I always checked them to make sure they were not ticking before I would open them.)

One year, before she moved permanently to Florida, the traditional shopping bag package arrived: a shirt for a 5K run sponsored by St. Ignatius Church in her hometown, Albany, New York. Of all the potentially cheap tee shirts in the world, this was just so wrong on so many fronts that I didn't even know where to begin. Above all, the thought of my obese, arthritic mother-in-law, who made walking into the kitchen her usual exercise for the day, attempting a 5K race on her swollen red knees, while limping along with a cane, was just too much.

A few days later, Norma, as was her wont, called to speak to Sandy—but her real reason was to find out how much I adored her present. When Sandy motioned for me to take the phone (usually after about 15 seconds), Norma asked me if I had indeed received the gift. I replied, "Yes, Norma. Thanks so much. It's lovely. But I'm a little surprised by the particular shirt. Did you by some chance participate or have something to do with that 5K race?"

"No." This one syllable was somehow drawn out over at least five counts.

"I'm not exactly sure who St. Ignatius is, I'm sure he was a lovely gentleman, but seeing as we're Jewish, I was curious if you might have anything to do with that particular church."

"No." Again, drawn out and ending on a downbeat.

Was the church near her? Not really.

"So, I'm a little curious. How did you happen to pick that particular shirt?'

"Welllll, I was going to the mall last weekend, and in the parking lot by the handicapped entrance, there was a table set up and it was piled high with these shirts. The women were starting to put them into boxes. So I said to them, 'How much are those shirts?' And they looked at each other and said, 'That's a good question, lady. Before the race, they were ten dollars apiece. But the race just ended and we've got all these left over. I don't know. I guess about fifty cents.' I said, 'FIFTY CENTS?! OH, OH! Let me have one for my son-in-law for his birthday next week!'

"Then when she started to give it to me, I said, "WAIT! I'VE GOT A BETTER IDEA! It's my son's birthday the week afterwards. GIVE ME TWO!"

I was really glad she didn't buy more—this could easily have been next year's present as well.

Chapter 70

It's My Birthday – Part II

Without my mother-in-law for inspiration, these memoirs could be considerably shorter.

Sandy—my lovely, intelligent wife, a terrific daughter (and later, wife, mother, grandmother and lawyer)—never got any praise from her mother, nor any gifts to speak of, for that matter. She was sentimental about gifts. One year, when visiting in Florida near her birthday, Norma offered to drive her to the store and Sandy would be able to pick out anything she wanted. Sounded like a good deal until Norma took her to Dollar General. (I'm not kidding.) Another year, when Sandy needed some intimates, they went to Victoria's Secret. Things went smoothly until Norma glanced at the price on the pair of panties Sandy had picked out and then started bellowing at the poor salesgirl for having the nerve of charging so much. They were both asked to leave.

Two years later marked the incident with The Blouse. Norma commanded Sandy to buy herself something she wanted, and Norma would reimburse her. Sandy found a blouse she liked for $50, but knowing her mother, told her she had only spent $25. Norma had started screaming. "Twenty-five dollars! Who spends twenty-five dollars for a blouse? I'm only giving you twenty dollars!" Sandy still talks about the sleeve her mother gave her for her birthday.

Ah, but these are my memoirs. So back to my presents, or should I say, my tee shirts, since that's what my presents evolved into. After the infamous St. Ignatius tee shirt, over the next several years, I would receive the same brown paper bag envelope with the address in crayon (purple was my favorite), and each year I would get a different tee shirt. They were uniformly hideous, poorly made, and unattractive.

Like clockwork each year, a few days afterwards, I would get a phone call from Norma to find out how I liked her present. My answer was invariable. "Yes, Norma, I got it. It's lovely. Thank you very much."

After a few years, as the shirts got worse and the phone calls stopped, I made the clinical decision that when a brown paper bag arrived around my birthday, it wasn't worth the effort of locating a pair of scissors and I just started throwing them away unopened.

That worked well for a couple of years. Until...

One year, around my birthday, Sandy was on the phone with her mother when she told me Norma wanted to say hello to me. Absentmindedly, I picked up the receiver.

"Gary, did you get my present?'

Uh-oh! I hadn't even remembered seeing a brown paper bag. A bead of sweat was starting to form. "Yes, Norma. It's lovely. Thank you so much." Boy, I hope that suffices.

And after a moment's silence, coyly from the other end, "What was it?"

What was it? What was it? It's got to be a tee shirt. What else does she send? Crap! "It's a tee shirt." I replied hopefully. The sweat was real at this point.

This time the silence was longer before she responded. "What color was it?"

OK, the game was up. Was she really asking this? Was the woman in the KGB or something? I was going to have to confess. Wipe the brow with a towel. Confess, or get myself in deeper? OK, going for broke here.

"It's white, Norma. It's white." I was sure the game was up as I waited to be caught.

"Oh, I didn't think you'd get it yet. I just mailed it this morning!"

Sometimes the forces of justice do prevail in the world.

Chapter 71

Norma Calls 911

This is a 911 story. No, not a medical emergency during my medical training or career, but a different 911 story: starring of course, my mother-in-law, Norma.

Norma was an unusual person, to say the least. She had a peeve against doctors (to be fair, she had a peeve against almost anything—but it was particularly pronounced with doctors). And you have to remember, she had a son-in-law and later a grandson who were physicians!

Despite her advanced years, Norma never actually went to the doctor. Now, you hear stories all the time of people who never see a physician, live healthily on no medications, and pass away peacefully in their sleep at 102. That was not my mother-in-law. This was an obese woman who limped along on swollen, hot, painfully arthritic knees, using a cane for support and would get breathless after five steps, pulling out a brown paper bag to breathe into. To walk across her small living room would usually involve at least three or four hits on the bag. Everything hurt her and her capacity to complain almost defied the human imagination. I'm not quite sure that any part of her body worked well, except her mouth.

She almost certainly had congestive heart failure, type 2 diabetes, severe osteoarthritis, depression, a tinge of paranoia, and several other diagnoses. Almost certainly, but we'll never know—as I said, she never visited the doctor.

Any medical care would be provided (with great reluctance) by yours truly, and always during phone calls: first from Albany and in later years, when she lived in Florida. She would usually describe horrible symptoms and my initial advice would always be the same: "See a doctor!" ("Norma, you can't breathe, you can't walk, your ankles are swollen, you have heart failure—see a doctor!" Or, "You say your knees are swollen and red and sore to the touch, you can't walk even with a cane—see a doctor!"). I would then get the same line each time: "The doctors never do anything. They just give me some pills and all they want is my money!" Any explanations on my part were futile and to no avail. Every once in a while, against all my training, I would give in and prescribe something from a thousand miles away with the provision (which we both knew to be patently untrue) that she would follow-up with a doctor—any doctor! The absurdity of me, board certified in Pediatrics and Allergy/Immunology, treating an 80-year-old unexamined woman with presumptive congestive heart failure using medical knowledge from my training decades earlier still boggles the mind.

(The only thing that eventually saved me from this farce that lasted my entire 40-year-plus medical career was the graduation of my son, Dan, from medical school. Dan was much nicer than me—or too inexperienced in early years to say "No" effectively to his grandmother. Thank you, Dan: I am truly grateful.)

Then again, this is a 911 story.

One night, Sandy took a distressed phone call from Norma's neighbor and after several minutes of tense conversation, handed me the phone. Norma had fallen in her living room, hurt her back severely, could not get up, but managed to phone her neighbor to come over. The neighbor was unable to lift her, realized Norma was in marked pain, and had called 911.

The paramedics had arrived, managed with difficulty to get her on a stretcher—and Norma refused to go the ER! When asked why she had called 911 if she didn't want treatment, she had responded that she just needed someone strong to lift her and place her in bed. (This was only the first 911 call.)

Now it was two hours later: the neighbor was angry that she was still there tending to Norma (who was still very much in pain), trying to roll my very overweight mother-in-law off and on a bed pan, with Norma yelling at her the entire time. The neighbor was not a nurse, not a relative, and had a life. She did not want to be there.

Sandy asked me to talk to her mother. My advice was obvious: go to the ER! She needed to be seen and treated. Characteristically, she insisted that if she remained at home, she would likely be much better in the morning. She would try to last the night but did promise if she were not better in the morning, she would call 911 again and be transported to the hospital. I began to realize that the elderly in her community thought of 911 as a taxi service. (I also learned that the hospital staff had to immediately see you if an ambulance brought you in, avoiding what otherwise might be several hours of waiting time.) I was dubious, to say the least, and given the pain and helpless condition she was in, it made no sense—but sitting in my living room in Atlanta, was in no position to insist otherwise.

Miraculously, Norma was much better through the night, the next morning and early evening. Or so Sandy and I assumed, since we heard nothing further and with Norma, decided to operate under the old adage: No news is good news. Except, of course, it wasn't.

The phone call came the next evening. Her extremely nice neighbor, thoroughly exasperated, called back. The day had been miserable, the neighbor had been called early, and good-hearted as she was, had watched Norma writhe in agony all day, struggling to roll her on and off bed pans, moaning the entire time and yelling continuously that the neighbor was hurting her. Finally, when the neighbor had had enough (we're all amazed at how long she lasted), they had called 911, taken her to the hospital, a vertebral fracture confirmed, and she had been admitted to the hospital where she now resided.

No, that's not the 911 call that's the subject of this tale. There's more.

Several hours went by, and Norma was miserable. Finally, she drifted off. At 2 A.M., the nurse came into her room to take Norma's vital signs. When she left, the nurse "forgot" to turn off the light. (Since Norma almost definitely would have been yelling at the nurse the entire time, "forgot" might be a euphemism.) In any case, Norma was apoplectic. She was miserable, she was in pain, the lights were on, she couldn't sleep. She had no idea how to use the nurse call button (pretty hard pushing that bright red button!) and her agony prevented her from sitting up. Luckily, she somehow managed to grasp her cell phone.

So, who to call? The hospital to reach the nursing station? A good thought, but incorrect. The neighbor? Not a great idea for the harried neighbor, but some logic there. Incorrect. Sandy or me? Pretty stupid idea to be calling Atlanta when we didn't even know which hospital she's in. Also incorrect.

Oh, that's right. This is a 911 story.

I admit I wouldn't have seen this one coming, as it would never have entered my thought processes. But it did enter Norma's. So, at 2:30 in the morning, lying in her hospital bed, the woman called 911! Twenty minutes later, the paramedics, obliged by law to respond, arrived at her bedside, accompanied by one very sleepy hospital administrator, to listen to the tirade from my mother-in-law about the nurse who wouldn't turn out the lights.

Our tax money at work.

For the rest of her life, Norma remained proud of her ingenuity and gumption in calling 911. Ouch!

Several months later, when Norma's usual labored breathing became more pronounced, Sandy and I finally convinced her to see a local physician. She went kicking and screaming.

When we called to find out his recommendations, she

complained that he hadn't said anything. When I continued that he *had* to say something, she said:

"He looked at me and then he said, 'Sit over there.'"

I persisted. What had he said afterwards?

"What did he say afterwards? What did he say afterwards? He said, 'Pay on the way out.'"

Chapter 72

A Fitting Fate

One of the old adages in medicine is that a doctor is likely to develop problems with an ailment in his chosen specialty. That was true for me—and certainly made me glad I chose a career in allergy and not in oncology.

I had bad allergies as a kid with chronic congestion, multiple respiratory infections leading to tonsils being removed, ears drained, mouth breathing, frequent doctors' visits, and finally had taken allergy injections. Although at the time I hated taking them, the injections brought good results and I had experienced no subsequent problems for 20 years afterwards. Until moving to Georgia, that is. By my second spring in Atlanta, I was as miserable as many of my patients, and after multiple sinus infections and episodes with ear congestion, required allergy immunotherapy injections for a few years. Happily, the results were outstanding and I've experienced none of these respiratory symptoms in the 30 years since my series of treatment was completed.

More interesting were my newly developed food allergies. A year after moving to Georgia, I broke out in hives within minutes of finishing a meal. A few days later, after eating a ripe peach (my dessert for that previous meal), I experienced tingling in the throat along with diffuse welts and itching, easily responding to an injection of epinephrine. A subsequent test did confirm sensitivity to peach. I thought it pretty funny that I had to move to the Peach State to develop a peach allergy. (This was in line with our moving to the city of Sandy Springs and Sandy taking an executive position with Southern Bell—you get the picture, Sandy from Sandy Springs, a Southern belle for Southern Bell. But I digress.)

This allergy lasted about ten years. After many years of avoidance and a negative test, I gradually reintroduced peach and experienced no further adverse reaction.

In more recent years, we have become aware of the Oral Fruit syndrome, or Oral Food Syndrome, where particular foods—usually fresh fruits or vegetables—and particular materials right under the skin or peel may trigger mild allergic-like symptoms, with most symptoms frequently being confined around the mouth (thus, the Oral). This can include itching or swelling in the throat or palate or some local hives and is sometimes more extensive. Some patients will experience this with many different foods, others with fewer. (In contrast, my peach reaction did seem to be a true allergic reaction to the peach.)

My more interesting food reaction came quite a number of years later. My son, Dan, was in medical school and happened to be in town for a short while, visiting with a buddy. We met at a Mexican restaurant, new to me at the time. As we sat and had a pleasant chat, accompanied by menus and water, we were served the traditional chips and salsa. We chomped and chatted, enjoying the snack, the salsa a somewhat a distinctive and unusual flavor. Five minutes into our conversation, I realized I was having an allergic reaction. While not yet externally obvious, I could feel tightness in the throat, tightness of the nose, and then, sensed the right side of my lip swelling like a balloon. I calmly exclaimed, "I'm starting to have an allergic reaction. My lip just swelled."

Dan, sitting opposite me across a small table, looked at me and said, "No, Dad. Your lip's not swoll…. Oh, my God, your upper lip just swelled in front of my very eyes." As my throat tightened a bit more, we jumped in the car and drove to my office five minutes away, where a shot of epinephrine and antihistamine reversed the process.

Curious as to the cause, I worked my way back to the Mexican restaurant a few days later. The candidates for my trigger were somewhat limited: chips and salsa, the salsa the more likely. We hadn't had time to order before my reaction, so I had eaten nothing else. Heck, there hadn't even been time to order a margarita!

The staff was extremely helpful. While I had taken the restaurant for a hole-in-the-wall, it was actually part of a chain, and as such, had neatly printed cards with every recipe— including the salsa. There were only five or six ingredients.

After convincing the manager that I was not looking to sue the establishment but just to figure out what ingredient I needed to be avoiding, he was extremely cooperative. He gave me a bit of salsa to take back to the office, and with one of my partners in attendance, we improvised a skin test, inducing a very nice itchy welt at the site, indicative of an allergic response. That confirmed the salsa as the culprit. Then I had to work my way through the several ingredients. Some were easy to eliminate, such as tomatoes. For sunflower oil, we did not have any current test material, so I ran to a nearby supermarket, picked up a small bottle and using this, induced a very nice positive test.

As with my peach allergy of 30 years earlier, my sunflower oil allergy lasted several years but was outgrown after years of avoidance.

That's two unusual food allergies. I'm waiting for the next act. What's that they say about things coming in threes?

Chapter 73

Who's Your Doctor?

I realize that medicine is complicated, and things can be stressful from a patient's viewpoint. Patients will often complain that their physicians do not take the time to explain things effectively. All these complaints at times may be true. But sometimes, the problems may lie with the patients themselves.

It was a Tuesday morning and I was in our Northlake office seeing patients along with my partner, Dr. Linda Guydon. We both had busy schedules; it was spring, a hectic time of the year for allergists, and the office was its usual crazy place. As the morning wound down, I was standing near the checkout desk, escorting a patient and chatting with the front desk staff.

Sitting beside me, Carolyn, one of our wonderful long-time receptionists, answered the phone. She and I had worked together for almost 20 years and by this point, we were good friends as well as colleagues. I heard the conversation from her side.

"Yes, ma'am. You just left the office a few minutes ago and can't remember how the doctor told you to take your pills. I should be able to help you with that, ma'am. I'll just need a little information. Which doctor did you see this morning, ma'am?"

Now, let me describe our practice a little. At that point, we had 18 physicians and almost as many offices. While the practice had been started in the early 1970s, and was originally diverse for white men in religious terms (the first five physicians were Southern Baptist, Roman Catholic, moderate Jew, WASP, and less-observant Jew), we now were much more diverse. Half of our physicians were female, and we had white females, Black females, Hispanic females, and Asian females. Our staff was also a diverse mix and at this particular office, two of the front desk personnel were Black, and two were white. Our nurses also were almost equally divided. Our practice worked well and if there were ever any racial tensions, I never saw them.

Similarly, our patient demographics varied greatly. Atlanta was a diverse city, the most heavily Black major city in the U.S. While our offices were in different areas of the metropolitan region and had different population characteristics, most were quite heterogeneous and we saw all comers. More than half the patients at this particular office were Black.

Dr. Linda Guydon and I had worked together every Tuesday for many years. Linda was a Black woman, a conscientious physician and a good friend, and we got on well professionally and socially. I would greet her in the morning with, "Hello, LG," and she would respond, "Good morning, GL." We would frequently consult each other and would share laughs over lunch.

My thoughts returned to Carolyn on the phone next to me. I stood around for a minute as she queried the patient on which physician she had seen; if it was my patient, I would save everyone time by answering directly rather than going through the more cumbersome office procedure with nursing contact forms, etc. "All right, ma'am. You're not sure which doctor you saw. Might you remember, was it Dr. Lotner or Dr. Guydon?" Carolyn glanced up at me as she spoke.

After a few seconds of silence, she continued. "Okay, ma'am, I'm sorry you're having trouble remembering the doctor's name. I understand they both sound similar. Let me ask you, was the doctor a man or a woman?"

By this point, all the receptionists and some nearby patients had turned in Carolyn's direction. She went on, "No, don't feel badly, ma'am." Then she leaned into the phone and proceeded in a seeming stage whisper: "Ma'am, do you remember if your doctor was a WHITE MAN or a BLACK WOMAN?"

Pretty much all nearby conversation had stopped.

"Yes, I'm sorry ma'am, I know it's been a few minutes since you left. I can look it up, that won't be a problem. Let me maybe ask you one more question. Do you remember if your doctor had a beard or not?" Silence for a minute. "You think your doctor DID have a beard, but you also think it might have been a WOMAN."

After Carolyn looked up the woman's name, I was glad the patient belonged to LG, not GL. Poor Linda. Based on that conversation, the patient clearly had more problems than not remembering how to take her pills.

Chapter 74

The Great Matzoh Conspiracy

I awakened at 4 A.M. on a Friday with moderately intense abdominal pain; not excruciating, but clearly I wasn't going to be able to fall back asleep. Five hours later, I was a little more uncomfortable and called the office of my young-ish GI doctor (anyone my son's age is at least young-ish, and my GI doctor was actually a friend of my son). He was tied up doing procedures all day, so I decided a phone call to my previous old-ish doctor (you got it, my age), recently retired, who confirmed my suspicions: the pain and tenderness I was describing warranted "the laying on" of hands. Indeed, two hours later, when I managed to see the young Dr. Singh in his practice (also a friend of my son), she did not like the tenderness she elicited palpating my abdomen and sent me for an immediate CT scan, promising to call me as soon as she had the results.

Waiting two hours for my scan, with the pain worsening to the point that I considered leaving the waiting area and going to the hospital ER, the discomfort finally eased a tad. I headed home post-scan and as I walked in the door, received the phone call from Dr. Singh that reminded me of drawing a "Go to Jail" card in Monopoly. "You have an internal hernia and a possible ischemic loop of bowel and need to get to the ER right away. Have someone drive you." But Sandy was at a funeral for our dear friend (I was supposed to be there as well) and wouldn't return for 45 minutes or so. Although as a physician, I understood the radiology report sounding ominous, I still tried bargaining for time until Sandy was available to drive me. Dr. Singh would have none of that. "You're not getting the seriousness of this situation. This is an evolving picture. You can't wait 45 minutes. Go there now and if you don't know a GI surgeon, I'll have one meet you there! From your study, you will probably require immediate surgery." Yes, ma'am! Do Not Pass Go and Do Not Collect $200.

Young-ish Dr. Wood, the surgeon who saw me shortly after my ER arrival, was extremely nice and helpful. (Of course, this was after his initial confusion as to who his patient was. As had been the case with Dr. Singh, he also had known a "Doctor Lotner," that being my son Daniel, and couldn't figure out why he was being called to see him since Dan had looked perfectly healthy when they had bumped into each other a few hours earlier.) Upon examining me, Dr. Wood—similar to the thoughts of Dr. Singh and myself—felt there was a disconnect between my X-ray picture (ominous) and my clinical picture (not so bad). The impressions didn't quite match up. In addition, a major complicating factor was that I was on Eliquis, an anti-coagulant, that made even minor surgery potentially hazardous, as I was well aware. (In retrospect, this was probably the only time in my life that I was happy I was on anticoagulants.) He decided we would watchfully wait, rechecking every few hours, realizing that he might have to perform exploratory surgery at any moment if I were to worsen.

I won't go into the course of the next three days in the hospital in detail—that is not the purpose of this story. Suffice it to say that the first 48 hours, there was some significant dissociation between my X-ray picture (improving) and my clinical picture (slowly worsening). I vomited several times and two liters of fluid were removed through an NG tube; but somehow, as surgery loomed, I got significantly better and seemed out of danger. While the scan had forced them to concentrate on the small bowel, it had also shown a totally impacted colon with hardened stool running its entire length. Could this all have been severe constipation—and if so, why was I so acutely constipated?

That was when I proposed the Matzoh Theory, initially half-jokingly and with everyone laughing, but as time passed, it began looming as a higher possibility. And, as I expounded, over time, all seemed (at least partially) to potentially accept what I came to call the Great Matzoh Conspiracy.

Two weeks earlier, as we prepared for Passover and expected a large turnout of over 40 guests for our Seder, Sandy had purchased many, many boxes of matzohs. As the holiday approached, she tasted a different type of matzoh, gluten-free (double ugh!), at a friend's house and bought some of those as well. However when Passover arrived, we had less of a turnout than anticipated, and for reasons unfathomable to me, Sandy had opened all ten boxes of matzohs.

While I suspect that anyone reading this is very familiar with matzoh, a short description is in order for anyone who may not be. Matzoh is an unleavened bread that comes in 7-inch squares, hard and dry. Think of old cardboard but without the flavor, or of three-week-old bread but without the mold or the moisture. If you are familiar with Elmer's Glue but have never read the ingredient list, matzoh is actually number one and water, number two.

Not really, but you get the picture. A great food: hard, dry, flavorless, and to be consumed with a lot of liquids. And for some reason, I like matzoh.

So there we were, with enough open matzoh boxes to feed a small army but no army in sight. Why they were all opened is a matter of conjecture and whether leaving matzoh open can actually make it drier might serve as the basis of a whole area of Talmudic debate. And while my wonderful wife has no problem with eliminating the middleman in the buy food, throw out food process, I am much too cheap to throw out that much uneaten food without giving it a good go first. Ergo, I attacked. During the eight days of Pesach, initially, I started out with one matzoh sandwich daily (two slabs of dried matzoh, separated by a slice of cheese). After two days, as many more boxes waited in the shadows, I increased my intake (but maybe not my output) to two or three sandwiches a day. Finally—and mercifully—Passover ended. But not the matzohs! Somehow, from the depths, Sandy found yet one more box and proceeded to open that as well. (We have only been married 42 years. I am certain with a little more time, I will better understand the female logic of why we were opening a holiday food after the holiday. But, again, I digress.) With some disgust and much consternation, I devoured the last box.

When I awakened that Friday morning, a few days after Passover, my theory was that all the matzoh had indeed turned into Elmer's glue somewhere (everywhere, apparently) in my colon.

The extent was massive enough that the matzoh glue had to be attacked from the top. Going at it the conventional route (i.e., from the bottom, with enemas) would be insufficient—something like trying to melt an iceberg with a blowtorch to the visible ten percent. The solution: several days of those horrible GI colonoscopy preps that everyone becomes apoplectic about. It seemed to work. A few days after my discharge, and with several days of GI prepping, I seemed to be fine and have stayed that way.

A major question is future prevention. Rabbi Analia, the female half of our married rabbi duo, had called me several times during the hospital stay. During our last call, while other possible causes were becoming less likely, I managed to extract from her a dispensation for the future that will spare me from eating matzohs. Of course, this came with a cost. On the third day in the hospital, I had started feeling better a couple of hours after her phone conversation with me. Later, she was convinced that her call turned me around (I personally think a more likely factor was the laxative my son prescribed) and wanted me to agree to more spiritual counseling in the future. I am currently weighing the choice between matzohs or spiritual counseling. Seems like a toss-up at this point.

So, what do we call this scenario? I have thought of a short book, perhaps to be entitled "Matzoh: The Eleventh Plague." In it, Pharaoh extracts his revenge upon the Jewish people from beyond the tomb and from past millennia. In fact, reflection on the entire Seder meal with matzoh, gefilte fish (an oily, fishy, malodorous glob when made by your grandmother) and homemade horseradish (used in several ERs in lieu of ammonia, to revive the unconscious) reveals it to be a likely anti-Semitic plot—in this case, self-inflicted.

While the resolution is still to be determined, Sandy has a much-reduced matzoh budget for future years.

Chapter 75

Electronic Medical Records

I hate electronic medical record (EMR) systems; I really do. I eventually retired from medicine largely because of them.

Unfortunately, when the government mandated that physicians transfer to EMRs around 2010, they did not do their due diligence and investigate what was out there for physicians to purchase. Particularly for smaller specialties, like allergy, there were no systems designed with our specific requirements in mind (in other words, there were none that handled the parameters that we needed to follow). EMRs were made even more challenging by the technology that supported them: the computers were slow, and largely MS-DOS-based—which means that they tended to "crash" and "lock up" often, like computers did two decades earlier.

Moreover, the systems were not integrated with each other as in Europe: for example, a patient in a Paris emergency room for chest pains who undergoes a cardiac catheterization, and then shows up in an ER in Lyons the next week, can have his records easily accessed, making the results from Paris immediately available to the next group of doctors. Conversely, while our systems were set up years later and this type of integration was theoretically an important goal, the government never set any standards for that integration. If I admitted a patient to Northside Hospital, where I was on staff, I could print out my notes and send them with the patient—but the records were not accessible otherwise (despite the other hospital being just a short distance away).

The EMR systems did have their lighter moments, however. Perhaps the most humorous ones revolved around the dictation systems, which were notorious for making errors. If you think Siri gets things wrong with voice commands, you should have seen some of the things that came out of the EMR computer.

My first one was just a few weeks after the installation of our very inefficient $1.5M system. As part of the inducement to have physicians install systems rapidly, incentives were created in which, if certain governmentally determined goals were met, part of the purchase costs would be rebated. One of these requirements was that at least 85 percent of patients had to leave with treatment plans printed off the computer at the time they left. Theoretically, this was a great goal—in fact, for years, I had personally hand-written directions to almost every patient to make sure that instructions were remembered. This became a challenge when using inefficient EMRs.

My patient that morning was an 82-year-old woman who, three months earlier, had experienced a short-lived rash that had disappeared after a few hours. She clearly did not need to see an allergist; a rash of such short duration in a patient of that age was almost certainly not an allergy and even if it had been, no evaluation or treatment would have been required. Yet her internist had referred her in. (He must have had a bad case of indigestion the day he saw her.) Even more unfortunately, her appointment, set up weeks in advance, happened to coincide with one of our busiest days of the year. Allergists' practices are largely seasonal; while we are busy year-round, pollen seasons are our busiest periods by far. The pollen count had gone crazy; new patients were frantically calling, desperate to be seen with severe seasonal hay fever or asthma. My office was scrambling to fit all of the needing patients into the schedule. In the midst of this chaos, I was seeing this charming elderly woman with no problems and no reason to be there.

Quickly ascertaining that nothing was required, I was ready to discharge the patient, who was just as happy to be leaving. She thanked me for my time, gracefully apologizing for having taken up an appointment space: "I have no idea why he sent me. I told my doctor I didn't think I needed to be seen." The only task that remained for me to dismiss her was to provide my government-mandated set of discharge instructions, which would help meet our quota to receive our $300,000 annual rebate. There was little to say. A terrible typist, I dictated: "You look fine. If it comes back again, give me a call."

I sent the instructions to the reception-area printer, brought the charming older woman to the desk, asked the receptionist to hand her the printed directions, and said goodbye. As I picked up the next patient chart to peruse before entering a room, I heard the woman read the directions aloud to my staff member. "You look fine. If you get pregnant again, call me." She paused for a minute before adding, "I'm 82 years old. You tell that nice doctor, if I get pregnant again, I'm calling everybody!"

Of course, it wasn't just me; I wasn't the only one having problems with our EMR, which slowed us down greatly. I was once again in the Northlake office, alongside my partner, Dr. Linda Guydon.

Linda, an attractive Black woman in her 50s, was seeing a young, athletic Black male in his twenties. The patient had moderately severe asthma, had been having some recent problems prior to seeing Dr. Guydon a few months earlier, and had apparently not responded adequately to the initial medications. She had dutifully seen him again, made some changes to his pharmacologic regimen, and was now seeing him once more to determine the effectiveness of the treatment. Thankfully, the newer regimen was working well and they were both happy.

Before he could leave, the all-important discharge instructions remained. She dictated: "I think you're moving in a good direction. Keep it up." As usual, she asked the front desk staff to print out the sheet and bid the patient goodbye, heading back to her office.

Before she could enter, Nicky, the receptionist, bounded over, paper in hand. She said, "Dr. Guydon, if you want me to give this to the patient, I think you should read it first."

Together, they glanced at the discharge summary, which read: "I think you're having a good erection. Keep it up!"

Chapter 76

How Did I Know?

Bob called from Arizona, out of the blue. As kids, we had been in the same neighborhood group, he a few years older—never the closest of friends but still, we had spent a fair amount of time together. That had ended around high school, when I was in a more academic crowd and several of my old buddies weren't. When I went off to college (City College of New York), most of the gang had gone more locally (Queens College), and we had drifted apart.

We hadn't spoken in ten years. I heard about Bob intermittently, married and no kids, living in Jersey in some sales position. For a while contacts were occasional, then more sporadic, and finally non-existent.

It was a wintry Sunday when his call came. I had been relaxing and watching a football game. I was surprised at the call and more surprised to hear the tone of Bob's voice. He was obviously in pain and his voice sounded decades older.

Bob wanted advice. His back had been hurting for a while and now he was in agony, an excruciating pain, which he described in great detail. He wasn't one to see doctors but wondered if he should go to the emergency room now, attempt to ride it out, or try some pain pills. He had moved several months earlier to the warmer climes of Arizona, had not yet established medical care and so had dug my phone number out to ask for advice. We chatted for a few minutes and it was clear that the ER was the only feasible course. (I had pretty much known that from his opening comments.)

As we neared the end of the call and his wife was going to call 911 (he wasn't able to walk), just before we ended, I said: "Bob, when you're in the ER and they get X-rays of your back, ask the ER doc to order a skull X-ray, too." He asked why and I mumbled something about some connection I had once heard about certain back pain and the head, not telling him what I was really thinking about.

It was many hours later when I got a call from Bob, very depressed but amazed. He hadn't had the typical disc problem, by far the most common cause of severe back pain, but instead they suspected multiple myeloma (MM), a serious cancer that can cause lesions in bones. It frequently can affect the back but many times there are lytic (eroded) lesions in the skull that can produce coin-like images on the X-ray, a diagnostic appearance. It was this that I had feared and this that they had found. "They wanted to know why you ordered the skull X-ray. They couldn't believe that you were looking for this in advance."

Confirming their amazement, I got a call from an oncologist the next day wanting to know what in Bob's phone call had made me ask him to request the skull film. Had I really been looking for MM? I said there was something in the quality of the back pain he was describing that made me think about multiple myeloma, not the much more common back-related problems. He asked me what it was specifically, since he had never heard of anyone ordering that kind of film immediately for back pain. I thought about it for a minute and said I wasn't sure but somehow, had no doubt in my mind that MM was the likely cause.

The oncologist went on, adding that he also had heard this was somewhat out of my medical specialty. I replied that my training had been in pediatrics and I had specialized many years ago in Allergy and Asthma. He laughed a little, muttered "unbelievable" under his breath, and said there were plenty of other tests I could have ordered to make the MM diagnosis. I told him I was sure there were better methods, but I was relying on something from my medical school days over 30 years earlier and hadn't kept up with this field, so far removed from my own medical specialty.

He had a last question or two for me. "I'm amazed. So how many patients have you taken care of with multiple myeloma that you thought of this? How often have you ordered a skull film under these circumstances?"

I didn't have to think long. "None and none. I've never had a patient where I would be the one diagnosing MM."

"Amazing," he muttered as he hung up.

Bob hung in for three years before he passed away from his MM and some other serious underlying conditions. He often thanked me for making the diagnosis; the oncologist said that his treatment was made easier by the speed in establishing the condition and when Bob visited, he was always greeted with some comment about "Here he is, the guy diagnosed by a skull X-ray." (I doubted that his diagnosis would have really taken long to make. With his level of pain, I'm sure it would have been made very shortly although maybe not on that first trip to the ER.)

Looking back, I've often wondered whether there was indeed a hidden detail in the description he gave that reminded me of something from very long ago in my training. This is most likely the case. At times in my career, something has triggered some long-forgotten memory that led to an unusual diagnosis. Or asking a few extra questions, omitted by another physician, has led to an obscure connection. During my career, on multiple occasions I suspected serious diagnoses (such as lupus or lymphoma) in patients seeing me for totally unrelated problems. There have been at least three young patients, recently examined and cleared by their family physicians, where my physical exam led to early diagnosis of Hodgkin's, the patients extremely grateful that I had helped diagnose this at easily treatable stages. (One came back to see me, both to thank me and to tell me he really wanted to treat his hay fever, the problem he had originally come to see me for. I told him I did too, but let's wait until he licked his Hodgkin's—which he did the next year.)

Over the years, I've realized that making a difficult diagnosis is done often based on training and hard work. However, for Bob, I can't honestly say why I "knew" this was MM, as the oncologist had wondered. As a physician, the truth is that the connections in a diagnosis aren't always clear—whether it's something the patient said, a long-forgotten memory, pure instinct or sometimes forces beyond our comprehension.

Chapter 77

They Make Stethoscopes for That

Sandy and I were visiting in Japan a few years ago on a long-awaited trip. After several days on our own, we met up with the small touring group with whom we would be spending the next ten days. Among us was Ed, in his mid-70s, a very nice lawyer from New York, who greeted me with a series of coughs. A few pleasantries were also met with further coughing. He had been in Tokyo with his wife on a pre-trip excursion for several days; 48 hours earlier, he had started with a bronchitic cough.

Shortly into our tour, during a visit to a small rural area, our group was walking uphill to an isolated village. I could hear Ed coughing along as he trailed the rest of us. When he caught up, he was audibly wheezing. Although I was not his physician and had no intention of assuming that role, I was also the only one with medical knowledge and didn't want the poor guy to die on the trip. A few questions revealed that he didn't smoke, didn't have known asthma or COPD (as his wheezing suggested), and he didn't have major heart disease. Without the ability to examine him or prescribe anything, I was limited to having him take it easy and wear a mask. While we had already been around him too long, a mask might prevent further exposure for the rest of our party. Unfortunately, Ed would wear the mask only intermittently and with frequent reminding. (Eventually, nine of the twelve of us would catch his illness, some becoming quite ill after we returned stateside.)

After another two days, as Ed showed no signs of improvement with frequent coughing spasms and seeming shortness of breath during an excursion, I decided it really behooved me to listen to his chest. He did not want to go to the local emergency room but agreed to have me listen when we could find an appropriate location. As our group was headed for dinner in our upscale hotel restaurant, I grabbed Ed and we ran into the spacious, empty men's bathroom together. Of course, I did not have a stethoscope with me. Realizing Ed was wearing a thick shirt which would make listening even more difficult, I asked him to strip from the waist. He looked at me incredulously, even after I told him this was how doctors had to examine chests before the invention of stethoscopes. With him now bare-chested, I lay my ear on his chest, and asked him to start taking slow, deep breaths—just as three middle-aged Japanese businessmen entered the bathroom.

Dressed similarly, in black suits, white shirts and black ties, they headed for the urinals along the rear wall, where they proceeded to go about their business. When I looked, all three heads were turned toward the two of us as I continued to have Ed breathe deeply with my ear glued to his hairy chest. (He sounded terrible, by the way, and I had to insist on him going to a local hospital the next morning.) The Japanese trio never stopped looking in our direction as they finished and washed their hands. Although they said nothing, we could certainly read their minds: *Crazy Americans!*

Having no idea if they understood English, I looked up and loudly proclaimed, "American male bonding!" They walked out quickly.

Ed's hospital visit was non-eventful, although he coughed for the next few weeks. Fittingly, in the category of "no good deed goes unpunished," my own subsequent case of bronchitis was worse than his and I required prolonged treatment back in the States.

Two months later, Sandy and I were in New York visiting relatives, located not too far from the apartment of Ed and wife, Ellen. We called and arranged a short reunion visit. Knocking on the door to their flat, we were greeted by a smiling Ellen and behind her stood Ed, proudly wearing his respiratory mask!

Oh, if only he would have done that while we were in Japan. I'm not sure if every foreigner thinks Americans a little bit odd, but I know for a fact there are three Japanese businessmen who do.

Chapter 78

Memories of Medicine

When I retired from full-time medicine in 2015, I knew that I had been blessed with a most satisfying career. I used to have a big box, long since lost from view. In it, I stored letters, photos, cards, and other mementos that I had saved from parts of my career and which provided insights into varying aspects of my journey through medicine.

It had been a long journey, including ten years of training before I finally made it into private clinical practice. As outlined earlier, the path had included some wonderful institutions: Albert Einstein College of Medicine, an excellent medical school in New York. Then pediatric internship, residency and an allergy immunology at the esteemed Children's Hospital of Philadelphia, the pediatric teaching hospital at the University of Pennsylvania and one of the premier pediatric institutions in the world. Finally, I completed a second fellowship in Pediatric Allergy, Asthma and Immunology for two additional years at the National Jewish Hospital and Respiratory Center in Denver to complete my training. As was frequently pointed out to me, that added up to a full ten years of medical training after college, some of the best years of my life (although certainly not the most lucrative, as I never had a salary of more than $17,000 annually during that decade). Ultimately, after moving to Atlanta, I was fortunate to have spent 38 years with a single medical practice, the Atlanta Allergy & Asthma Clinic, P.C. This group evolved into one of the largest and most respected practices in the field of allergy.

While my career wound down slowly from my partnership in 2015 with some part-time work filling in for my old practice and then some time as the medical director of a tiny company that dealt with the pharmaceutical industry, finally ending completely four years later, it was in 2015 that I viewed some of the contents haphazardly thrown into my box. Ah, but what memories! Several items in particular caught my attention.

The first were two letters from Turkey, dated several years apart and from much earlier in my Atlanta career. In the first of the pair, a mother thanked me for taking such good care of her son and apologizing that they would not be able to see me on a regular basis in future years. I, of course, remembered them well. While I had patients from a large geographical area, Turkey was beyond the norm. The family had spent several years in Atlanta and I had seen the son, an early grade-schooler, two or three years into my practice. He had a history of moderately severe asthma back home before moving to Georgia, including several hospital-izations. Subsequently, he had worsened after moving to Atlanta, which had heavier pollens and other airborne allergens, along with exposure to different viruses becoming major triggers for fre-quent asthma attacks.

As was frequently the case back then, the child had been treated by his pediatrician with frequent antibiotics during attacks and with short-acting medications. Again, he had several ER visits and even more disturbingly, two hospital stays. After I started seeing him, he had been switched to longer-term asthma medications (called controller medications) and since there was a major allergic component, had gotten onto an effective program of allergy immu-notherapy injections (a non-drug therapy that alters the body's allergic sensitivities). He had done very well with almost no flare-ups during his next few years in Atlanta prior to the family's return to Turkey.

To my surprise, two years after their move to Turkey, the family came back to see me for a check-up, the mother explaining that the doctor they had seen upon their return to Istanbul had stopped most of her son's treatments. His asthma, quiescent for years, had started to flare once more. They were returning to get him under control. While I offered to help them find a specialist in Turkey, the mother explained that she still had family in Atlanta. As they were relatively well-off financially, she preferred to see me annually when they visited relatives that remained in the area, if I didn't mind. Mind? What an honor!

And they did, returning each year for five years until the aunt had moved home and continued visits were no longer feasible. The child was doing great and they had found a younger Turkish doctor who was agreeable to carry on treatment along similar lines. It was at this point that she had written the letter I mentioned above.

The succeeding letter, almost ten years afterwards, was a picture of a young man graduating college in Turkey as an engineer and a shorthand-written note thanking me for changing his life. His asthma, an overwhelming factor in his earlier days, was no longer an issue. He still took a benign preventive inhaler but had almost no symptoms. He could not have envisioned such an outcome for himself as a young child when he had first come under my care so many years earlier.

While I've not read these in over five years, the recollection still warms me on both professional and personal levels. Medically, of course, it was the ability to help take care of the disease that led me into my specialty in the first place: asthma. Asthma was such an important disease, particularly in the pediatric age group, that I almost preferred to call myself an asthmatologist rather than an allergist.

Why care so much about this particular illness? Part of the problem was the mystery of the disease; part was its frequency and severity. When I started my career, asthma was far and away the most important and perplexing common chronic pediatric disease. It is a frustrating ailment. While allergies, viral infections, exercise, strong odors, pollution and many other factors can set off attacks, these are all triggers, not causes. No one really knows the cause, but the disease is still increasing in frequency. In fact, of all the chronic diseases of children, there were more hospital admissions for asthma than any other illness; indeed, at times it seemed there were more stays for asthma than all the other chronic diseases combined. (I emphasize the pediatric age group, although asthma can be equally devastating for the adult patient. Indeed, throughout my career, I cared for as many adults as children with the illness. However, adults can be afflicted at some point by so many other disease categories that can even be more devastating than asthma—heart disease, cancer, diabetes to name a few—whereas in the pediatric population, it is asthma and other allergic diseases that predominate.)

Moreover, when my career started, we had few effective medications to treat the asthmatic. Nowadays, everyone is familiar with asthma inhalers and nebulizers. Back in "the day," we had neither in large quantity. The only inhalers for providing quick help ("relievers") were relatively more dangerous and less effective compared to the ones we typically use today. Nebulizers, ubiquitously available today for both hospital and home, were only just coming into use and were too new and expensive for the average family. We were also beginning to realize then that asthma was a chronic inflammatory disease and the reliever medications that were used did little to control the underlying process.

This child's earlier care was typical at the time, having seen pediatricians in two countries. Despite advancements in the knowledge and the development of effective anti-inflammatory treatments ("controller" medications as opposed to "relievers"), he had only been treated when symptomatic and the result had been a sickly child, fearful of all too frequent attacks, unable to participate in sports and depressed with the whole situation.

My greatest joy in my career was the ability to impact someone's life like this on a longer-term basis, indeed, the lives of an entire family. Some of these concerns about chronic illness related back to my own earlier life experiences. My late brother, Larry, had a severe congenital heart malformation, that he struggled with his entire life before ultimately succumbing as a young adult. (Possessed with a tremendous spirit, he lived happily and fully despite his condition.) Our entire family life was affected by his illness. Thus, I knew the hardships that any chronic ailment placed on a family and not just the patient.

While I would love to think the results achieved with some of my asthmatic patients resulted from my own brilliance, it was more the willingness to devote a little more time with a family to initiate effective treatment and to better make them understand what needed to be done to keep the patient's asthma under control. I was just doing what I was trained for, but that was why I had gone into medicine in the first place. Conversely, the most discouraging part of my career was my frustrations with some of the primary care doctors, particularly a number of otherwise excellent pediatricians, who were slow to adapt to the newer advances in this, their most common serious disease. Thinking on asthma had changed, but for some reason, the importance of initiating longer term control measures seemed to catch on more slowly with asthma than with most other long-term illnesses.

To encourage patients to take the appropriate medications, I developed an oft-repeated analogy comparing asthma to hypertension that patients seemed to intuitively grasp, even if they did not suffer from blood pressure problems themselves. Consider a hypertensive patient whose blood pressure rose so markedly that she experienced severe headaches. She might have two different medications, an analgesic such as Tylenol, which she liked because it gave her some quick help with her headache (her "reliever"), although doing nothing to bring the underlying blood pressure elevation under control; and secondly, her blood pressure pill, that would not give her any quick relief if taken only at the onset of a headache but, if used routinely, would help prevent the headaches in the first place by stabilizing her BP (obviously, the "controller"). For some reason, patients seemed to grasp this example readily and understood the need for the more important daily medication more easily than they did with their own asthma. They were also able to understand the idea that just asking about symptoms (in this case, headaches) did not reflect the control of the underlying issue (blood pressure). Similarly, just asking about asthma symptoms, as was the custom with many of the primary care physicians, in many cases failed to truly characterize the disease status.

Thus, when taken together, the two letters reflected what I felt to be the most important aspect of my career from a medical viewpoint: helping to improve the lives of patients and families with one of the most troublesome of chronic pediatric diseases.

The other great satisfaction that the two letters emphasized to me was the personal closeness which I felt with many of my patients, particularly in the earlier part of my medical career. I would sometimes amaze even myself with how much I recalled about a very large portion of my clientele—without the need to look into their charts! I often remembered not only their history, but lab tests, medications, and considerably more from a medical viewpoint—but just as importantly, often knew about jobs, families, hobbies, and their travels. Sandy sometimes commented that I knew more details about patients than I did of our own two children, and she was probably correct.

The second item to catch my eye in my box, not surprisingly related to asthma, was a short letter accompanied by a picture of a pretty young woman. Also not surprisingly, it was from someone I hadn't seen for years. Without having to be reminded, I remembered her circumstances very well.

I had taken care of the then pre-teen girl with mild asthma for quite some time. Her illness was never severe, didn't require much medication to keep under control, and while she had some allergies that affected her throughout her respiratory system, they were mild and required little specific treatment. Her only strongly positive allergy was to cats and the family had assiduously avoided pets for years. Her asthma remained quiet—until mysteriously, it didn't! Mysteriously, that is, because nothing seemed to have changed but suddenly her asthma was out of whack, with many more frequent and severe symptoms than ever before. She required additional and stronger controller medications. Despite this, she had her first-ever ER visits. Adding stronger medications did not suppress the disease.

Nothing had changed, ostensibly. No recent nasty viruses, no moves to a new location, no new pets in the house or environs, no floods or mold, no other illness, no new foods or change in diet, no obvious sources of stress. Nada! Ancillary lab tests were normal and allergy testing, repeated for the first time in years, showed only mild reactions to the same inhalants (i.e., dust mites, pollens) as before and no food reactions. The only difference was a dramatically larger reaction to cats—but there was no cat in sight.

I'm not sure what motivated me, but I embarked upon one of the three home visits that I was to make during my career. My academic training had taught me that when an allergic medical problem doesn't offer a clue, a very good idea was to examine the source, whether the home or the work environment. A great idea but in practice, who does that?

Frustratingly, the home inspection was unproductive—at least at first. I knew the family, so I wasn't surprised that the house was as described: fastidiously clean, no pets of any sort, no damp or moldy areas, etc. A wasted visit. Or at least it seemed that way until the mother and I walked into the back yard.

About to leave, I glanced over at the adjacent neighbor's yard and saw a scrawny cat skulking around, off to the side—barely visible in bushes, a bowl of milk where someone had obviously been feeding the cat surreptitiously. Whose house was it? None other than the house of my patient's best friend, and one which she visited almost daily.

Interviews with the appropriate suspects revealed that the friend had found the cat wandering nearby several months earlier. She had started feeding and playing with it frequently, always outside, but the cat had never been in the house. This went on daily. The friend, aware that my patient was highly allergic to cats, made sure never to let the stray enter her home, a fact confirmed by her mother. Questioning my patient, she had omitted saying anything about the cat because it wasn't hers, sure in the knowledge that it couldn't be causing her a problem if exposure to it was only outdoors (she tried never to be too close to it while outside) and most of all, because she loved cats!

On the other hand, I was familiar with multiple studies that confirmed that cat exposure could be high indoors, even in homes that cats had never entered. (In one well-known study done years earlier in rural Finland, a cold place, in a town where the large majority of households had cats, researchers had found high levels of cat dander in ALL homes, including the ones that never had held a cat. The source was traced to coat racks in the elementary school classrooms where all children hung their winter coats in rows touching each other. The transference of cat dander from all those cat owners' coats to those of the other children was enough to make their homes contaminated as well. Similar results were not seen in a nearby town that had very few cat owners, despite the same arrangement of the coat hangers. I suspected something similar was operating here.)

Following our discoveries, the neighbors (with difficulties) were able to make their back yard inhospitable to cats (over the protests of both girls); the house was thoroughly cleaned several times with my patient no longer visiting for a while, medications were continued; and in part to placate my young patient, she went on allergy injections for a few years, mainly to cats.

It took a few months to see any significant changes, but the patient's asthma gradually started to improve back to its previous quiescent status. Once it did, she never had any issues again and I stopped seeing her a few years later when she was in high school and doing great, off of everything. I sometimes wondered why I hadn't done more site visits. I'd rather enjoyed imitating Sherlock Holmes.

Oh, the picture with the letter? Why, it showed my former patient sitting in her apartment in New York where she had moved after college, smiling and with both of her roommate's cats snuggling in her lap!

The third memento I'll mention was a giant Hallmark card given to me by my office staff shortly before I retired. Inside was a giant photograph with the gleeful faces of more than 15 different people, all grinning and doing silly things. It's a pretty mixed group, a few more Blacks than whites, and an occasional Asian and Hispanic—a fairly good representation of my staff at various offices over four decades. What a great group of people and I miss them!

I'm quite proud of my long career in medicine but one thing that was very clear to me was that my career actually belonged to many people. I never felt that I was treating a patient by myself; I felt that WE were treating the patient. It always seemed like a team effort. I might have been the one making diagnoses and prescribing treatments, but my nurses and front desk staff were the ones performing the tests, talking to the patients, handling the phone calls, greeting the patients. I was very lucky to work with a group of people that usually sounded as if they had smiles on their faces—lucky, because they were the ones who interacted with the patients more often than I did. Whatever I was able to accomplish during my career was in large part due to all these good and caring folks.

Two things that I'm proud of during my medical career spanning five decades: gratitude and acknowledgement. Almost daily when I would leave the office, I would thank my staff for the work they had done that day (often adding facetiously that I had no idea what that work might have been). Secondly, that when our practice started annual patient satisfaction surveys, I was always at or very near the top for all the many physicians in our very large group. That last part meant a lot to me and I know that wasn't necessarily because I was the smartest doctor in the practice. I tried to treat patients the way I would like to have been treated myself. Thus, these ratings meant a great deal to me. While they may have been in my name, they likewise mirrored the dedication of the fine people I was fortunate enough to work with.

Chapter 79

A Most Satisfying Career

I retired from medicine a few years ago and to be honest, there's a lot I miss. Not enough that I want to go back, but definitely enough to feel like a big part of my life has somehow faded just a little. Of course, medicine has been replaced by many other things with benefits of their own, including more time for sleep, considerably more time for the travel that Sandy and I love (at last count, over 60 countries visited) and the opportunity to explore new ventures. Most importantly was more time for the small bevy of grandchildren we continually find underfoot.

The grandkids seemed to be well-placed and well-spaced; physically, placed within half-hour commutes, and as for spaced: while my daughter's two children head towards pre-teendom and no longer need us quite as much, no longer laughing at all my silly jokes, they are succeeded by my son's three very young children (the oldest of whom approaches the age of 4 as of this writing). With my son and daughter-in-law both busily involved as young physicians, I have a very strong feeling those kids are going to need us for a while. Happily, these younger ones find EVERYTHING I say to be funny!

As mentioned at the beginning, this memoir was not intended to be a compendium of my medical cases but more as a means of hopefully introducing my grandchildren to a different side of me, rather than the achy older man that my mind has inconveniently chosen to inhabit at this stage of my life. This was an image that I first developed from a long-ago conversation with my mother. One of my favorite memories of her, a wonderful, warm woman with a wry wit, universally loved, involved a phone call I made to congratulate her on the occasion of her 69th birthday. I was 42 and while she had a wonderful spirit, her age seemed rather ancient to me on that day. Her body had begun to betray her with severe arthritis and chronic back problems. "So Mom, how does it feel to be turning 69 today?" I asked. She slowly replied, "Well, I feel fine, but I look in the mirror and wonder: how did my 18-year-old brain get trapped in this old lady's body?" That was years ago. Now, as I've left 69 in my own rearview mirror, I wanted to give my grandchildren some memories of me from the part of my life they never knew, particularly the part as a physician, the part I clearly cherish the most. (As for my mother, who lived a wonderful life into her nineties, I often wondered what she thought about, contemplating her reflections in those later decades.)

Regarding medicine, there are questions I'm often asked: If I loved medicine, why did I leave? And, if the medicine has changed so much, would I have made the same choice again? Or would I indeed recommend medicine to young people as a potential career? Surprisingly, these questions are easy for me to answer.

As to why I left: simply stated, it was time. Time to leave, time to make a change. Clearly, I had loved my lifetime profession but over many years, enough small things had started to add up that I found myself focusing more and more on unpleasantries than concentrating on the things I loved about being a physician. I will spend only minimal time here, since my career was so positive for the most part.

My largest concern was with the increasing domination of medicine by large impersonal corporations, changes that resulted in the patient's medical care too often becoming secondary to financial considerations. These considerations were handed down by anonymous bean counters rather than caring medical personnel. Although the public sometimes believe that physicians enter medicine for purely material reasons, this is most definitely not the case. Of the very many fine doctors I know, few would have spent the six to 12 years after college pursuing their training with insanely long hours and ridiculously low pay, just for the money they might make later. No, they did it because they truly cared about their patients. So, later in my career, as I too often watched the most effective medications being denied to people, other treatments withheld, or extra staff hired just to argue with insurance personnel trained to say NO, I resented the changes.

Secondly, I did not like the electronic medical records (EMRs). Certainly necessary in the long run, sadly, these systems were forced upon physicians by the government years before they were up to the task, largely outdated and ineffective. After our very expensive but maddeningly inefficient system had been in place for two years, I found that I was in the office late every evening but seeing fewer patients than previously. Realizing I was spending far more time with the computer than with the patients I loved, I knew the time to leave was at hand.

Given the grievances, why would I do it again or even encourage young people to consider a career in medicine? Simply because there is no profession better. I am very proud of my son, Daniel, who made the decision (with only moderate parental urging) to go into medicine. He is now a hospitalist at the hospital of his birth, one to which I admitted most of my sick patients over several decades, and on whose staff many of my friends still remain. By all accounts, he is an excellent young doctor. Similarly, his wife Monique is also a physician, an anesthesiologist. I'm equally proud of her and the good reports I've heard from surgical colleagues with whom she interacts. The two work long hours and provide quality medical care, but their world is different from the one in which I started my career several decades ago.

Younger physicians of today start off with a different mindset. They have only known an increasingly corporate medicine. They have always worked with EMRs, which are slowly improving, gradually becoming the helpful tools they were originally envisioned to be. Today's young doctors get to participate in a world that is constantly evolving with incredible changes in technology that will intensify over the coming decades. I follow these innovations closely and find myself enthralled. Indeed, with good insights and some luck, I have recently done far better financially with some well-placed investments in start-up medical companies than I had done in my own practice of medicine.

I expect these will be exciting times to be in medicine for young doctors and know many of the issues that had troubled me will be worked out. On the other hand, when I respond to young adults who ask my thoughts about medicine, I am always cautious to add the proviso, "if you are so inclined." There will be frustrations, there will be long hours, and there will be less control to individually manage patients; medicine is a field to be entered only by those devoted and willing to make the necessary commitments. But for those who want a wonderful profession offering the ability to actually help people, one in which they are not just looking at the financial considerations, there can be no career better.

As for me, among the many highlights of a 50-year career:

Foremost, the chance, indeed, the privilege, to take care of people. A sacred trust that, hopefully, I did my best to meet throughout my career. As I well knew, people and families come to doctors in times of need, with their health on the line. I would like to think that I met their trust to the best of my abilities.

Next, the chance to know people on a longer-term basis. I loved that I had a chance to know families over extended periods, and was even more honored when I saw children as new patients whose parents had themselves been my patients years earlier. Eventually, I found families in which I had treated three generations of patients. What an honor!

A third highlight, of course, was the exposure to the intellectual challenges offered by medicine. An unexpected treat for me late in my career was assuming a position as the part time medical director for a tiny pharmaceutical-related start-up. While the company ultimately was unsuccessful, the position afforded me the opportunity to refamiliarize myself with the many advance in fields of medicine outside my own. While I had always attempted to keep up, the changes had been both amazing and staggering. I experienced the same sense of awe that I could see reflected in my grandchildren visiting a planetarium for the first time.

Lastly, I loved the chance to find humor in a very serious world around me. The old adage holds that laughter is the best medicine. I'm not sure if that's true but it's pretty high on the list- for the doctor as well as the patient. My life was made richer by the finding of humor in the world, both medical and non-medical. As an example, Papa Doc is the name I chose to have my grandchildren call me. It is a moniker that combines two of the great roles of my life, as a father and as a doctor. However, it represented a pretty risqué choice, since the name was appropriated from that of an infamous Haitian dictator of a generation earlier. Most of my friends thought it hilarious until by happenstance, I made a new acquaintance from that Caribbean country who upon hearing the name, initially took offense. But even he began to laugh uproariously upon seeing my oldest granddaughter, then aged 18 months, as she came running towards me, both arms extended, crying "Papa Doc! Papa Doc!"

Harkening back to my souvenirs of the last chapter, the fourth and last memento I recalled from my box was a letter from a long-term patient, written at the time of my retirement. In many ways, it was similar to so many other notes that I'd received during my career, thanking me for many years of care and for helping to improve his life. There was nothing remarkable about the patient or his treatment; his asthma had never seemed particularly severe. He was not anyone famous, but he was someone I had come to know well over a prolonged period. Originally, he lived in the Atlanta area but at some point, work had caused him to relocate to the Northeast. In his thank you letter, he noted that while he had been under my care for nearly two decades, the last ten years had involved traveling from Connecticut annually, seeing me while passing through Atlanta, even though he had found an excellent physician at home. He realized that our visits were no longer warranted medically. I realized that as well. He came more as a friend than as a patient.

That's exactly the way I had thought of him towards the end — a friend, rather than just a patient. I went into medicine looking to heal people but in many ways, I think my patients and staff helped to heal me. Funny — I hadn't even realized I was ill. When I looked back on my career, perhaps one of the best things that I could say was that I could no longer always separate patients from friends.

BIOGRAPHY

Gary Lotner is a physician living in the Atlanta area. Born in New York, his medical training began at the Albert Einstein College of Medicine in that city. This was followed by internship, residency, and fellowship training at the University of Pennsylvania (Children's Hospital of Philadelphia) and subsequently, by a second fellowship at the National Jewish Hospital and Respiratory Center in Denver. Afterwards, he had a long and satisfying career in the private practice of medicine that spanned four decades as a partner with the Atlanta Allergy & Asthma Clinic, P.C., one of the nation's largest and most respected medical groups in that specialty. Dr. Lotner is board-certified in both Pediatrics and Allergy and Clinical Immunology.

Upon leaving clinical medicine, Dr. Lotner served as the medical director of a small pharmaceutical start-up before retiring a few years ago.

He is delighted in recent years to have his two children, Jessica and Daniel (the latter a physician) have chosen to return to the Atlanta area with their families. Currently, Dr. Lotner and his wife, Sandra Cuttler, have indulged their love for travel with visits to over 60 countries, are involved in diverse activities, and find themselves particularly delighted to have all five of their wonderful grandchildren so close at hand.

This is Dr. Lotner's first book, borne from his warm reminiscences, many of them humorous, of his long medical career. The time to sit and write is the only positive thing he can see for himself personally resulting from the isolation of the COVID pandemic.